NEW DIMENSIONS IN JUDAISM

NEW DIMENSIONS IN JUDAISM

A CREATIVE ANALYSIS OF RABBINIC CONCEPTS

by

Rabbi Phillip Sigal

An Exposition-University Book

EXPOSITION PRESS   NEW YORK

EXPOSITION PRESS INC.

50 Jericho Turnpike   Jericho, New York 11753

FIRST EDITION

LIBRARY OF CONGRESS CATALOG CARD NUMBER: 72-186485

0-682-47429-0

To my beloved father
MOSES SIGAL
whose life has been a constant inspiration
and whose memory I consistently
cherish, this book is dedicated with
affection and reverence.

CONTENTS

PREFACE

THE GREAT MASTER of Talmudic-Rabbinic literature, Louis Ginzberg, once termed *halakha* "the really typical creation of our people." In a lecture at the Hebrew University in Jerusalem he stated that his purpose then was "to demonstrate that the development of the *halakha,* at least of the most ancient *halakha,* is not a creation of the House of Study, but an expression of life itself."[1] (Halakha throughout this book denotes "religious forms.")

This point of view is one that I share. First of all, I believe that there is nothing so singularly characteristic of Judaism and the Jewish-faith community as halakha, and second, I believe that halakha at its best and most appealing is a halakha that is an expression of contemporary life and experience.

My intention in this volume, the first of a number to follow, is to provide the student and the curious layman with a background and a contemporary approach to the history and development of the halakha as well as to the current problems and proposed solutions in the field of halakha. The book is rooted in an intuition that Judaism cannot survive in a free Western environment with its present halakha, and that without a discipline of halakha it cannot survive at all. Consequently it is my belief that it is our task in this last third of the twentieth century to move in on the crisis in a two-pronged drive.

First of all, we have a responsibility to update the old halakha, to prune dead branches in the orchard, to clear the medieval thicket, and thereby prolong the life of the healthy portion of the plant. Second, we have a serious obligation to create new halakha in consideration of our changing environment and in anticipation of the space age, in harmony with new psychological, intellectual, socio-economic and historic insights. If Louis Ginzberg was correct, as I earnestly believe he was, our generation has the sacred and difficult obligation to do for Judaism what Moses, Ezra, Yose B. Yo'ezer, Rabbi Yohanan B. Zakkai and others in the course of Jewish history did for their generations. Essentially what they achieved was a successful response to the intellectual and social climate of life in their times. They enabled the halakha to express the highest ideals of self-discipline and communal discipline within the context of their societies.

This preliminary volume, I pray, will contribute in some measure to a similar effort in this restless and rootless age which, perhaps more than any other, cries out for the discipline of halakha.

Some of the material herein has appeared previously in print, as articles. (I thank the *Reconstructionist* and the *Jewish Spectator* for having published "The Problem of Halakha Re-examined," "Jewish Law Still in the Making," "Revelation and the Halakha," "The Rabbis and Divorce," "Neurotic Fixations" and "Halakha in Crisis.") But the themes have been comprehensively revised, updated and expanded so that in effect they constitute new material.

It is in order at this time to offer my appreciation to the Rabbinical Assembly for the opportunity it has given me to further my work through my association with the Committee on Jewish Law and Standards both as a member of the committee and in the capacity of secretary.

While this book is intended for students and laymen, I nevertheless feel that it will perform a useful function for Rabbis and scholars as well. For this reason it has been copiously annotated. But to avoid undue distraction, the notes have been relegated to the end of the text, as has any complex or extended excursus.

The manuscript has gone through a number of hands over a period of two years, but to Mrs. Harold Gaffin, my secretary at Temple B'nai Zion in Bloomfield, New Jersey, I owe a special debt for her patience and for her willingness to take on extra burdens. I am also grateful to my students at the Academy for Jewish Religion for stimulating me to sharpen many of my thoughts and compelling me to buttress and document my suggestions.

My labors in halakha began some thirty years ago, when my teacher in Toronto, Rabbi Jacob Kamenetsky, taught me that there were alternatives in halakha. I am thankful to that master of the halakha, now Rosh Yeshiva at Mesifta Torah Vodath in Brooklyn, New York, for my earliest insights and for the recognition that authentic halakha must be inspired by ethical motivation. I am naturally also grateful to all my other teachers, but most especially I owe a debt of gratitude to the master of them all, Professor Saul Lieberman of the Jewish Theological Seminary, at whose feet I sat for four years.

It had been my aspiration that my first published volume in Judaica would include a foreword by that outstanding classical scholar, Fritz M. Heichelheim of the University of Toronto. Alas, Professor Heichelheim was recalled to his Creator in an untimely hour. But I am deeply grateful for the hundreds of hours we spent in conversation which provided me with a wealth of stimulation and insight. Though Professor Heichelheim was a specialist in classical economic history, his wide range of knowledge in Judaica was of inestimable interest, and I cherish his memory.

This book is dedicated to the memory of my beloved father, whose life was one of my profoundest inspirations. To my dear mother I owe her original permission to leave home at the age of fifteen and to pursue my halakhic odyssey in New York, in more advanced and sophisticated circles than were then available in Toronto. This she did at considerable self-sacrifice.

But if anyone has really challenged my halakhic ingenuity and compelled me to refine my every response in day-to-day life, it has been my precious daughters Sharon and Sabrina. They also helped me with the Index; and to them I owe much. And finally, in the sense of the Talmudic *aharon, aharon, haviv,* "the last is most precious," I feel a sense of awe when I attempt to express my profoundest gratitude to my life's partner. Lillian is a remarkable person whose constant patience and whose unerring sense of what is right for me have been a consistent source of motivation. This preliminary offering is truly the product of her encouragement, stimulation and constructive criticism.

Prayerfully I join with the Psalmist:

> That I may sing Your praises and not be silent,
> Lord my God, I am forever grateful to You.[2]

February 24, 1971   —PHILLIP SIGAL
Bloomfield, N.J.

Acknowledgment for practical assistance in the publication of this volume is appreciatively made to Benjamin Bussin, Dr. Morris Harris, Albert Hochberg, Harold Kaplan and the Hon. Carl Stier of Bloomfield, N. J.; to Charles LuBow, Albert and Henry Schrank, of Bridgeton, N. J.; to Herman Leitzow and to the family of Arthur Reckseit.

NEW DIMENSIONS IN JUDAISM

Chapter I

MEDITATIONS

THE TURN OF THE eighth decade of the twentieth century marks a watershed in the history of mankind. All around the world, in Christendom, in the Communist societies, in the lands of Islam, in the East and in the West, there is insecurity and frustration, with consequent restlessness and turmoil. Profound socio-economic and intellectual transmogrification is in process. Spiritual upheavals, from tension in the papacy to new frontiers of space-age thought, make the intellectual seismographs shudder. Judaism will inevitably not emerge unaffected. Jews must consequently begin to turn from their preoccupation with sheer physical survival to the great spiritual questions. They must begin to grapple with the intellectual challenge that inheres in a serious commitment to faith.

What has long troubled me is the apparent confusion in many minds between Judaism as a permanent on-going, classical expression of life and Judaism as a transitory, ever-changing contemporary expression. We suffer from a historical time lag. Thus our generation identifies one form of Judaism, essentially that which reached its apex in nineteenth-century Eastern Europe, as Judaism par excellence, evidently oblivious of the elementary historical reality that Eastern Europe merely possessed a given expression of Judaism. It was a meaningful and spiritually enhancing form in its time and for its adherents, but it has long been apparent that it is no longer meaningful or spiritually enhancing. Somehow we have to recapture the idea that each socio-historical epoch thrusts forth a new expression of Judaism. This is then embodied in a halakha which becomes the contemporary expression of the Jewish spiritual commitment.

It is my conviction that the transhistorical essence of Judaism —"Revelation"—requires an ever-changing and ever-current evolving human interpretation, a living form into which is molded the essence and through which the spiritual commitment is concretized in a real community in actual history. Frequently, as even a cursory study of the Bible, the Talmud and halakhic literature will reveal, "forms" of specific halakhot became obsolete and were discarded, or at times were found to be potentially salvageable and were transformed. The ever-recurring challenge has been how to understand this historical truth in each successive contemporary setting. In our own time the same challenge should inspire us to present a thoughtful and reasonable modern approach by which the sophisticated Western Jew living in the free societies, and most particularly in North America, can fulfill the Torah's injunction "that you may live by them."[1]

There is much merit in the argument that Judaism crosses frontiers and that it is questionable procedure to particularize a North American Anglicized Judaism. But this is not an irrefutable argument. The Rabbis of Babylon did not legislate or decide for Palestine. Spanish and North African scholars were the mentors of Jews residing in Islamic lands, while the Franco-German sages served the Jews in Christian Europe.

Each of the three great modern centers of Jewish life—Israel, Western Europe and North America—like Babylonia, North Africa and Spain in the tenth or eleventh century, or the Franco-German center and Eastern Europe in later centuries, has particular needs and requires reasonable solutions pertinent to its needs.[2] As a Rabbi in North America, committed to raising my family here and committed to the Western democratic tradition of an open, an integrated, society, the responsibility I have is vastly different from that of a spiritual leader in Israel, or for that matter in the Soviet Union, a potentially great center presently deactivated.

My thoughts cannot be concerned as strongly with how to save Judaism in the Soviet Union or how to transmogrify the stifling monopolistic orthodoxy of Israel into a dynamic twentieth-century expression of free religion. They may be of some value, assuming the language barrier is overcome, in helping our fellow Jews in Western Europe. But basically my meditations, reflections and researches are devoted to the problems of English-speaking North American Jews.

When Maimonides wrote his *Guide for the Perplexed,* he addressed himself to a particular time and place in history, seeking to make viable an eternal essence in a temporal setting. Nahman Krochmal essentially strove for the same objective in his *Guide for the Currently Perplexed* (incidentally, in my opinion, the correct translation of his Hebrew title *Moreh Nevukhai ha'Zman*). I refer to these works in order to justify a particularist approach—particularist in the sense that I may be addressing myself to a limited community within the context of a specific cultural setting during a particular period of history.

The fact that it takes up the problem of halakha constitutes a major difference between this book and the other books cited and is also at the root of my philosophy. Although Maimonides also published a halakhic code, this was not designed for the "perplexed" or for those seeking an intelligent and reasoned faith. Both Maimonides and Krochmal, concerned about new directions in their respective periods, wrote works of theology for those who were in search of a philosophy of religion. It is my contention that what the perplexed Jew of today needs is a work on halakha. We are more pragmatic. We are interested in the how more than in the why of Jewish religion. Halakha is the response. Yet the why emerges from halakha subtly and richly, as will later in this book become evident.[3]

Unfortunately, instead of anticipating events and planning wisely for them, man often reacts to vast socio-political changes only after they have brought him to the brink of spiritual disaster. The Reformation is a classical expression of this in Christendom. The present difficulties encountered by Rome provide us with a window on history. We are witnessing a process in which a vested institution is reluctant not only to anticipate further great changes in our epoch but even to respond to them after they have occurred. The collision between change and tradition then becomes a shattering experience.

This has happened in Judaism as well. What I am worried about is Judaism's expiration by default. I would like to see us accept the revolutionary changes that have occurred in our world, in government, in science, in human interests, and strive to adjust Jewish forms accordingly. But I am concerned with more than merely getting off the collision course with technology upon which Judaism is now drifting. We should plan for the end of the century; and even more, we should look deeply into the future, into what cybernetics and the great population explosion will do to our world half a century hence. We should strive to ascertain what the spiritual needs of North American Jews will be at the end of our century and begin to move in the direction of fulfilling those needs.

Meeting the future challenge will require that we become what someone has called "loving critics" of Jewish life and thought. But this will be infinitely superior to being "uncritical lovers" of all things Jewish. While a sina qua non of Judaism is continuity, an equal prerequisite of the future is change. Neither discontinuous change, which is anarchy, nor an unchanging continuity, which is stagnation, will be acceptable. It will require no less than fashioning a new Yavneh and beginning the production of a literary heritage that will be our modern Talmud. Short of this, we will suffer spiritual catastrophe. The defection of our grandchildren will not necessarily be to Christianity, nor to escape their identity out of self-hatred as in bygone generations. The fears of yesteryear and the solutions for the problems of the past are no longer the fears or the solutions of the problems of the morrow. The defection of the future will more likely be toward an aimless and spiritless secular life that will leave despair in its wake and enshroud our grandchildren in spiritual darkness. As marriage between Jews and non-Jews increases, there will be a drift into Unitarianism as a sensible and pragmatic alternative to an obsolete and hostile Jewish community and an obsolete and theologically untenable Christian church.

An omen of our times is that while all around us every religious community grows in sheer numbers, the American Jewish religious community not only remains rather stable but is actually decreasing in proportion to the whole. Yet I am not concerned with whether we will number 3 percent or 2 percent of the American population. I am concerned with whether the lack of growth of our actual numbers does not portend a significant spiritual problem.

Halakha is the quintessential characteristic of Judaism. For this reason halakha will have to be the key instrument in the coming decades through which we renew the spiritual vigor of Judaism. The halakha of the future will have to deal radically with the problems of the future, including intermarriage—or what we might preferably refer to as "exogamy"—the dietary laws, the irrelevance of traditional forms of worship, and corporate morality, or what someone has fortuitously called "white-collar crime." Halakha will have to consider the intrusion of man into outer space, the challenge of cybernetics, the medical revolution related to transplants, in vitro embryology, the freezing of terminal patients for future revival, a host of other already known problems and a myriad of unforeseeable challenges.

When Louis Ginzberg called halakha "the typical creation of our people," he indicated it was not merely the inspiration of sages locked in an ivory tower. On the contrary, a most remarkable ivory-tower scholar who epitomized them all was one of the giants of Rabbinic literature, Elijah Gaon of Vilna. Yet because he specialized in textual criticism and commentary he was not a historic figure in the evolution of pragmatic halakha. Halakha is the process of developing norms in the arena of real life. It is necessary to differentiate between ends and means, essence and forms, ideals and norms. Halakha is the complex of guideposts to observance, the product of the fusion of the creative imagination of seers and sages with the socio-political reality. It is the attempt, so far as humanly possible, to express God's will. Judaism is not the existential corpus of halakha in any given epoch. Judaism is an attitude toward life and death, nature and man, the universe and society. The major facets of this attitude or philosophy constitute the essence of God's will. Halakha is the "form," or the ongoing historic manner in which we express this essence in life. For this reason any discussion of Judaism and its future, or of Judaism and its significance for man, must center on halakha and its promise for both our time and the era to come.

Cosmic events have shaken Jewish life in our time in a manner unequaled since the biblical period. The shattering experience of the destruction of Jerusalem in 586 B.C.E., contrary to all Jewish expectations in those days, or again in the year 70 of the Common Era, was as traumatic as the Holocaust of the twentieth century. Trauma cannot be measured in the quantity of human lives involved. Trauma is a qualitative thing. The Book of Lamentations, the evolution of Tisha B'av, the numerous rites in Judaism associated with both biblical-era Destructions, all testify to the penetrating role that trauma has played. The modern Holocaust, subsumed under one dread rubric, "Auschwitz," has had a shattering impact upon contemporary Jews but not a similar impact upon Jewish history or religion.

There is a significant and troubling distinction between the impact of the Destructions and that of Auschwitz. Throughout the centuries Jews referred to the biblical Destructions as *hurban ha'bayit*, "the destruction of the house of God." The phenomenon was seen as a theological calamity. Dazed and trembling, the sages saw it as the consequences of sin. For centuries we confessed *mipnai ha'ta'ainoo*, that we were expelled for our sins. The bizarre element in the aftermath of the contemporary Holocaust is that we have been so stunned that no vindication or justification of God has yet been enunciated. We have not yet said what is Jewishly normal, *Barukh . . . dayan emet,*

> The Lord gives and
> The Lord takes back.
> Praised be the name of the Lord.[4]

Perhaps this theological gap which has come to exist between Judaism and the Jew also explains why this overwhelming cosmic event has had no consequence for halakha.

There is also the possibility that we were caught off guard. Before we could cry out in anguish in 1945, the Holocaust was followed immediately by an even greater cosmic event, the establishment of the republic of Israel. As once before in history, as many facets of the halakha were intimately connected with *yetziat mitzray'im,* the Exodus, so again we might have expected a halakhic revolution, related to the renewal of Israel, that would have significant consequences.

That neither the Holocaust nor the Re-establishment had an impact upon halakha might be somewhat related to the spiritual vacuum of our time, to the dread stagnation that hangs precipitously over Judaism, to the inability of our generation to articulate a philosophy, an essence, which can be expressed in theological terms amenable to the technological twentieth century. Jewish fate and history were cemented into the halakha with myriads of strands binding the halakha to *yetziat mitzray'im,* the Exodus from Egypt, and the *hurban,* the Destruction of 70. Similarly, in the coming epoch of Jewish history, the Holocaust and the Restoration, Auschwitz and Israel, will have to become an integrated segment of the historic consciousness of Jews and Judaism. To meet the challenge of that day, the halakha will have to rediscover within itself or create anew such forms as will give expression to the ultimates of Jewish life.

A paradox of Jewish history can be read in the strange fact that the miracle of the Exodus was betrayed by the golden calf and the *hurban* was dignified by the faith and dedication of Pharisaic-Talmudic Judaism. The Jew did not recognize the role of God in Egypt. As in later history, his eyes did not see, his ears did not hear, and his mind did not perceive, as the prophets expressed it. Throughout the biblical period the Jew betrayed monotheism, the essence to which he was to be witness, by paying homage to pagan deities. The first Destruction by Babylonia and the subsequent Restoration of Judea appears in retrospect to have been a divine warning and reprieve. Subsequently, though monotheism was salvaged and the Jew abandoned his pagan heresy, he nevertheless seemed incapable of rising to the moral challenge of his faith. The consequence of this was the second *hurban,* the Destruction of 70 C.E. There seemed to be an inescapable conflict between the building of a specific human kingdom defined within geographic bounds and the spiritual Kingdom of God which was to transcend time and space.

Instead of seeing the "death of God" in the flames of Jerusalem, our sages recognized that it was "because of our sins." The trauma of the *hurban* inspired a mass historic repentance that crowned Judaism with some of its finest centuries in Babylonia, Spain and Western, Central and Eastern Europe. The new Holocaust has hardly been analyzed. Some see in it the "death of God." Recently a Canadian philosopher, Emil Fackenheim, saw in it what he called God's "commanding voice," the command coming out of the fires being that every Jew is to strive to survive as Jew.[5] Assuming this suggestion to have some merit, one is nevertheless compelled to inquire into its meaning and to determine how one "survives as a Jew."

Like Fackenheim, who confessed it took him twenty years to confront the scandal of the Holocaust, I must confess that I have not yet discovered a meaningful interpretation of the event. Nevertheless, I can accept it as part of the general mystery of life and am compelled to ask with the author of Job,

> Shall we accept
> Only good from the Lord,
> And reject misfortune?[6]

Misfortune cannot be measured statistically. For Job sitting on a dung heap the mystery of personal adversity was just as tremendous as the mystery of Auschwitz for the collective Job of 1945. The insanity that produced the abomination of Auschwitz has no theological meaning in itself, but it certainly is an organic element of the teleology of history.

Undoubtedly there is a causal relationship between the Hitler aberration and the Restoration of Israel. The historic interplay of challenge and response obtains between Auschwitz and the subsequent emergence of Israel as an independent Jewish republic. Causal relationships are secular history, not religion. For us, both Auschwitz and Israel must have religious impact.

As a preliminary hypothesis I would regard Israel's emergence as God's *Redeeming Return,* His renewed manifestation in the historic process, after His *hestair panim,* the eclipse of His presence, the abandonment in which He left us during the black night of Auschwitz.

We can see the post-Auschwitz era as the first faltering rays of a rising sun which may ultimately appear as the blazing messianic fulfillment. But if this age is to be crowned with this glory, we will have to take to heart more than did our biblical precursors the prophetic admonition that we are God's witnesses.

The "commanding voice" out of Auschwitz may be a call to the heart and mind of every Jew to avoid a future *hestair panim,* the eclipse of divinity in the world. This is not to say that Auschwitz was punishment for our sins, any more than Job's suffering was for his. Suffering is a mystery, as life itself is a mystery and as Redemption is a mystery. But while an Auschwitz is a mystery, it can only occur when divinity is in eclipse. The Restoration of Israel, like the Exodus from Egypt over 3,000 years ago and the Return from Babylonia 2,500 years ago, is a fact of history. But so were the *hurban*—the Destruction of 586 b.c.e. and again of 70 c.e.—facts of history. The Return from Babylonia was a reprieve, but for some strange reason the Jews again remained insensitive to the prophetic admonition and experienced a progression of agony through the darkness of Antiochus, the dim light of the early Hasmoneans extinguished by their successors, and the subsequent eclipse of 70. How can we avoid a repetition of this type of encounter between our hopes and our frustrations? Theologically speaking, or put another way, religiously speaking, we must accept the idea that only righteousness will avert the cataclysm, that only when Jews give witness, are servants of the Lord, when they become crystallized as the "kingdom of priests and a holy people," will messianism be possible. It is elementary in our tradition that in every age it is incumbent upon us to see ourselves as having left Egypt, which means not only to be grateful for our freedom as a consequence of that redemption but to absorb within ourselves the purpose of that redemption: to stand at Sinai and receive the Revelation.

The Revelation was the initial discovery by Israel of the will of God. In the Ten Commandments we have a rudimentary form through which God's will was to be fulfilled. Revelation began to provide form for essence. The Revelation was to be put into human hands, and man's interpretation of the will of God was henceforth to prevail. Man had to meet issues, make decisions, relate himself to God and live with his fellow man. The forms and norms which the Jew devised were his halakha. The word halakha has been loosely translated as "law," but this is neither accurate nor adequate. Perhaps the Greek term *nomos* properly defined Greek law, but the Rabbinic usage of the term halakha cannot be considered an equivalent of what we call law in Western civilization. Thus, to see Judaism as a "nomistic" religion and Christianity as "anti-nomian," or to see any segment of Jews which strives to modify the halakha as "anti-nomian" for discarding some halakha, is inappropriate.[7]

Biblically the concept of "law" is expressed in several terms. *Mishpat* is a law of equity, *hak* is a statute, *torot* are procedural instructions, *mitzvah* is an obligation. All these were subsumed under the Rabbinic term halakha. As Professor Saul Lieberman has helped to understand the term, we might translate it "guideposts"—for halakha constitutes the guideposts to observance of the forms or norms of the tradition.[8] These guideposts undergo change as the historic terrain in which Jews function changes.

It is to adumbrating the problems of the existing halakha and the challenge to fashion a futuristic halakha that this book is devoted. There is serious need to discover new forms that will once again appeal to the hearts and minds of Jews. When existing guideposts fail to point the way, it is prudent to erect new ones.

Chapter II

DIVINE REVELATION
AND HUMAN AUTHORITY

THAT GOD MANIFESTED His presence at Sinai has been the authentic, historical Jewish belief down through the ages. We cannot ignore the belief that at a magnificent moment in the wilderness all of human history was illuminated by a flash of divine lightning. The crack of Sinai's thunder and the accompanying blast of the trumpets, reverberating through the corridors of history, became the cornerstone of Jewish religious life. All halakhic authority traces itself to Sinai. That Revelation was the medium through which the process of halakha began to unfold itself.

There can be no doubt that any discussion of practical halakha and its claim to authority in our time must take into account this origin of halakha. In the past the claim of halakha to authority always rested ultimately upon the assumption of its divine character. It was believed, and was so presented in Scripture, that at a given point in the history of Israel, God revealed laws, statutes and rites to Moses at Sinai, and at other junctures during the journey from Egypt to Canaan.

A system of law may be the fiction that cements a society, as the Roman jurist Cicero put it, or it may be the road to salvation or life abundant as a people, if we put it within the framework of discourse used by Mordecai Kaplan. But whatever may be the consequences of a legal system, halakha was always more than this in Judaism. It was not conceived merely in humanistic terms as a road to salvation or the cement of society. It was the mode by which the Jew served God because he believed that God willed He be served in this mode. It is the second half of that proposition, that God willed these forms, which is by far the more significant in opening any discussion of halakha in modern times. Revelation and the consequent problem of authority are intimately interwoven with the problem of how or whether halakhic change can be instituted by man.

There is no need here to recapitulate the many biblical references to the effect that God chose Israel as His witnesses, or servants, as an ensign to the peoples of the world to be a kingdom of priests and a holy people and that Israel affirmed its covenant at Sinai. This theological fundamental in Judaism need be neither belabored nor elaborated. The prophetic concept of the "mission" of Israel is the equivalent of the idea of the "suffering servant." These are merely two distinct ways of enunciating the objective of Judaism: to make saints of ordinary men, or to elevate man to the status of the priesthood. Halakha, in these terms, is to be primarily conceived as the force which would draw man closer to God.[1]

In the light of this it is essential to examine the attitude of the Rabbis toward the concept of Revelation and from there to proceed to spell out its meaning for us. We find that the Rabbis of the Pharisaic-Talmudic period had no compunction in declaring a law obsolete or in instituting new practices and modifying old ones. As Professor Abraham Joshua Heschel has said, "The will of God is eternal, transcending all moments, all events, including acts of revelation."[2] The "act of revelation" was merely the seed. Firmly rooted in the well-tended garden of Judaism, it produced many a fruit or flower. The Rabbis understood that because the will of God is eternal, it requires a variety of forms of expression to meet the varying needs of changing circumstances. If the Torah was to be livable, it had at repeated stages in time to be amended, expanded or contracted. If the eternal will was to be done, it had to be reunderstood and reinterpreted in each age and applied in a manner which made it currently functional.

The Talmudic Rabbis did not accept a blanket version of Revelation to include all the written and "Oral Law" as a definitive divine message complete for all time and hence immutable. They were perfectly aware that law evolves. They realized that Jewish religious practice, halakha, had grown over the ages. The Rabbis were so astute about this that they even risked the anachronisms of expressing what the biblical Patriarchs had observed. They believed that the Patriarchs observed certain mitzvot prior to the Sinaitic Revelation. Thus Joseph was said to have observed the Sabbath. There is a difference of opinion on the extent of patriarchal observance, but all were agreed that some Torah was observed prior to Sinai, even if only the ethical and moral dicta summed up in the Noahide laws, in addition to circumcision and the Sabbath.[3]

Obviously the opinions of the Rabbis may be relegated to the sphere of *agada*—"lore"—and as such are not binding upon us in a halakhic sense. But in history it is not always the significant or the true that is believed. What counts more is not the fact but what the people believed to be the fact. So in Judaism, what is of ultimate concern is not whether we want to accept such statements about patriarchal religion as historical and true but that the Rabbis believed them to be so. In these terms, therefore, this agadic material indicates that our Rabbis believed that portions of Judaism known to us in the Pentateuch were already known to and lived by our ancestors before Sinai. The Sinai Revelation, according to this, served the purpose of introducing new elements of Judaism, as well as crystallizing, expanding and reaffirming a pre-existent halakha. The divine will was therefore manifest since the times of Noah and Abraham, and expanded at Sinai, according to Rabbinic theory. The parallel thought to this was that what they termed the Oral Law, the normative, Rabbinic halakha, served as a further extension of the divine will.

The Rabbis, furthermore, attributed *takkanot* (special enactments) to a series of historical personages such as Solomon, Ezra and Rabbi Yohanan B. Zakkai, to mention only three.[4] It is apparent from these references that our forerunners in the science of halakha were conscious of a whole realm of Jewish practice that had not been known or operative previous to having been enacted as *takkanot*.

Perhaps one of the most intriguing statements in all of Talmudic literature related to the origins of halakha is a paragraph in the tractate Hagiga.[5] That passage is not agada and hence not subject to possible relegation to a minor position. The Mishna lists various halakhot that lack dependable scriptural foundation.

It is said that all the laws related to nullifying a vow are suspended in midair, resting only upon indirect references in the Torah. Yet a whole body of law has grown up in this connection. This aftergrowth is considered *gufai Torah,* as valid as Torah itself. The Sabbath halakhot are called "a mountain resting upon the foundation of a hair," almost entirely constituted of Oral Law or Rabbinic halakha. Lest we question their authority, the Talmud reads the Mishna text to indicate that whether the halakha is explicit in Scripture or largely dependent on the Rabbinic process, both types are *gufai Torah,* as if they were an integral segment of Torah itself.[6]

The Mishnaic admonition concerning the complex corpus of Sabbath halakha is even more troubling in our time. The Sabbath itself appears to hang as if by a hair. The observance of the Sabbath, in terms of traditional requirements, has greatly diminished. It is apparent that a new concept of prohibited and permitted *melakha* (work) is long overdue. It is evident from the lack of respect accorded the Sabbath among Jews that a radical Sabbath-observance campaign is long overdue. But such a campaign would be a futile gesture in our society if it were rooted in the existing halakha. The Rabbis of the Talmud always emphasized that one should not enact regulations that the public finds troublesome or burdensome. In matters of prayer, for instance, they emphasized that one should not fatigue the congregation. These are ideas that should be employed for twentieth-century man, and looking beyond, most particularly to escort Judaism into the twenty-first century. Moderns, even those of "Catholic Israel," as Solomon Schecter called the community of believers who sought to preserve the halakha and were committed to it, are unable to scale the mountain of restrictions that make the Sabbath a day almost impossible to observe. To neglect this problem is to be guilty of serious indifference to the principle of "Live by them."[7]

The Rabbis were obviously conscious of the growth of a halakha supplementary to the Torah. They were also conscious of being involved in its evolution. Our Talmudic sages, therefore, were not Orthodox in the present-day sense of the word when it designates an attitude toward the halakha that eschews change and adjustment. They were equally not "unconscious," as those theorists propound who claim that the halakha went through an unconscious evolution. The evidence in our literature sustains the idea that the pre-Mishnaic Rabbis, then the Tannaim, in turn followed by the Amoraim, and finally the Gaonim, were all as fully aware as we are of participating in the fashioning of Jewish destiny. The statement *lo ha'midrash ha'ikar elah ha'ma'a'seh,* "not inquiry, but action, is primary," can be extended to include the idea that while academics should enjoy a central place in the scheme of things, it is also vital to legislate for action.[8] This principle the Rabbis followed in abundant measure.

Considering that it is axiomatic that the Rabbis legislated anew, and were conscious of doing so, how are we to understand their attitude toward divine revelation? Obviously how the Rabbis reconciled the doctrine of divine origin of halakha with the fact of human legislation is pregnant with meaning for us. Their point of view is clarified in a number of sources.

Levi b. Hama quoted Resh Lakish of the third century to the effect that *Torah m'Sinai* includes the "Oral Torah." R. Yohanan, a contemporary of Resh Lakish, echoed this idea. But in the latter instance it appears that *Torah m'Sinai* was revealed only to Moses. This source evidently suggests that Moses knew all future Oral Torah, but that Israel, an actual people living in real history, was yet to evolve it, regardless of and indifferent to Moses' prior knowledge. Yet even this should be qualified further with a Rabbinic opinion that Moses received only a general outline of the halakha, with the untold mysteries contained in the Torah still to be uncovered in future generations by men like Rabbi Akiva. In the world of reality the people had to unravel anew the complications of life in a halakha of which Moses may already have been apprised at Sinai.

What these remarks must suggest to us is that the sages believed Moses had been granted a brilliant revelation through which he was enabled to preview the future unfolding of halakha. In the eleventh century R. Solomon b. Isaac of Troyes (Rashi) noted that Moses was given to understand the exciting methodology of the Rabbinic scholars and the halakha that would flow from the interpretations and exegesis they would apply to their antecedents.[9]

Students of Talmudic literature will note that neither R. Asher b. Yehiel (Rosh) nor R. Isaac of Fez (Alfasi) included these Talmudic utterances in their commentaries, thereby alluding to the fact that they are not binding upon our credulity. Nevertheless, the idea that agada is optional as authoritative doctrine, though correct, should not be overstressed. Whether authoritative or not, such statements reflect Rabbinic doctrine and are therefore quite interesting in their own right. Above all, in relation to a discussion such as ours on the question of how to reconcile divine revelation and human legislation, the Rabbinic attitude toward revelation is central. This attitude seems to be that Moses was cognizant of the ultimate evolution of Jewish religious practice, but that each generation was to adapt and supplement the halakha as it understood its own requirements. Undoubtedly the Rabbis were often hard-pressed by the "orthodox" of their day to justify themselves. It was probably for such a purpose that they expressed the hyperbole that when Moses died, three thousand laws were forgotten and that at the same time one thousand, seven hundred hermeneutical proofs were also forgotten. The Rabbis saw the necessity for human halakhic development as originating immediately upon the death of Moses. They indicated this awareness when they said that Joshua, through the process of his own reasoning, arrived at the same halakha as was revealed to Moses at Sinai. Their point was that successive generations of sages "rediscovered" some of the methodological elements as well as the reasoning and decisions of their predecessors. Because they had done so, they could properly lay claim to the legitimacy of their halakha. The purpose of the very first paragraph of Mishna Avot can be understood only in the same sense. Pharisaic Judaism was seeking legitimacy, striving to vindicate its authority. And so, as an heir to a throne would trace his genealogy, the Mishna traces the authority of the Tannaim through a chain of tradition to Moses himself.[10]

The Rabbis acted with self-confidence, but nevertheless occasionally paused to justify themselves for enacting either positive or negative decrees. For such justification they cited Ps. 119:26, giving it their own peculiar interpretation. The verse declares that God should do something, since His law has been transgressed. The Rabbis, however, interpreted it to mean that it was time something be done for the Lord, even to breaking His law in order to preserve its spirit and intent. In commenting on this justification, Rashi explicitly interprets the Talmudic meaning to be, "If a time comes when a *takkanah* must be enacted for the sake of heaven, we may violate Torah itself for the required period."[11]

The above citations are really only a fraction of the many possible selections in Rabbinic sources that indicate:

(a) The Rabbis were conscious of what they were doing.

(b) The agadic idea that the Oral Law in its entirety may have been known to Moses applies at most only to Moses and nevertheless implies that Israel had to rediscover it through human agency and supplement it in each generation.

(c) One can modify the letter of the law in the interest of the spirit of tradition.

(d) Medieval halakhists and scholars, such as Rashi, went along with these propositions.

Thus the Rabbis claimed that the Sinai Revelation was a privilege granted to Moses as dean of the Prophets. But to affirm this is not to affirm anything more. The other side of the coin is that the post-biblical halakha remained an unknown quantity in Judaism until in each phase of development, the sages assembled in the academies, or the rabbinic judges in the course of handing down decisions, forged the new halakha. This was incorporated in the body of literature that has come down to us in the form of Tannaitic Midrashim, the *Midrashai Halakha* (works of halakhic exegesis from the schools of both Rabbis Akiva and Ishmael, such as Mekhilta, Sifra or Torat Kohanim, and Sifre), Tosephta, Beraitot and Mishna. All these were further elaborated in the Talmud, the conclusions being consistently arrived at in the rigorous debating fields of life. Some of the data included in these works naturally came down as inherited tradition—tradition, we might even concede, that dated from Abraham. But a very large portion of it was case-law legislation and transformation of precedent into norm. Additionally a goodly segment of it consisted of affirmative *takkanot,* enactments of new practices, or *gezerot,* the enactment of prohibitions. *Takkanot* and *gezerot* are different from other evolutionary segments of the halakha in that they resemble "executive decree" more than legislation or the products of judicial review.[12]

The Rabbis felt no compunction in continuing this work. Although from time to time we encounter, as I remarked previously, what appears to be a felt need to justify their activity, this was more probably a response to Sadducean prodding. Outside of Sadducean circles, there never really arose a serious challenge to the basic Rabbinic prerogative to be a partner in the expansion of divine Torah law.

There is a well-known story of how R. Joshua triumphed over R. Eliezer on a question of halakha with the argument that Torah "is not in heaven" and therefore not even God can sway a Rabbinic decision. R. Jeremiah expanded upon this and noted that the Torah, having already been given long ago at Sinai, was not to be replaced by another heavenly voice. Thus, if an issue arises for which there is no precedent in the Pentateuch—or so it appears from the words of R. Jeremiah—we are to seek guidance in the Torah, such as the provision that one should follow the majority. But the actual halakhic conclusion must be left in the hands of the Rabbis living in a particular period of history.

Another related item to bear in mind is the Rabbinic belief that once the Torah was given to man, it became subject to human authority. As in the case of Joshua, successor to Moses, when the Israelites threatened his life and urged him to ask of God the laws forgotten when Moses died, he replied, "It is not in heaven." There is a further facet to this question of human authority. The Talmud stresses that patience and consideration for the masses are marks of priority in authority. Thus the words of Bet Shammai (the school of Shammai) were considered as inspired and as sacred as the words of Bet Hillel (the school of Hillel), yet the halakha usually remained in accordance with the latter because its adherents evinced patience and leniency.[13]

Finally, it is extremely illuminating that the Rabbis themselves used the term *somkhim* or *asmakhta,* signifying that we may rely on a certain verse or that a given nonscriptural halakha is supported by scriptural warrant. They therewith taught us that these laws were not Torahitic but merely related to Torah by an ingenious hermeneutical methodology. They were nevertheless called *gufai Torah,* the essence or substance of Torah, the equivalent of scriptural law, and for that reason they enunciated the hyperbole that everyone who violated Rabbinic law was guilty of death. The Rabbis reasoned that since the Rabbinic halakha was "man-made" and often contemporary, the public might not be wholly responsive, as we have good reason to know in our own day. They therefore sought the additional moral weapon to induce quicker and more widespread acceptance.

From the foregoing discussion of only a fragment of the literature that can be marshaled to sustain this point of view, there are many among us who conclude that a belief in Revelation does not impair modern Rabbinic power or authority to modify Jewish practice. Whether we believe that only the word *Anokhi,* "I am," shattered the stillness of Sinai and constituted the totality of the mystery of divine communication with the mind of man, or that the entire Pentateuchal legislation represents the inspiring radiation of God into the mind of Moses, or whether we argue that certain distinctly limited passages of the Pentateuch are the words of God, has no ultimate bearing upon the right to champion the mutability of Jewish practice. To put it perhaps more cogently, what I am here propounding is that acceptance of the dogma of Revelation does not imply acceptance of a parallel "orthodox" doctrine, the immutability of Jewish religious law. In the words of Professor A. J. Heschel:

> The word was given once, the effort to understand it must go on forever. To study, to examine, to explore the Torah is a form of worship, a supreme duty. For the Torah is an invitation to perceptivity, a call for continuous understanding.[14]

We may conclude further that not only may the modification, supplementation and expansion of Jewish religious practice be

undertaken by human agency, but more, it is upon human agency
that the wreath of authority has been placed. It is clear that the
ancient and medieval sages were not merely "interpreters" or
"commentators" but innovators—bold, imaginative and courageous
men who accepted the Torah's "invitation to perceptivity" and
thereby enabled Jews to live by Torah for two thousand years.
There are any number of post-Talmudic innovations that we can
point to in the realm of *orah hayyim* (ritual practice). It was
such innovations in the realm of synagogue worship customs and
the liturgy itself that enabled us to introduce such modern practices as the use of instrumental music at worship and the right of
confimation for our young people. There are similarly a large
number of Talmudic practices that have become obsolete or pre-
Talmudic laws that have been legislated out of existence by the
Talmudic Rabbis or their successors, which equally enable us
to assert that we are in the authentic tradition when we discard
certain obsolete or unreasonable practices or allow others to fall
into desuetude. Nobody would today seriously attempt to enforce
the ban on *mamzerim* (children of adulterous or incestuous relations) entering into Jewish marriage, and very few would consider
prohibiting the remarriage of a widow without her having undergone *halitza* (ritually freeing the encumbered sister-in-law from
the necessity of levirate marriage). We would no more stress the
priestly prohibitions, such as a person of *kohenite* descent being
forbidden to marry a divorcee. As a matter of fact, both the
Reform movement in its abandonment of this segment of halakha
and the Conservative movement in a series of responsa in recent
years have already transmogrified the practices here referred to.
The problem of the *agunah,* the woman bound to a husband who
is for all practical purposes nonexistent, was debated for decades
without seriously pondering the Talmudic statement *m'shoom
agunah akiloo bah rabanan,* that because a woman may be doomed
to the status of an *agunah,* unable to remarry, the Rabbis instituted certain leniencies in the laws of testimony. Other leniencies
could long ago have been introduced as well. Nevertheless, although this was an agonizing area of halakha and relief was long
overdue, the necessary adjustments have now been made within

the tradition. Many another example crying for reasonable adjustment can be cited. History alters conditions. Changed circumstances and environments under which Jews live inevitably influence and stimulate departures and innovations in religious practices and procedures, and these ought to be reflected in the official halakha of the time and place.[15]

The belief that Jewish law is in a special category which renders it unchangeable by human agency (as distinct from the doctrine of the immutability of the Torah itself as expressed in the thirteen principles of Maimonides) is not historical. It is not warranted by tradition and is a late medieval and early modern form of Sadducaism or Karaism. The present-day "Orthodox" insistence that Jewish religious law cannot substantially be modified in accordance with a modern perceptivity to meet twentieth-century standards of aesthetics and the psychological needs of modern man is not at all orthodoxy in the true sense of that word.

Essentially, there were always historically at least two major schools of thought, and so it is on the contemporary scene. There was the Sadducaic, or static, Judaism, and the Pharisaic, or dynamic, Judaism. The former rejected change; the latter accepted and welcomed ongoing adjustment. The essence of Sadducaic error was not that it was what might be termed a heresy. On the contrary, Sadducaic Judaism was conservatively traditional. Sadducees insisted on a literal interpretation of Scripture and used the principle *dibra Torah k'lashon b'nai adam** to reject Pharisaic methodology of deriving new interpretations for the halakhic innovation from unusual expressions, repetitious terms or superfluous words. Furthermore, they objected to giving post-scriptural halakha an authority remotely as compelling as that of Scripture. They admitted that post-scriptural traditions had arisen but insisted that these were in accordance with Deut. 17:9, which gave the right of legislation or judicial change only to the priestly teachers and judges and not to the lay scholars who were emerging during and after Maccabean times. Basically this is the problem of Orthodoxy in our era. It eschews reinterpretation and ad-

---

*The Torah speaks in the language of men.

justment of its own "written law," the sixteenth-century code, the *Shulhan Arukh,* and although it will admit that new approaches have been taken since 1565 and new practices introduced, it reserves the right to make such innovations to members of its own class, scholars who have received ordination within the Orthodox sphere.

The lay teachers who became Pharisees interpreted Deut. 17:9 not to limit the right of interpretation to priests alone but to include any teachers who served the people in that capacity. They conceived of the Torah as sovereign and of the Torah's allowing for the discovery of hermeneutical rules by which to apply it to life in all ages. But to establish the full and compelling authority of the post-scriptural halakha, they insisted that everything that was derived from the Torah through the legitimate means of interpretation and application was the equivalent of Torah, or as sometimes expressed, *gufai Torah,* the substance of Torah.

This, again, is the position of dynamic Judaism in every age. It recognizes the supremacy, not of a class but of tradition itself, and affirms that all evolving tradition is equally sacred and compelling. As Lauterbach has written of the Pharisees, they "did not become the slaves of the law, but rather the masters of it." This was the singular distinction between the Sadducees and the Pharisees, and this remains the singular distinction in modern times between the so-called Orthodox and non-Orthodox.[16]

The chain of development in Judaism has been the dynamic one from Torah through Mishna and Talmud through medieval codes to the modern exegesis and innovation in non-Orthodox circles where scholars strive to keep Judaism viable. It might appear to the average lay reader a paradox, but in truth it is the non-Orthodox segments of religious Jews, whether they are Conservative or Reform, Reconstructionist or Transcendentalist, who strive to transcend all the denominations, in which segment I count myself, who are the truly orthodox Jews of our time.[17]

The whole principle of halakha is based on the idea of erecting a limit beyond which we must not go or of setting standards for the infusion of piety in our midst.[18] But the fabric of halakha is worthless if our limits are so restrictive as to result in everyone's violating them, or if the requirements of halakha are so impossible of attainment as to meet with wholesale neglect. We must not adopt a stance of modifying simply on principle. The philosophy of flexibility in halakha should not be construed to imply chaos. It may be necessary at times to balance permissive legislation with new restrictive boundaries or to replace abolished rites with new customs. A recent example of this very process was evident in the Rabbinical Assembly's Law Committee. A permissive attitude has been in vogue for years toward weddings during the Sephira period from Passover to Shavuot. While so-called Orthodox tradition has for the most part prohibited marriages during the seven-week period, Conservatives practice the restricted weddings only during the second of Iyar to the day before Lag B'omer, the 33rd day of the 49-day period. The Orthodox restriction was based on the old notion that these days were calamitous ones, when, according to legend, the ever-quarreling students of Rabbi Akiva died of a plague. On the other hand, in 1969 the committee, recognizing that this explanation of the Sephira period is not historical, expanded its permissiveness and allowed marriages for the entire period. However, the committee also instituted a hitherto nonexistent restriction on marriages during the weekend preceding and including the 27th of Nisan in remembrance of the twentieth-century Holocaust.[19]

Permissive legislation is a desideratum for our time. But because an evangelism for higher standards in Jewish life is also a profound need, we should look to new halakha in order to both discard old, obsolete restrictions and create new, spiritually meaningful customs. In either case, the proponents of dynamic Judaism will do a disservice to twenty-first-century Jews and Judaism if they keep an ear to the ground for organized Sadducaic opposition. We must be original, bold and creative and act on the presupposition expressed by Heschel, that Judaism is based "upon a minimum of revelation and a maximum of interpretation."[20] Judaism is a fellowship of faith, and we must emphasize that this faith will not be maintained as an effective instrument in our lives unless we bring God into our daily life-style through the process of an imaginative halakha.

Chapter III

HALAKHA AS
A MODERN PROBLEM

A FUNDAMENTAL TRUTH that inheres in every civilization is that it grows, even if only imperceptibly. A concomitant of this axiom of history is that a variety of factors inspires diverse insights and stimulates the society's evolution into a particular direction. If Sophocles did not jar Athenian civilization, Solon did; and while the legacy of a Sinclair Lewis might remain ambiguous, there can be no doubt that the school of John Dewey will long remain a determinant in the evolution of American education, and consequently of the American philosophy of society. A novelist or dramatist might merely mirror the tenor of a given period of history, but the philosopher sometimes and the lawgiver usually provide real direction to society. The people are frequently moved to bring forth a folk custom; but more typically, a "law" or a suggested procedure for doing something a certain way or reacting to a given problem in a particular manner originates at the top and percolates downward. The great scholar of American law Roscoe Pound has similarly commented that "to a certain extent, greater at some times than at others, custom is formative law."[1] This is true in all cultures and in Jewish halakha.

In the midst of more recent cultural interpretations in which the "people" and such elements as "folk custom" have been overemphasized, social anthropologists and cultural historians have often overlooked the "great man" element in history. When undervaluing the individual personality as a decisive force in history, it is not difficult to lose sight of such men as Moses, Akiva, Hillel and Rabbi Yohana B. Zakkai in Judaism, or their ancient equivalents in pagan and Christian society, such as Solon, Augustus and Paul, to mention only a few directors of history who were more than mere expressions of their societies.

Halakha, as has been indicated in a previous chapter, is the characteristic feature of Judaism. But it is not unique to Judaism. All ancient societies possessed a halakha that governed religious, civil and criminal law. Furthermore, we have sufficient knowledge of the evolution of all these ancient codes to be able to asseverate that they were directed by the sheer weight of individual sages or lawgivers. When English "common law" was formulated in the twelfth century, it was not composed simply of the practices of some nebulous "folk" but included the law of the old Anglo-Saxon tribes, church law, Roman law and Norman law. The Angevin Henrys "directed" this law in no small measure, as did Frederick II, for example, in his Sicilian domains. "Direction" and "evolution" are therefore two supplementary aspects of development, two independent ingredients of social growth that harmonize to give fullest expression to a particular civilization. This conception holds true in Judaism no less than in other systems of thought and life.[2]

History is defined by the philosopher Woodbridge as "the career of things in time." He conceived history as having pragmatic purpose, as material used for the progressive realization of spiritual ends. History helps man to live in the light of the past and therefore contributes to his living a life of intelligence. Woodbridge insisted that continuity in history is not necessarily movement from the lower to the higher and that the chronological positon of an event or idea gives it no claim to preeminence. For instance, science, as we understand it, is later than what we call superstition. But what we term superstition was, after all, the science of previous ages. We have no right, from the standpoint espoused by Woodbridge, to make the value judgment that science is better. Man in every age proceeds with what is at hand, and because human history is largely aspirational, man makes a conscious effort to make life what it might be and is not. Thereby man participates in history. "History is, then, not only the conserving, the remembering, and the understanding of what has happened: it is also the completing of what has happened."[3] This, in another way, asserts the role of man in directing the evolution of a society.

The axiom of history is at the root of the problem halakha constitutes in our time. It has been previously noted that in the matter of halakha, we are immediately confronted with the conflict between divine revelation and human authority. But the confrontation also takes place on another level. The question that must be answered is, To what extent may men direct the halakha to respond to the parochial needs of a given society in a particular period, and to what extent shall we leave it alone so that presumably, like water, it will find its own level? The crucial fact is that although we may prefer catholicity in our halakha, so that Jews throughout the world and through history will enjoy horizontal and vertical unity, the North American community is challenged by unique problems owing to the intellectual milieu of our time and the socio-political ideas of our place. No Jewish community in history has ever been faced with precisely the same loss of faith both quantitatively and qualitatively, nor lived in an environment utterly alien to the authoritarian Jewish *kahal* system. This means that neither the corpus of belief and law nor the social organization of the past can be renewed and revived. It means that something new, a new direction, must be fashioned.

Matthew Arnold once wrote:

All the world is, by the very law of its creation, in eternal progress; and the cause of all the evils of the world may be traced to that natural, but most deadly error of human indolence and corruption, that our business is to preserve and not to improve.[4]

This is no less true in Judaism and in particular in the realm of halakha. There can be no doubt that Judaism was saved during the Babylonian Captivity after 586 B.C.E. because our Prophets of the time understood the universal possibilities of Judaism and transcended the older territorial and cultic limitations of ancient religion. The generation of the sixth century before the Common Era neither attempted to preserve the past nor despaired over its disappearance, and thereby saved the future. The same may be asserted for the generation of the second century of the Common

Era. Despair or a conservative narrowness bent upon saving what was left would have ended, like Samaritan Judaism, in a cultural indolence that would have caused Judaism to perish. The great new intellectual, technological and socio-political developments since the nineteenth century place before us once again the alternative of "preserving" or "improving."

We cannot escape the fact that the new intellectual currents of the nineteenth century opened up such avenues in philosophy, anthropology and archeology leading to profound new studies in comparative history and religion that, in the words of the historian Freeman, it marked "a stage in the progress of the human mind at least as great and memorable as the revival of Greek and Latin learning." The reference, of course, is to the late-medieval enlightenment that brought forth the modern era. But perhaps the famed classicist Jowett came even closer to the cogency all this has in halakha when he said, "The diffusion of a critical spirit in history and literature is affecting the criticism of the Bible in our own day in a manner not unlike the burst of intellectual life in the fifteenth and sixteenth centuries."[5]

These men, on their more rarefied level, anticipated the great cultural explosion through which we are living today: the accumulation of vast masses of information: archeological, documentary and interpretive. This has been true of the halakha no less than in the disciplines of history or biblical criticism. The sixteenth century required significant strides, and men of the stripe of Joseph Karo and Moses Isserles provided the felt need of that day. The traumatic expulsion from Spain had taken place; Jews were in the process of migration and new settlement in North Africa, Eastern Europe and the Middle East. Poland and Turkey had invited the migrants, and many accepted the welcome. The chaos and confusion during the transition century constituted a challenge that was met by the Karo-Isserles response, supplemented by a burst of vigorous secondary commentary and codification. It is not at all accurate to assess their efforts as merely an attempt to "preserve" the tradition in a time of confusion. On the contrary, they presented all the new data in their works to update and contemporize the halakha for the common man. A similar effort is needed in our time. The Holocaust, the Restoration of Israel, the information revolution, all constitute a distinct challenge in our time that requires that the most earnest endeavor be to re-examine the whole vast realm of halakha with a view to updating and contemporizing Jewish religious practice in the home, in the synagogue and in the community, as well as to present to Jews the halakhic view of current public issues of general moral significance. Jews ought to reflect in their behavior that which halakha teaches on such questions as new sexual morality, medical science, war and peace, poverty, the pollution of God's world, and efforts in outer space. If Judaism has nothing to say to modern man, to what avail is the preservation of the heritage?

This problem must be given thought because we believe that the improvement of Judaism is a prerequisite for preserving it at all. The halakha is the key to this proposal because halakha is the form which expresses the essence of Judaism. Halakha will help direct and guide man on how to react or respond to the problems and issues of the day, how to fulfill what we regard as man's noble aspirations or the will of God, and how to expand the blessings of the universe. It is theology, or the philosophy of religion, which will help those with the intellectual curiosity to satisfy their search for a "why," but it is the halakha which will make possible the "how to live" in our world and the concretization of the moral imperative.

It is a commonplace to affirm that the significant interdenominational struggle in Judaism today is precisely on this question of how to express the essence, what should and should not or need and need not be done to express one's "Jewishness." Even halakhic libertarians sponsor some form of halakha because it is utterly impossible to live a way of life without what Rabbi Finkelstein has called "action-symbols."

Obviously "action-symbols" imply acts which have their symbolic value. Unless the symbolism is cogent and inspiring, it loses its value and the action is no longer a symbol. It therefore becomes axiomatic that for halakha to be spiritually meaningful, we must take a pragmatic-historic attitude toward it. We can no longer afford the luxury of the obsession of working within the framework of halakha as that was understood until the middle of this century.

When the Committee on Jewish Law of the Rabbinical Assembly (Conservative) added the term "standards" to its name, it was implicitly signifying that there was a realm beyond the framework of halakha that required our searching inquiry and serious attention.

To inaugurate a new era in halakha, however, will not be simple. The first task will have to be a comprehensive program of what the Talmud calls *pok hazi ma d'ama diber,* "examine what the public is practicing." This will have to commence with a comprehensive survey of what is still meaningful and renewable in Jewish life. Once a relatively extensive understanding of the common core of halakhic observance is acquired, it might be possible to analyze and evaluate it so that we might more scientifically approach the future halakha. We would naturally find that some facets of the halakha are wholly neglected by the overwhelming majority of Jews who profess adherence to denominations other than the ultratraditionalist segments. We will also find that certain elements of tradition, such as the Passover Seder or an awareness that a Jewish divorce ought to be acquired before remarriage in the event of a civil divorce, are still widely observed among all segments of Jews. Once this data is appreciated, we will better understand what we can extend or reinvigorate, and what we must allow to fall into desuetude or even actively discard so as to preserve intellectual integrity and spiritual credibility. We will then also begin to fathom the most serious facet of the problem: what significant areas of Jewish observance require totally new rituals, and what vital areas of socio-political morality require totally new halakhic guidelines.

Naturally, a set of criteria will be required to help us in evaluating the old halakha and in recommending the new. These various criteria, as I grasp them, would basically be oriented toward two all-embracing spheres. The first is the historic and the second is the personal. The historic sphere is concerned with the vertical relationship between Jews or Jewish communities in any given time and those of previous and future ages, as well as with

the horizontal relationship between contemporary Jewish communities in any given place and Jews and Jewish communities of
other places. There must be continuity and coordination with
what we do today and what other Jews did yesterday, with what
we do here and what other Jews do elsewhere.[6] Even a cursory
examination of history will reveal that while there have been
sudden and distinct shifts in Jewish practice from one period to
another, the reality of continuity always provided authentic historic legitimacy for the change. For instance, the cessation of the
sacrificial cult resulted in a new form of worship: prayer. But
prayer had been used with the sacrificial cult, and the synagogue
in which prayer was thenceforth conducted was an institution
which existed simultaneously with the Jerusalem Temple and its
cult. The priesthood lost its prerogative and function but retained
certain vestiges of its role, such as *birkat kohanim,* the blessing
of the congregation by the descendants of priests during Musaph
services, or in the Holy Land, even at daily worship. When this
ritual was eliminated from the modern liturgy, the Rabbi, the
spiritual leader who stood in the place of the old priest, continued
to use the ancient priestly benediction as the form in which to
invoke God's blessing upon the congregation. This is what is meant
when we speak of continuity. The blessing ordained in Scripture
to be used by the spiritual leader of ancient times, is still used
by the spiritual leader today, albeit in a different setting. This
same awareness of the need for continuity was undoubtedly behind the Rabbinic wording of the *Amidah,* the silent devotion
which is said in a standing position. This was a totally new prayer
which was unknown in biblical times. But the Rabbis devised
the sense of continuity if only by arousing a relationship to history
by using the formula "God of our fathers, the God of Abraham,
the God of Isaac, and God of Jacob." Although these words were
not a usual formula in blessings, which normally contained the
words *melekh ha'olam,* "king of the universe," rather than "God
of our fathers," they not only connected the Jew with the Patriarchs, they evoked the manifestation of God to Moses at the
burning bush. Continuity, therefore, does not require "sameness"
and does not induce "unchangingness." It merely signifies that

what we do today and here should relate us to the past and to other places.[7]

The second major sphere of criteria for halakha should be the Personal. This has to encompass the relationship of individual experiences, both intellectual and emotional, toward the act required by halakha. We must also consider the spiritual benefit that may accrue to the person fulfilling the mitzvah, the halakhic obligation. Obviously a halakhic particular cannot be taken seriously if it does violence to our intellectual honesty, just as Jewish institutions should not be supported if they do violence to our ethical norms. Another facet to the Personal criteria will be, as a matter of course, the aesthetic. This has its effect on our emotions. Our observances should naturally be designed to satisfy the normal human craving for beauty and symmetry, for harmony or even dissonance, depending on the individual. Music should be able to speak to the modern soul. Synagogue architecture, art and drama would have to be explored as a means of coming to grips with the problem of aesthetics in the modern halakha. This is all most certainly in accord with Rabbinic emphasis on the concept of *hidur mitzvah,* "beautifying a mitzvah."[8]

Finally, modern halakha, no less than ancient halakha, will be well directed into channels that elevate and inspire man to moral motivation. It should enhance the individual and provide him with ethical insights and objectives. In another chapter of this book there is more fully discussed the underlying philosophy of halakha that obtained in Talmudic times. That philosophy can be summed up in the phrase *imitatio dei,* "the imitation of God," seeking to fulfill those attributes by which we characterize the Lord, in recognition of our being in the divine image. This is in a sense the summary provided by Abba Sha'ul. When the Israelites safely crossed the Sea of Reeds after the Exodus from Egypt, Moses led them in the famous song recorded in chapter 15 of Exodus. On the verse "This is my God and I shall glorify Him," an unknown sage inquired, "How can man glorify God?" And Abba Sha'ul replied that it meant, "We try to approximate Him; for example, as He is gracious and compassionate, we too should strive to be gracious and compassionate."[9] This is the objective of halakha, to approximate the divine image through human behavior. This alone leads to the fulfillment of God's purpose at Sinai, the creation of the Kingdom of God on earth which means also to create a "Kingdom of Priests and a Holy People."

Although this problem of how to approach halakha, which agonizes us today, is peculiarly modern in certain aspects of it, nevertheless it has always constituted a challenge in Jewish life. We must understand that there has rarely been any question in any segment of Judaism about the need for a form of halakha, the idea that Jewish life requires some form of halakha as its basic structure. The dissension throughout history has been rather over whether halakha is to be static or dynamic, over precisely how the halakha is to be dealt with in any given period. The Sadducees had their halakha as well as did the Pharisees, and the Karaites had their halakha as well as did the Rabbanites. In modern times all the denominations within Judaism have their own halakha. The question, therefore, was not whether or not Jews have halakha, but how to go about meeting the challenge that halakha confronted them with at any moment in time.

In this latter third of the twentieth century, it is probably prudent to inquire into whether the nature of the dissent has changed. In other words, has the question in some circles of believing and committed Jews—"Catholic Israel," as Solomon Schechter termed the faithful community—now become, Is halakha any longer valid or necessary as a concept? To determine our answer to this question we must examine the nature of halakha as a concept or as an instrument in Jewish life. This, in turn, might contribute to our improved comprehension of how to adumbrate its future. Halakha connotes stability and regularity. Professor Saul Lieberman has indicated that the term halakha was used for a fixed land tax in Babylonia. In Sifre the term halakha was used to connote a boundary marker. Taking these etymological elements into consideration, we can perhaps understand why the Talmudic Rabbis termed their case decisions and academic conclusions halakha. Aside from the generally accepted figurative implication of halakha as derived from the verb "to walk," thus implying "a way of life," it also denoted a boundary marker, a line that guided man's path in life.

Halakha, in other words, marks the spiritual guideline for piety. If one does not stay within the fixed area, or put in another way, if one does not practice a given suggestion or if one violates a prescribed act, one is disregarding guidelines for piety and loyalty to faith, and is risking one's spiritual life.[10]

This connotation of halakha as "guideline" is, in my opinion, precisely what the Rabbis had in mind when they advised "make a *si'yag* [hedge] for the Torah." It is my contention that this was a positive and not a negative admonition. The sages were not urging the establishment of cumulative restrictions. They were simply suggesting "guidelines." Such "hedges" or lines that fix the spiritual area can be positive as well as negative. Thus, to further the Torah's admonition to observe the Sabbath, the sages evolved a positive form of observance aside from the prohibitions. In other words, the *si'yag,* the elements that fenced in the Sabbath, were not merely restrictive but positive, enhancing the Sabbath with beauty and expanded worship to add to the feelings of piety and holiness. This meaning of "hedge" can and should be understood in the connotation of a hedge for a property: to beautify it and add to its grace and color. I am not unaware of the negative meaning historically given to that phrase "make a hedge to the Torah." But the exclusive validity of this meaning can be questioned. Most especially can we raise the question of how we shall employ it as halakhic advice in our own time.

Let us consider when and by whom this advice was uttered. It is quoted in the Mishna in the name of the "Men of the Great Assembly." Regardless of who these men were or when and whether the "Assembly" as such existed and functioned, historically the sayings attributed to them are to be understood as pre-Maccabean. Probably these sayings originated during the third century before the Common Era, but they could have originated as early as the fifth century, from the time of Ezra. The religion of the Torah entered into its development and expansion from the time of Ezra, and the vital endeavor that preoccupied the sages, as it still does today, was the development of a post-scriptural halakha. This in itself was creating a "hedge," a system of procedures and practices that was to adorn, not only protect, the Torah. All the advice given in that same paragraph of the Mishna, to deliberate, to set up disciples, and to create the hedge, was advice in the field of methodology transmitted from the Sopherim, the "Scribes," as the sages were called during the pre-Pharisaic period, thence to the Pharisees and on to the Talmudic teachers. It can be understood basically as the program of the post-biblical school of scholars who were the forerunners of Talmudic Judaism.

It is apparent that even the early Rabbis of Tannaitic days were concerned about the meaning of erecting hedges to the Torah. Thus we find that Rabbi Hiyya of the third century admonished the scholars not to make the fence more important than the substance to be protected. And his son, Hizkiah, probably having learned the lesson well from his father, taught that he who adds, detracts. The idea expressed by Rabbi Hiyya was, as is clear from *Avot of Rabbi Nathan,* that if the fence is too high it may become top-heavy and collapse upon the plant it is intended to protect. There can be no doubt that the restrictive encumbrances of the halakha, accumulated over the centuries, had this effect on the substance of Judaism in the nineteenth and twentieth centuries. Halakha must therefore be seen as that which adorns our spiritual values and assists us in acting out the drama of religious symbolism. This is a compelling reason to retain halakha as a functioning concept in Judaism at the same time that we labor to bring its particulars into consonance with contemporary spiritual insights.[11]

The problem then becomes how to modify and adjust the halakha with a view to raising the standards of Jewish spiritual life and coming closer to the spiritual fulfillment for which we strive. To arrive at a meaningful process, it is useful to examine how a practice became halakha in ancient times. Herman L. Strack has a useful and succinct outline of four major procedures which led to halakha. This first was a relatively elementary development, alluded to previously in this book, that custom developed into law. The second was that the strength of authority possessed by an individual scholar was such that when he vouched for a halakha, it was declared to be such. A third way a given practice was elevated to the status of halakha was to find a scriptural support for it. And the fourth way reviewed by Strack was that a majority vote determined it.[12]

All these four ways to elevate a practice to the status of halakha are still open to us. Orthodox Judaism may not yet be prepared to accept the premise that halakha must be dynamic, requiring constant supplementation. But those who are zealous for the survival of Jewish spiritual values will have to recognize this as "a time to do for the Lord" even if it results in unfortunate polemics and temporary disruption of cooperative efforts in the areas of general public issues. There will always be a challenge to the authority of any man or group proposing active adjustment or innovation in halakha. But in reply to this we must invoke the statement of Hillel, who told his generation in Palestine, "What caused me to come from Babylon and become your *Nasi,* your presiding scholar? Your own indolence: the fact that you ignored the two great men of your generation, Shemaya and Avtalion."[13] Those who prefer the static concept of halakha lead too somnolent a religious life to be justified in opposing the diligence of others.

As we learn from many Talmudic sources, and as was discussed in the chapter which considers the paradox of divine revelation and human authority, once the Rabbis supplemented ancient practice they regarded their new halakha as equally binding with previous halakha, even that of the Torah. This is illustrated with particular force in the formulas we use for blessings. We praise God for sanctifying us by ordaining certain rites, when it was actually the Rabbis who instituted the practices.

Beyond adaptation and adjustment there was *minhag*—custom —and *takkanah*—special enactments. In this the principle of public practice was especially active. New customs arose that were considered equally legitimate with those of greater antiquity. And variety rather than uniformity was the historic reality. Geographic locale often determined the halakha. Spanish Jews never accepted the *takkanot,* the enactments of the synod called by Rabbenu Gershom of Mayence. Or, for another instance, Moses Isserles, who typified the Ashkenaz point of view, that of Jews who resided in Christendom, discussed certain practices related to burial and mourning, as well as other areas, which were apparently unknown to Joseph Karo, author of the *Shulhan Arukh* who reflected Sephardic practice, the custom of Jews generally residing in Islamic lands. Isserles approvingly cited an earlier authority, Maharil (R. Jacob Moelln), to the effect that "the customs of our fathers is Torah."[14]

The critics of a dynamic halakha forever misread history. When Lord Acton, an otherwise erudite scholar and philosopher of history, saw the Civil War descend upon the American states, he wrote an essay in 1861 wholly predicated on the mistaken notion that the Union was dead. So too the critics of dynamic halakha constantly foretell the demise of halakha and of Judaism itself as the inevitable price of change and innovation. The recurring erroneous argument is the spurious question, Where will we draw the line? But history teaches the contrary. In contrast to Sadducees and Karaites who disappeared because they defended a static concept of halakha, the proponents of change and dynamic halakha always flourished as the mainstream of Jewish history. It is wrong to think that by preserving a static approach to halakha, at least a "saving remnant" of some supposed "authentic" Jews will be preserved. For when the Prophets used the term "saving remnant," they actually spoke of a group of "modifiers," people who came up from Babylon to revolutionize and transform Judaism.

The Rabbis of the past did not hesitate to effectively abrogate Torah provisions when necessary. Throughout this book examples will be encountered. Two illustrations at this point, one touching upon ancient and the other upon medieval Judaism, will suffice. Rabbi Yohanan, the High Priest, tampered with Temple ritual even to the point of eliminating the tithe declaration called for in the Torah. His motive may have been to purify the ritual of pagan influences, as Professor Lieberman indicates. But whatever his motive, it is the fact that he eliminated a formula required by the Torah that is of utmost importance to us. In the tenth century, when Rabbenu Gershom influenced Jews to abandon polygamy, a practice permitted in the Torah, and prohibited a man from taking more than one wife, or when he and his synod required a woman's consent for a divorce, which the Torah did not require, he was blazing a path for the twentieth century. Obviously Rabbenu Gershom was convinced that the spirit of the Jewish religion which called for respect for women and constantly ameliorated their lot now validated his abrogation of Torah halakha.[15]

These examples also help us to emancipate ourselves from what is almost a metaphysical obsession that we must modify halakha "within the framework of halakha." This is not always feasible and was not always adhered to. It was often the spirit underlying Jewish practice which motivated a change beyond the framework. There are, as has been suggested previously, the two spheres of halakha, History and Personal. It is our task to preserve historic continuity and enhance the human personality. But when it is necessary to go beyond the "framework," as Rabbi Yohanan and Rabbenu Gershom did, we must.

The Rabbis examined public practice both in the positive and in the negative sense. They sought to define certain practices by suggesting *pok hazi,* that the sages examine how the people practice a given custom. This was the positive facet of the criterion of public practice. The negative facet was in their ascertaining that the public was totally indifferent to a given prohibition, in which case the Rabbis removed it.

Certain Rabbis were undecided about a ritual. For instance, in the case of which thank-you blessing should be offered after partaking of a glass of water, Rabbi Joseph suggested that they see what the people did. This is a limited situation in a minor ritual. Students of halakha might object to utilizing it as an example of the broader principle of giving consideration to public practice. They might argue that *pok hazi,* to see what the people practice, cannot affect halakha beyond relatively simple private rituals such as the one offered.

There would be objections to applying it, for instance, to the Sabbath, with the argument that if we examined public practice we could be led to abandon Sabbath observance altogether. But actually public custom and the people's will played a role in Rabbinic legislation even in relation to the Sabbath. Rabbis followed the wise policy of desisting from maintaining an *issur* (a prohibition) when it was clear that the people were no longer obeying it. An illuminating example is the prohibition of bathing in the hot springs of Tiberias on the Sabbath. The people violated this prohibition repeatedly. This led the Rabbis to categorize the prohibition as *davar she'ain omed la'hem,* "a rule that no longer mattered." Subsequently the sages permitted the people to bathe. Rather than have a law on the books consistently violated, the Rabbis felt it was both more consonant with piety and more practical to remove it. As a matter of interest, it might be noted that in this particular instance we have the combination of two criteria: public practice and public indifference.[16]

Public custom was thus one criterion for the ancients, and it can serve as a criterion for us. This is the essential meaning of continuity, for continuity cannot be limited to mere continuation of a particular ritual in its traditional form. Continuity must also apply to the method of arriving at halakha. Rabbinic concern for the public will went beyond mere consideration of the wording of a prayer. It concerned itself with their respect for the halakha and expressed itself in various ways. Here the Talmud had indicated that the sages saw that the prohibition "no longer mattered." Such indifference impressed the Rabbis who took immediate action to remove a prohibition. Another aspect to this question of the public will was that the Rabbis did not legislate too severely, always keeping in mind the principle that whatever the public could not accept was not to be enacted.[17]

Another criterion in our approach to halakha must be its harmonization with the state of our scientific or technological knowledge. The Talmud is witness to the Rabbis' consideration of their physical environment. Glass was a new product in postbiblical times. The glassblowers of Tyre and Sidon exported their wares to Jewish Palestine in early Maccabean times. The question that arose regarding these new vessels was whether glassware attracted impurity like metalware or earthenware. Scriptural halakha on purity and *kashering,* the process of making a vessel ritually fit once again, had not provided for glassware. Since glassware offered serious competition to earthenware, which could not be purified at all, the sages issued a decree that glass becomes ritually impure. Nevertheless, the Rabbis took a long, hard look at glassware as a new technological item and also decided that although it attracted ritual impurity like metalware or earthenware, it might be kashered. It is interesting that in *kashrut* too, glassware was given an independent status for use with both meat and dairy.[18]

We too must consider the modern state of knowledge, new technology, the economic environment and similar matters. We cannot fly directly in the face of science. When science operates with electricity as a form of energy and not fire, when we know that even the Talmud regarded as "fire" only that which undergoes combustion and oxidation, which are not involved in the flow of electrical energy, we most certainly should operate with this knowledge relative to the Sabbath. Similarly we would have to rethink many other traditional Sabbath restrictions regarding travel, the enjoyment of recreational facilities, perhaps even the use of money, for *oneg shabbat,* the enjoyment of the Sabbath, as distinct from commercial exchange. There is, after all, the halakhic consideration given to a variety of ideas such as *melakhah she'ain tzreekha l'gufah,* a "work" which is not needed in itself. Such ideas might be employed in our time, not to speak of more boldly applying modifications to those areas which come under the concept of *shevut,* a Sabbath prohibition which had its source in Rabbinic law and not in the Torah.[19]

Another element which has extensive application at home, in the synagogue and in the community is the question of aesthetics. Rituals should measure up to our standards of beauty and decorum. They should be so designed as to bring warmth and joy into our homes and color, drama, poetry and music at worship. The Rabbis stressed *hidur mitzvah,* the performing of a mitzvah in a beautiful manner. This principle is enunciated in no uncertain terms when Jews are urged to buy the most beautiful *lulav,* build the most decorous Sukkah and supply an ornamental Sefer Torah.[20]

Perhaps most basic of criteria would be to consider the spiritual value inherent in the halakha. In other words, when pondering the preservation of a particular practice or the introduction of a new one, we should evaluate its spiritual effect on us. Will it develop within us a greater tendency toward the fulfillment of our humanity, or will it contribute to deadening our sensitivity to God, beauty and man? The real justification, for instance, in permitting man to turn an ignition key and indirectly cause combustion in his automobile engine on the Sabbath is to allow him the opportunity to drive to synagogue, because public worship is so essential to the virtuous life. There are prohibitions in our halakha which are no longer conducive to the spiritual life, which, on the contrary, contrive to make the halakha appear so obsolete as to be unattractive as a modern guide to religious practice. These will have to be reconsidered, re-evaluated and revised. The Talmudic Rabbis sought to foster piety, to satisfy a need in people and to avoid overburdening them with standards far above their reach. They met the needs of their day, as we will see in later chapters, by taking into account public custom, the psychological need of human beings, economics, technology, aesthetics and holiness. Judaism's purpose, the Talmud averred, was "to purify man," and so the all-embracing criterion, which would incorporate many sub-criteria, was whether Judaism would make of Jews better individuals. To this end, our religious law and standards, our halakha, must contribute to purging us of the dross of our daily lives. Where halakha must be readjusted, abrogated or innovated, steps must be taken to pursue the necessary course. We must naturally approach the task with great humility and pray that the founding of a successor Talmud will meet with the blessing of God. We can no longer afford the whimsical denial of change. We cannot safely embark upon a course which will reduce our action-symbols to a quaint expression of an ethnic group, nor abandon altogether the quest for a modern halakha which will attract the personal commitment of Jews and thereby acquire historic authority.

Related to this criterion of the inherent spiritual value of a given halakha is the question of obsolescence. Halakha may be obsolete for any number of reasons. Perhaps it is a changing life-style which makes halakha obsolete. But whatever it may be, whether the style of life, intellectual growth, economics or new technology, when a rule is obviously obsolete, it ought to be abandoned. The Rabbis never hesitated to do this. For instance, it was permissible to save sacred Scriptures from a fire on the Sabbath. But this rule was a very limited one. It extended only to Scripture written in Hebrew and referred only to the Pentateuch, Prophets and Hagiographa. The same source explains that one may rescue the Hagiographa from the flames, although it is not permitted to read it on the Sabbath; and the reason it was not permitted to read Hagiographa was that indulging in such interesting and speculative literature would keep people away from attendance at the Sabbath afternoon sermon.

In the course of time both these practices were changed for compelling reasons. It became permissible to read the Hagiographa on Sabbath afternoon. And in time it was permitted to rescue from the flames even such copies of Scripture as were not written in Hebrew. Since the Hagiographa was considered a rival to afternoon sermons, it followed, as Rabbi Joseph Lifshitz, author of the commentary *Tiferet Yisrael,* indicated, that when reading it no longer prevented attendance at such sermons, reading it became permissible. He argued that in his day, the nineteenth century, since everyone came to hear the Sabbath afternoon sermon or to join a study group, or since there were places that had no Sabbath afternoon sermon, it was no longer necessary to proscribe the reading of the Hagiographa or to proscribe saving Scripture written in any language from the flames on the Sabbath. Rabbi Lifshitz considered whether such modifications of halakha were a violation of the precept that a later court cannot reverse the decision of an earlier one and concluded that rather we might consider this as a time "to act for the Lord." In other words, it would achieve more for the halakha and for piety to abandon those restrictions. Rabbi Lifshitz cited the earlier opinion of *Ba'al ha'Ma'or* as his authority on rescuing Scripture written in any language, in spite of the Mishna's having restricted it to Scripture written in Hebrew.[21]

Here we have a clear instance of extending a permissive

halakha: rescuing books from a fire and carrying them from one domain to another on the Sabbath. It was extended from limiting the permission to Scripture written in Hebrew to Scripture written in all languages. And we have a clear instance as well of a restriction: the reading of Hagiographa on Sabbath afternoon, entirely abandoned. The reason for extending one halakha and abandoning the other was the spirit of tradition. The Rabbis were not interested in barring Hagiographa, or they would have declared it apocryphal. They were simply interested in having attendance at afternoon sessions. Once the study of Hagiographa no longer constituted a threat to their objective, their prohibition lost its force. Smilarly, when it was essential that Jews be encouraged to read Scripture in any language to maintain a modicum of knowledge among them, it was considered vital to allow them to rescue their books from flames on the Sabbath. For this reason we find the law so codified in the Middle Ages.[22]

What is of some significance in these two examples is that they are both *koolot,* relaxations of the original law. This refutes the oft-repeated notion that only in modern times have changes become permissive and that we ride so roughshod over the halakha that before we know it we will have permitted ourselves out of all halakhic restrictions. In our own time we operate with any number of obsolete restrictions analogous to those we have just discussed. The traditional halakha required post-menstrual use of the *mikvah* by all Jewish women. Today very few non-Orthodox Rabbis, if any, insist upon this for their own wives or urge it upon the members of their congregation. They no longer demand the immersion of a new bride as a prerequisite for sanctifying the marriage. Yet all so-called Orthodox Rabbis and most Conservative Rabbis require *mikvah* for a gentile woman who applies for conversion. This is a limited restriction which perhaps ought to be discarded. Conservative Rabbis do not require immersion of those who have been converted without it by Reform Rabbis. The requirement of immersion in a *mikvah* for a proselyte is not biblical. It might perhaps be considered as obsolete as the prohibition on Sabbath bathing in the hot springs of Tiberias.[23]

The purpose of halakha is the idea of erecting "markers"

within which we ought to guide our spiritual life, by adorning our Torah and by setting standards for the infusion of piety in our midst. But the fabric of halakha is worthless if it becomes so restrictive as to result in everyone's neglecting it, or if there is such an excessive and complex array of practices to fulfill as to cause most people to despair of attaining the objective. We must not abolish or modify merely for the sake of change. But when necessary, for reasons of enhancing Judaism both in the sense of history and in the personal sense, for the Jewish community and for the individual, it behooves us to take the steps required. These steps will not necessarily always involve abolition or modification of old practices. There will be times when we innovate steps, both restrictive and permissive, to set the stage for the unfolding of new and meaningful traditions. Judaism is a fellowship of faith, and we must emphasize that this faith cannot be maintained as an effective instrument in our lives unless we bring God into our daily patterns through the process of a halakha that is creative and imaginative.

Chapter IV

A PROFILE OF JEWISH
RELIGIOUS PRACTICE

IN CHAPTER I, "Meditations," I wrote that Halakha is the quintessential characteristic of Judaism. For this reason halakha will have to be the *key instrument* in the coming decades through which we renew the spiritual vigor of Judaism. This chapter stresses that we require a portrait that defines the profile of halakha as it appeared in the classical Pharisaic-Talmudic age. An "instrument" must meet the needs of the task it is to perform. And the instrument we call halakha, which alone can enable the Jew to express an authentic form of Judaism, must be so developed that it will enable the coming generations to find meaning and joy in their religion.

Halakha, the guide to conduct, did not appear in the world full-grown. The Talmudic Rabbis recognized it as a constantly evolving system of practice. It is safe to say that it began in primeval times and found its first historic codified expression in the Torah. The agada records that when Joseph's brethren left Egypt to return to Canaan to prepare their families for migration to Egypt, he gave them traveling advice. The sages there imaginatively suggested that one of the tidbits of wisdom he imparted was that they not become preoccupied or distracted through discussing halakhic subjects lest they lose their way.[1] In this and many similar agadic sayings the classical sources attest to the concept that halakha was always the instrument through which the Jews and their forerunners, the Abrahamites, expressed their religion, whether in matters related to God or in matters related to their fellow men in society.

The halakha of the Torah was an attempt to formulate a constitutional framework for a wholly new set of circumstances: the emergence of a nation-state on a specific territory. We have no way of knowing precisely how much of our Torah Moses actually claimed as divine and how much the people knew to be the product of Moses and others. In accordance with the usages of the Ezra and post-Ezra period, the Torah halakha was regarded as a divinely revealed halakha and canonized as Sacred Scripture. Nevertheless, the scribes and sages continued their labors and brought forth a monumental literary legacy which not only legislated new halakha, reinterpreted old halakha and even abrogated certain obsolete practices but also defined the criteria of halakha. A survey of our Tannaitic and Amoraic sources, a legacy that spanned seven centuries from 200 B.C.E. to 500 C.E, will enable us to infer the underlying motivations that impelled the sages to act. These criteria and motivations of halakha determined what specific halakhot there were in any given generation or year and in any given geographic area. In other words, the Jews fulfilled certain norms of practice and forms of observance depending on the respective criteria used or the motivations at work, these often differing in accordance with the exigencies of time and place.

It is not difficult to portray a broad canvas of these criteria and motivations. They range from doing honor to a deceased in the halakha of *avelut* (mourning) to the consideration of economic need; from the desire to beautify religious practice (*hidur mitzvah*) to a belief in the supremacy of liberalism. My list of criteria, which tentatively number over twenty, is merely a personal preference. Others may discern more. The classification I choose to make is found in the notes to this chapter and will be discussed in following chapters.[2]

Louis Ginzberg preferred to define halakha as "conduct." He wrote, "Judaism, however, is a religion of deeds; it wants to elevate through action and so strengthen man's likeness to God." He went on in this same vein, "The *halakha*, the 'conduct of life' then, is not a mere external form; on the contrary, it is the spiritualization of everyday life."[3]

When we see halakha in this way, we can better understand the reason the sages were motivated by humane criteria that

ranged from the desire to preserve social harmony to the impulse
to honor the dead; from economic concerns to the aesthetic drive.
Halakha was the instrument through which man's life was spiritualized and beautified, and it was therefore so interpreted and
arranged that man would love it and find just reward in living
according to its recommendations. Halakha was not a yoke in
the sense of a burden. When the sources speak of the "yoke of
heaven," the "yoke of the Torah" or the "yoke of the Mitzvot,"
the term yoke must be understood as that which guided entities
that might move in potentially different directions to move in con-
cert. In other words, the "yoke" placed upon the Jew was at
once a source of self-discipline and communal identity. The yoke,
or the halakha, guided him in life's path and also enabled him
to function as a member of a faith community which practiced
similar forms. The yoke did not hold the Jew in thrall, frozen
into a stiff, unyielding routine. It allowed for flexibility and was
never permitted to become a burden. Precisely to prevent its becoming a burden the halakha was determined by the various historical, humane and aesthetic criteria.[4]

The Rabbis did not codify their halakha in the usual sense of
the word. The Mishna was not so much a "code," as conven-
tionally understood, as a handbook of reference, designed to preserve the data of the time. For the Rabbis understood what a
contemporary lawyer has written of law: "The more it is codified,
the more it is in danger of petrifying. Its primary function, to do
justice [or in Judaism, to spiritualize conduct] becomes circumscribed by rules and precedents which all too often interfere with
its attainment. . . . The journey through the forest which was to
give us shade and shelter, becomes a hazardous undertaking in
itself, and so diverts us that we may forget our original destina-
tion. . . . To become so enamored with the paraphernalia of law
as to lose sight of its noble objective is the great legal disease. I
believe the true legal philosopher tends to simplicity. He uses his
technical knowledge to clear away the obstructions. . . ."[5]

For this reason the Rabbis did not codify the halakha after
the canonization of Scripture. They preferred to allow the halakha
to grow like a luxuriant plant, flourishing and growing, and allow-

ing each generation to pluck the flowers and enjoy the fragrance exuded as it could. In their hands halakha was a living and organic process. As a matter of fact, although the theory persists as a supposed fact that the Mishna was codified by Rabbi Judah the Prince around 200 C.E., there is some question whether it ever was really published as an authoritative book such as one would expect in the case of a code of law. Professor Saul Lieberman has indicated that there is no mention anywhere in the entire Talmudic literature that a Mishna text was consulted in cases of controversies or in cases of doubtful textual renderings. Yet it was an established practice of antiquity that an authoritative volume, once published, was deposited in official archives in a temple or a library to serve as the permanent, authentic version against which any copy could be verified. The conclusion Lieberman reached, therefore, was that there was no official Mishna, and that all the references to written Mishna and statements of halakha were to private notes which carried no real authority.[6]

Compilations of such notes with brief halakhic statements began to appear as early as the third century. They were necessary as the academic material and court cases proliferated. Among the originators of it may have been Simon the Just, or Simon II, who is mentioned in Avot 1:2 and probably was a proto-Mishna teacher. The Maccabean uprising, coupled with the Antiochean persecution which produced Vietnam-like conditions in Palestine, with populations uprooted and widespread guerrilla warfare, had its ramifications in the neglect of study and the suspension of stable religio-socio-economic conditions. Undoubtedly this imperiled the preservation of halakha and the continuity of Judaism. The Mishna form of reference manuals would provide an easier memory-system and quicker access for the harried student. Simon II was an active religious leader, the mentor of the earliest Mishnaic teachers, such as Antigonos and Yose b. Yo'ezer and the latter's colleague, Yose b. Yohanan. Yose b. Yo'ezer is the earliest scholar in whose name a halakha is cited.[7] These men lived through the Maccabean upheaval and undoubtedly early perceived the need for developing what they later came to call Mishna. The third century B.C.E. was one of great tumult and hazardous conditions of life. It was a period of much violent contest between the Ptolemaic and Seleucid empires of Egypt and Syria, a century of oft-repeated historical competition between East and West. The Mediterranean world was Hellenized, and there were vast new changes in technology, industry, art and politics. In Jewish life the priesthood declined and lay leadership emerged, synagogues proliferated, and the people increasingly turned to nonpriestly religious leaders for advice and guidance. Furthermore, these halakhic notes were required even more during the first century B.C.E., when controversies between Pharisees and Sadducees deepened and the Pharisaic student needed an easy reference and a pithy and cogent formula with which to counter Sadducaic arguments about what the halakha was.

Professor Lieberman has indicated further that the "official" Mishna recited by the Tanna in the Academy became controversial after the divergence of the schools of Hillel and Shammai. The consequence was that a revision or updating of the compilation was undertaken by Rabbi Akiva. He strove to systematize a correct compilation. After this each Tanna recited the text as decided upon by Rabbi Akiva. In effect this meant that a new Mishna was in circulation. The disciples of Rabbi Akiva produced variants of this Mishna, and subsequently Rabbi Judah the Prince arranged for a new edition, largely utilizing the version of Rabbi Meier. It was his Mishna that, as Lieberman wrote, "was virtually canonized," and all the other Mishnayot were declared *beraitot,* that is, extracanonical, or unauthoritative.[8]

Why did the Mishna of Rabbi Judah not share the fate of previous collections? It would appear to me to be the consequence of power. As the effective governor of Roman Judea, he was able to establish his Mishna almost as a virtual code of law, Roman style. This Mishna, declared authoritative, was disseminated in Babylonia as well and became the source of all future discussion and interpretation.

The pupils of Rabbi Judah who disseminated his Mishna, however, disseminated it not as a "code of law" but rather as a "law text." They and their Rabbinic successors did not recognize a truly canonical halakha and even altered the text of the Mishna when necessary.[9] So far as halakha was concerned, they fully expected their own findings and decisions to carry the same weight as those of previous scholars. For in truth the process, as Lieberman has interestingly shown, was similar to that of the Greek and Roman commentators of juristic texts. They cited the text and interlaced the citations with their running commentary in much the same way as our halakhic *midrashim* did with Scripture.[10] The Mishna and Talmud, therefore, should be seen for what they really were, vast literary compilations embodying the halakhic literature but not codifying a conclusive or authoritative halakha. The Rabbis expected that out of their deliberations viable halakha would be inferred and practiced. To make this halakha viable they allowed themselves the luxury of being influenced by a large number of criteria, all of which might be subsumed under the general heading of humanitarian and historic concerns and all of which would meet the test of the scientific data available to them. The Rabbis regarded the halakha not as mere duty but as a mitzvah. As R. Travers Herford has written, "The duties enjoined in the halakha were called *Mitzvot,* i.e., commandments. And the essence of a *Mitzvah* was that it was a thing which God willed to have done. It was an occasion of service, a means offered man by which he could in a given instance please God."[11]

Just as the vast material that emerged during the Persian and Hellenistic periods had to be epitomized, so too the newer Talmudic literary material had to be abridged for practical use. This task was probably first undertaken during the Gaonate (a period which lasted from about 650 to 1050) by the Gaon Yehudai of Sura during the course of the eighth century. Scholars of the period often kept private notes of the lectures they heard. These notes were called *megilot starim,* literally "secret rolls," but probably signifying "private" or "apocryphal," with the intention of conveying the idea that they were not for publication and not for inclusion in what might be considered the "canonical" literature, the Talmud.[12] Louis Ginzberg inferred from a statement made by Hai, the Gaon of Pumbedita (947-1038), mentioning the "secret rolls" before Yehudai, that Yehudai was the first who turned to publication of the post-Talmudic halakhic material.[13] The product of his activity was the *Halakhot Gedolot,* the "Major Halakhot," which became the basis of much halakhic literary activity as well as of actual religious practice and observance in both the Franco-German and Hispano-Provençal centers of Jewish life.

It is instructive for our own time, when there is much confusion about proper religious practice in Judaism, exacerbated by the questionable institutionalized denominationalism from which we suffer, that Yehudai undertook his work during the period of the Karaite schism. There was a need for ready access to correct tradition, and it was impossible for the average Jew to infer a halakha from the complex Talmudic material. But again, it is evident that Yehudai did not mean his work to be some kind of ultimate "code of law," for his method was to abridge the Talmud, to epitomize its major halakhic statements and omit all the non-halakhic material. Another interesting feature of his work was that he excluded all the irrelevant halakha, that segment of the halahka which through the intervention of history or Providence had become obsolete, and was especially unrelated to the Diaspora.[14]

Yehudai's efforts were duplicated on a number of occasions during the Middle Ages. In all these cases modern literature in English refers to these works as "codes" to distinguish them from commentaries or responsa. But the term *code* too often conveys the idea of a finalized decision which *must* be obeyed. *Code* has a ring of authority about it which is unwarranted in halakha. Even the *Mishna Torah* of Maimonides, which reads like a law code, is basically an extract of the Talmud but grouped in themes and carefully organized. Though monumental in scope, it carried no special authority. On the contrary, it became a source of much controversy. The selections of halakha preferred by Maimonides often were not accepted by all scholars, and right into modern times practice follows his opinion no more than that of others. The authority of a halakhic work was only as great as the reputation of the author or his ability to persuade other scholars that his view was either historically correct or currently practical. All these "codes" were really books of reference, manuals of practice, *guides* to observance, digests, and nothing more.[15]

It is important to understand this in order to be able to accept the vast halakhic literary legacy as *not* possessed of the nature of authoritative codes. Rather, the religious practice suggested in the books of halakha should be seen as the contemporary sum total of religious experience still relevant and out of which selection may be made. Inevitably authentic Judaism will require that this selection be based on criteria that match the profile of halakha portrayed in the classical works. Thus when the Gaonim ruled that a husband might marry a second wife only with the consent of the first, in an age before polygamy was banned, they were quite aware that they were acting contrary to the Talmud. But as Louis Ginzberg put it, in this and other cases, "They felt secure in the other consciousness that they were acting in its spirit."[16] The spirit of the Talmud and the historic trend of the halakha of domestic relations was toward alleviating the disabilities and elevating the status of women.

Considering that it was in this spirit that halakhists always operated, and should still govern themselves today, every halakhic change which is within the spirit of its own history and of the Talmud is legitimate. It is therefore no surprise that the sages of the Talmud never contemplated themselves as ultimate authorities, nor were they prepared to accept subordination to the Torah. Thus we have examples where the Torah might require one course of action and the Rabbis set that aside for another. Even if they rationalized that the halakha was not a Torahitic one but a Rabbinic one, they insisted on the strong power of the Rabbinic halakha as equal to the force of the Torah's with the phrase *asoo hizook l'divraihem,* "they fortified their words," and the consequence was the same as having violated a Torahitic halakha.[17]

Quite a bit more interesting and relevant to our modern halakha is the question of the absorption of substance by vessels. Meremar, successor to Rav Ashi as head of Sura during the fifth century, was asked whether all-year glazed vessels might be used on Passover. He replied that since they absorbed liquids, they could not be used for Passover, nor could they be prepared for use through a kashering process. That is, glazed vessels as they knew them in Talmudic times were to be adjudged simply as earthenware and were too absorptive to be kasherable. The question was then raised why it was that he permitted Jews to use glazed vessels that had been previously used for forbidden wine. The premise of the question as elucidated in the Talmud was that although forbidden wine was only a Rabbinic enactment, it nevertheless had the force of a Torahitic enactment, becausen *kol d'tikun rabbanan k'ain d'oraita tikun,* "all that the Rabbis enact is as if the Torah had enacted." This would imply that there could be no further use for such absorptive earthenware vessels even if what they had absorbed was only prohibited by the Rabbis. The explanation given for the permission was that wine is cold and its absorption into the walls of the vessels is not similar to the problem of the absorption of hot liquid cooked and served in the glazed vessels under consideration for Passover use.[18]

Seeing halakhic development in this light enables us to understand that great changes took place in the light of certain values. These values ultimately constituted the profile of the instrument we call halakha. Halakha is a great stream that flows on. Like a great river it continually adjusts itself to the topography, following the contours of the land through which it flows. When it must round a bend, it does so gracefully; when it must shed its tributaries, it does so smoothly. Halakha, the great river of Judaic expression, must also adjust itself to historic contours, and at times is called upon to shed certain of its practices from the mainstream to be expressed only in given geographic centers or in certain ages but not elsewhere in other times. A serious contender against traditional reluctance to relinquish forms of observance is common sense. This elementary ingredient associates itself with the movements of history and molds those movements or adjusts to them as logic and humanity require.

All this is not to neglect the caution of our sages, "make a hedge for the Torah." But one must not take that caution to the point where it becomes a disaster. The old Tannaitic commentary on *Avot* indicates that Adam made a hedge for the Torah which brought disaster upon the human race.[19] The story in Genesis relates that God enjoined Adam from eating of the tree that provided the power of moral discernment ("the tree of knowledge of good and evil") but that Eve, upon repeating that admonition to the serpent, seems to have received an additional injunction from Adam never intended by God: not to touch it.[20] The midrash explains that the serpent used this "hedge" as his opening, confounding Eve and challenging her faith and obedience by touching the tree all over and showing that nothing happened. He then issued his *coup de grâce,* urging her not to fear eating of the fruit any more than touching the tree. The consequent history of mankind is known to all of us. The "hedge" erected by Adam to prevent Eve from violating the core of the one simple halakha they had in Eden was thus the source of disaster. The point is expanded in *Avot de Rabbi Nathan,* which goes on to admonish man not to erect hedges. It uses the phrase "hedge his words," a perfectly modern expression, for then he cannot fulfill his words. Man must be lucid and explicit, set his goals and aim at them and not encumber the path with all forms of brambles supposedly set there to protect the garden, as some would interpret the nature of erecting a hedge. The same midrash also comments that a person should never make a fence more significant than the original lest all the effort be directed to the fence and when it is broken the planting be cut away.[21] In other words, when the added restrictions are found to be too onerous and are toppled, the Jew's erroneous assumption that halakha is an "all or nothing" phenomenon leads him to abandon the "all" for the "nothing." The fence having been regarded as vital and now having been breached, a despair sets in which results in the garden's decimation. This was expressed by the third-century Palestinian Amora, Hezkiah, when he said that the story of Adam is evidence that "he who expands, diminishes."[22] Possibly Hezkiah, who stood close in time to the Tannaitic period, whence the famous saying "Make a hedge for the Torah" originated, understood its real significance better, in that it probably meant, as I have elsewhere indicated, to fulfill the Torah's essence through the creation of forms, but *not* to encumber the core with a thicket.[23]

The effort to fulfill the Torah's essence through the creation of forms appropriate to time and place carries forward the metaphor of the flowing river which adjusts to the contours of geography as it wends its way toward the great sea. Moses Isserles made it clear that "when new circumstances develop which were unknown to the ancient authorities it is permitted to institute new enactments."[24] The limitation we accept on this is that all new enactments must be in consonance with our classical profile of halakha or else they are no longer in the historic spirit. But as long as we strive to fulfill the profile, we have not only the right to dissent from frozen traditionalism or stifling fundamentalism but even the duty to do so. Milton Konvitz once expressed the idea that the "strength of a dissenting opinion is, like words of the prophet, a plea to the future."[25]

The task before the halakhist, therefore, is to select and classify the features that make up the profile of halakha. And it is to this task that the following chapters are devoted.

Chapter V

RELIGIO-HUMANITARIAN CONCERNS IN HALAKHA

EVERY GREAT IDEA requires forms through which it is expressed. This was first perceived by the Greek sage Plato, who understood and defined in his *Republic* the concept of the Ideal and the Real, or Idea and Form. Judaism, broadly speaking, is a philosophy of life as well as a means to concretize that philosophy. It has conceptualized objectives for human love, compassion, mutual aid among men—the whole realm we call "ethics." It has also expressed certain theological doctrines concerning Creation, how the world came into existence, Revelation, how the moral imperative, or ethics, was first brought to man's awareness, and Redemption, the destiny of man. All these elements of Judaism are its essence, its ideal, or the Idea. What is real, or Form, is the halakha. The halakha is the Form which serves as an instrument through which we express and live Judaism. Put another way, society must make its great ideas work, and it does this through a discipline that preserves its ideals. This is the function of halakha.

Nevertheless, despite Judaism's being a halakhic system, a system of action-symbols rather than dogma, in which greater emphasis is placed upon concretizing theology and morality than upon ideologically systematizing them, it should not be mistakenly impugned, as it sometimes has been, as a pedantic formalism which retarded or perverted prophetic ideas behind the brambles of trivia. The halakha was designed as an earnest search to express the true prophetic spirit of authentic religion. Rabbinic Judaism is not inferior to prophetic Judaism but is rather its expression. That minutiae over the ages often obscured the real design of halakha was the product of historical error, not evidence of the inferiority of halakha as a system. It is precisely to make a contribution toward overcoming this error that I am writing this book and explicating the original halakha, its purpose and its profile, and hoping that in our time we will recapture that profile and further its purpose. Above all, the Rabbinic profile was a masterly exercise in what we hear so much of today: "religious relevance."

The classical Rabbis emphasized conduct leading to ideals, and they shunned mere lip service. They therefore admonished their people that study is vital because it leads to *action,* and warned them that if one studies without intending to act it would have been better had he not been born.[1] The Prophets taught the objectives; the Rabbis showed how to get there. In this sense, as expressed elsewhere in this book, halakha can be defined as the "way," with or without its mystical overtones.[2]

The Rabbis expressed this lucidly when, in reference to the dietary regulations, they said, "The mitzvot were only designed to refine men," to teach kindness and self-discipline.[3] The first purpose of halakha, therefore, was moral perfection. And to underscore this they banned the observance of a ritual which involved disregard of ethical values. They denied man virtue for a *mitzvah ha'ba'ah b'averah,* a mitzvah that was the product of sin. In other words, the instrument whereby one rises to moral perfection cannot be stigmatized by unethical behavior, for that would be a contradiction in terms. The end does not justify the means. Therefore, for instance, the Rabbis prohibited the use of a stolen *lulav.*[4]

The ancients instinctively realized that if the Form were to be true to its divine nature, it had to be developed within such guidelines as were humane and intelligent, and yet provide historic continuity both in a temporal and in a spatial sense. Each faith community of Jews should be identifiable as a sister community with other contemporary ones, and should also be recognizable as a historic continuation of previous ones. In essence such an effort was merely another way of saying that since halakha served man, it must be like man in its broadest outlines. Man, created in the image of God, possesses humanity and intelligence, and is the only creature among nature's infinite variety that has a sense of time and a real sense of the interrelationship of communities in space. Not only do horses have no sense of time but horses in America know nothing about horses in Africa. Animals experience no drive for communion with animals elsewhere. But human beings, since the beginning, have had a strong impulse to unite with other communities and have had an expansive attitude toward spatially extended identity. Thus the hallmark of halakha has been horizontal identity among communities round the globe as well as vertical identity with communities of the past. A sense of humanitarianism, intelligence and the awareness of the need to preserve historic unity in time and space were therefore always among the criteria that determined halakha. It is these criteria which infused the profile of this instrument throughout classical Talmudic times and must remain the motivation and rationale into the future.

The Talmud is replete with reference to the features that compose the profile. Although the Talmudic Rabbis, having been pragmatists rather than theorists, did not philosophize about these matters and never drew up a summary or classification of them, their constant appeal to such motives speaks for itself. They did not sit about the Academy dreaming up new halakha but created it by interpretation of current halakha, or by enacting new halakha to meet new situations that arose out of litigation before the courts when existing halakha proved to be inadequate. But in either case the halakha was the product of life, and because it was, and because it was for real people with real problems and real aspirations, the sages applied their intelligence and sense of compassion to their findings. Halakha was the instrument by which the Jew met his needs in contemporary society. It was never necessarily conceived as a permanent practice. There were, of course, certain observances that were designed *l'dorot,* "forever," but these were all highly expressive of a significant historic event, such as Passover, or of the covenant, such as circumcision. In such instances the Torah makes it clear. It becomes evident from the context that the practice was designed for all generations.[5]

The Rabbis applied their intelligence and compassion in these matters and were never governed by mere ideology. They were not doctrinaire. Thus, although they were quite knowledgeable in economics and understood the forces and ramifications of commercial competition, they favored it at some times and opposed it at others, and not all the sages thought alike upon it. Sometimes those who desired to limit competition in the market were able to impress their view upon the halakha; at other times the view that favored competition prevailed. It depended on the nature of the product and the need of the poor. Thus when it involved food and the price of a product, the halakha favored free competition so as to bring the price down.[6] Such considerations have their implications for modern times and should be carefully scrutinized with a view to applying them. The area of *kashrut,* which includes the broad questions of chemical ingredients, the methods of food processing and new technology in glazing vessels, is related to economics. The burden to be borne by young people or others of modest income is often a discouraging factor. But more concerning this will be said in a later chapter when I take up the matter of Economics as part of the profile of halakha.

In chapter 4, "A Profile of Jewish Religious Practice," I suggested that there were over twenty possible criteria or ideas that motivated the classical halakha.[7] Others may formulate them in some other fashion and may compute more or less than that. The figure is purposely vague because, as I indicated, the expansion of each criterion into its subdivision may perhaps yield as many as fifty. The number is purely arbitrary, as are the precise formulations. They are sometimes the product of my inferences from the classical halakha. In some cases they are stated explicitly in the sources. But it is not a matter of any grave consequence whether they are formulated precisely as I have done or what the accurate count of the criteria may be. The summary presented here is merely suggestive and can serve as an anchor for our evaluation of presently operative halakha and as a takeoff point for the halakha of the future.

There is no attempt here to comprehensively and individually delineate the precise twenty-two criteria I enumerated in my previous chapter, because these twenty-two do not exhaust the Rabbis' philosophy of halakha. Indeed, as I have suggested, if each were taken into consideration along with its subdivisions and ramifications, the list might conceivably become endless. Instead, therefore, I am attempting to establish a tentative series of overriding considerations that motivated the classical halakha and found expression in any number of such Talmudic epigrams as *kol d'mekadesh al datah derabbaan mekadesk:* when a man takes a wife he is doing so on the premise that he has fulfilled the halakha in accordance with Rabbinic requirement. Otherwise his act of *kiddushin,* his act of marriage, is faulty and retroactively of no consequence.

The halakhic literature of the Talmud is full of similar pithy principles. To explore each one, to define it and to evaluate it, would require a work in itself. The task would prove to be as exciting as mining an inexhaustible vein of ore. It is a task which undoubtedly requires doing, and perhaps I will undertake it one day, because it would be invaluable for future halakhic discourse. Such an analysis would certainly place the entire field of halakha on a far more scientific footing.[8] But it would be going too far afield in this book to attempt such a comprehensive analysis. Instead, therefore, I will classify the central motivations of Rabbinic halakha as I see them. This is what I call the "profile" of the instrument —the profile of halakha as it should also appear in current Jewish practice. The intent is to establish the underlying and overriding considerations that allow a given practice or observance validity and should therefore evoke our continued observance.

It is my conviction that all the underlying motivations out of which sprang the classical Rabbinic halakha may be subsumed within five primary categories: I, Religio-Humanitarian; II, Historical; III, Intellectual; IV, Aesthetic; V, Economic.[9]

By Religio-Humanitarian I have in mind all those aspects of Torah which inspire the humanitarian impulse, through which man seeks to fulfill the ultimate aim of religion: love of man and the establishment of God's Kingdom on earth. By Historical I denote the impression history has made upon Judaism or the transformations in Jewish life resulting from events. It also denotes the natural human impulse to create rituals which will ensure survival of the identifiable group in history, and to remember great events, to recall high points or to thank God for the providential moments of redemption. The term Intellectual used for the third category is merely the best I could locate to, first of all, describe the desire of the Rabbis to be intellectually honest, and also to indicate that they followed where their reason led them in formulating halakha. They also took science and technology into consideration. The Aesthetic is well epitomized by the concept of *hidur mitzvah,* that it is the Jew's obligation to observe his mitzvot in a context or environment of beauty and dignity, using beautiful objects, expressing himself with sincerity, and maintaining a high sense of decorum. The Economic category is self-explanatory and includes both the religio-humanitarian impulse to be concerned for the poor and how the general welfare is affected by trade and commerce, finance, labor supply and other general economic considerations.

Although I am attempting this fivefold identification of Rabbinic criteria, I am not disposed to neat categorization. I would therefore not vigorously expound the thought that a given halakha is to be attributed to only one specific area of concern to the exclusion of others. Frequently there are overlapping halakhot that were derived from more than one of the five categories. To fulfill the Torah's moral imperative "Love your fellow man as yourself," which they considered of primacy, the sages arrived at conclusions which reflected their love of, and respect for, the dignity of living men, as well as their respect for those no longer among the living. Their concern for all forms of harmony, whether in the family, in the country at large or internally among Jews, and their pursuit of the general welfare and tranquillity, which had primacy in their deliberations, were also due to intellectual conviction or economic need. Bidden by the Torah to be concerned for the poor, the widow and the orphan, the framers of later halakha always exhibited a deep awareness of the human condition. The masters of Rabbinic halakha sought to fashion a halakha that was predicated on the protection of the defenseless and underprivileged, and in large measure they succeeded in alleviating human anguish. Since they were concerned for the welfare of man, their concern was comprehensive, encompassing his physical and psychological well-being and his economic well-being. This led them to consider also man's responses to ritualistic requirements and led them to leniency in decision-making and to concern for man's intellectual as well as religious capacity to respond. Therefore they took into consideration the other areas I will discuss separately as well: the Aesthetic and Intellectual. All these concerns—Religio-Humanitarian, Historical, Intellectual, Aesthetic and Economic—were interrelated and frequently overlapping. All were related to man. The Aesthetic concern was also related to God: it was designed not only to satisfy man's taste and refinement but to honor God. They strove for beauty in the observance of ritual. And so, in their Aesthetic criteria, as in their Historical criteria, in which they remembered and thanked God for His function in history, the halakhists were aware of and conscious of their relationship to God. It was, in sum, this twin expression of their love of God and of man that provided the halakha with meaning and purpose. One thing the halakha was not: a pedantic legalistic formalism. One criterion above all did *not* motivate the Rabbis: sheer legalism.

Among the criteria, however, undoubtedly the Religio-Humanitarian and Historical were the most significant. They probably accounted for more halakha than all the others, infusing personal practice and communal observance, accounting for all the festival observances as well as the Rabbis' ability to find intellectual validity to frame halakha.

In this chapter we can only hope to examine a sampling of this halakha under the rubric of Religio-Humanitarian. In the following chapters we will examine the other categories.

THE RELIGIO-HUMANITARIAN CRITERIA

The Religio-Humanitarian considerations served a wide variety of purposes, from the halakha of joy to the halakha of bereavement, from protecting the underprivileged to cementing society, from elevating the status of women to conserving life, from showing respect for the dignity of the living to dignifying the dead. And informing all this was the determined attitude to fulfill the ethical imperatives of Judaism.

The Rabbis were constantly aware of the need to concretize and actualize Torahitic and prophetic Judaism through a viable halakha. Their major interest was to apply the halakha to life and to derive from life the needs and wants of real people and fit these into the context of halakha. Thus theory and life were woven together into a functional fabric. Each Rabbi or each generation of sages was born, as we were, into a given halakhic context. But their responsibility, like ours, was to see to it that it worked. And in this task they used, among other tools, intelligence and compassion with a proper regard for historical continuity and for current usage, or *minhag*.

Whether the halakha was related to the dead or to the bereaved, or to the socio-economic concerns of the day, or to the practices governing domestic relations, or to interfaith relations, or to the dignity of one's fellow human being, or to the status of women, the Rabbis thought in terms of the humanitarian injunctions of the Holiness Code or in terms of other moral imperatives expressed in the Covenant Code.[10] The ethical maxims of their faith underscored their halakha in both civil and criminal law as well as in domestic relations and ritual. They were concerned for the preservation of life before the conservation of tradition and allowed their understanding of human psychology to influence their halakhic conclusions.

Preservation of human life, the recognition that man is created in God's image and is therefore entitled to respect and dignity, and the general welfare of society might therefore be seen as three major subdivisions of this philosophic posture which I have called the Religio-Humanitarian. And this whole field of halakha, as we will see in projected references, was informed and transformed by the general tendency toward leniency. It is this which gave it such remarkable relevance, a characteristic we too often miss today.

One of the interesting leniencies of the Rabbis was the principle of *shev v'al taseh*, desisting from an overt action. This meant that the Rabbis allowed one to neglect the mitzvah or injunction by inaction. This prerogative the Rabbis exercised even in cases which called for *karet,* the "cutting off" of the person from the community of Israel. Whether *karet* signified excommunication in this world, the alienation of the soul in the next or the untimely and premature death of the sinner has never been really satisfactorily expounded.[11] But in any case, for our purpose it is important merely to indicate that when *karet* was threatened for violation, the Torah thereby signified that the matter was a very grave one. Yet the Rabbis saw fit to permit a passive avoidance of certain injunctions. *Rashi* (Rabbi Solomon b. Isaac of Troyes, 11th century) was troubled by the idea, but he innocently explained that when the Rabbis suggested the person refrain from acting, they were not "uprooting a Torah halakha by *hand*"; it was "uprooted of itself," which was the Rabbis' objective.[12]

The Rabbis used several other formulas to sustain their practice of circumventing Torah halakha by imposing new actions or prohibiting certain actions which made it impossible to observe the Torah's halakha. They argued *hefkar bet din hefkar,* "the court has a right to declare property ownerless," and therefore could nullify a marriage which a man had presumably contracted with a sum of money. They prohibited the use of the *lulav* or the shofar on the Sabbath, although the Torah required these rituals, on the basis of *shev v'al taseh,* that passivity is not a violation of the Torah. They argued that on the basis of the Torah itself, parallel to Elijah, the prophet at Carmel who offered sacrifices to the Lord in a place where it was forbidden, a sage might virtually abrogate Torah halakha in order to improve the religious condition of the people as Elijah did.[13]

The leniency of the Rabbis was extended to become a general principle in certain procedures. In matters that affected the bereaved in the event of death they decided *halakha k'divrai hamaikil b'evel:* the halakha follows the opinion of the liberal or lenient scholar.[14] They enunciated the same rule in matters of domestic-relations practice when there was the possibility of a woman's being abandoned to the netherworld of being husbandless and yet formally subject to a married status—an *agunah.* To mitigate the consequences of this the Rabbis introduced safeguards and decided certain halakhot on the grounds of *takkanot agunot*, enactments to prevent the hardship from arising.[15] In general, in the practices related to domestic-relations halakha the Rabbis protected and extended the rights of women and sought to elevate their status and reduce their disabilities.[16]

One explicit formulation which directly or indirectly led the Rabbis to leniency in halakha and unquestionably constantly affected their decisions was that they ought not to require anything of the community which, according to one reading, "the community cannot abide," or according to the reading of Elijah of Vilna, "unless the majority of the community can abide by it." This statement is in the context of a ritual matter. Rabbi Ishmael b. Elisha, who flourished shortly after the destruction of Jerusalem, remarked that since the Jerusalem Temple had been destroyed, it would be appropriate for the sages to enact a ban on meat and wine. His reasoning was not given in the Tosephta, but probably it was considered meritorious as a remembrance of the altar offerings and the altar libations. He refrained from doing so, however, on the basis of the aforementioned formula, that it would not be feasible, since the community could not live up to that requirement.[17] It was also Rabbi Ishmael who enunciated the idea that "the Torah speaks the language of men."[18] He did not accept the meticulous and infinitely minute inferences that Rabbi Akiva was wont to make from words and phrases. It is not my task at this juncture to attempt an evaluation of their respective points of view. Suffice it to say that both Akiva and Ishmael had a profound effect on halakha and the history of Judaism, their successors having engaged in both Rabbi Akiva's ingenious methods and Rabbi Ishmael's thirteen hermeneutical rules.

The intuition that the sages should not attempt to compel the public to accept what is beyond their piety or capacity reflected itself in a large number of halakhot.[19]

The overall Talmudic inclination to be lenient was undoubtedly the product of what was originally a Pharisaic reaction to the fundamentalist conservatism of the Sadducees. This tendency toward liberating the pious from the Sadducean straitjacket by revising and updating the halakha expressed itself in many other forms. The Rabbis emphasized what we might today term the "general welfare" or the "public good" in preference to tradition or historical practice. The cases which are reflected in the Talmud, elucidated in modern terminology, would include the idea of "improving" the status of women, or "women's liberation." They expanded social harmony, promoting interfaith or interracial relations, and provided for a happier society by introducing "new deal" anti-poverty legislation to uplift the poor, the defenseless and the underprivileged of any class of citizenry. The corpus of halakha affected by this concept of legislating for, or making judicial decision in the interest of, the "public good" encompassed again all branches of the halakha: civil law, domestic-relations practices and ritual.[20]

The sages went so far in one instance as to state that the entire Torah is given only for *darkai shalom:* to make possible human society's welfare, for the expansion of tranquillity.[21] For this reason they could anticipate that if their objective was ever to be realized, the mitzvot, the observances of Judaism, would become unnecessary. They too understood that it matters little to God how we kill an animal or what we eat, and they emphasized that the dietary regulations were provided for human refinement. Eating meat in itself was undoubtedly of deep concern to them, since originally man was intended to be a vegetarian and only after the Flood was animal food permitted. The Rabbis therefore looked upon the dietary procedures as refining men by teaching them kindness to animals and self-discipline for themselves, and perhaps providing Jews with a medium of communal solidarity and identity. When the Rabbis emphasized, therefore, in the first instance that Judaism (the "Torah" as they put it) existed only to promote peace in the world, and in the second instance that "the mitzvot were only given to refine man" (they used the word *man* and not only *Jew*), they were expressing the religio-humanitarian concept that the purpose of halakha was the elevation of humanity.[22] All halakha must meet that test. If it separates people, if it casts a pall of boredom and ennui upon Jews during what ought to be a joyous festival, owing to undue restrictions, if it deadens spirituality through boring repetitiousness, or if it entangles man in a web of minutiae so that he loses sight of the spiritual vision, halakha is failing. When, for instance, the insistence on the observance of two days of Yom Tov brings crowds to the synagogue to honor the deceased through Yiskor on the second day but keeps them away on the first day, which is the Torah's prescribed day of sacred convocation, we are guilty of a travesty and halakha is failing. For in essence it is then elevating homage to the deceased above pure religious dedication, and we are guilty of placing man above God, which is the precise opposite of the purpose of faith, in which man, never God, strives to reach God.

All these considerations, as we have already seen, often led the Rabbis to sanction the abrogation of Torah practices. But they profoundly, and correctly, believed that sometimes the abrogation of an undesirable or obsolete practice, like the pruning of a dead branch on an otherwise healthy and beautiful tree, is its salvation. They stated this explicitly in one place, and in another they argued that sometimes the abolition of the Torah's halakha is virtually necessary for the sake of God or to attain a superior value.[23] This was expounded by even so conservative a halakhist as Maimonides, who, although he advocated unquestioning obedience to the Great Sanhedrin in Jerusalem and in general circumscribed the freedom of later halakhists, was willing to accept a less conservative position in times of emergency. It is my guess that even by his reticent standards we can consider our modern condition one of religious emergency. Maimonides wrote, "Just as a physician amputates an arm or a leg to save a person's life a Bet Din may advocate at times the disregard of some of the *mitzvot* [obligations of Judaism] as a measure to preserve the whole. . . ."[24]

Out of deep sensitivity and respect for the poor the Rabbis modified a whole array of halakhot. These ranged from such ritual observances as the size of the *sukkah,* and from the right to remove shop shutters on Yom Tov to supply the poor with their meager needs on credit, to the minimum to be spent for festival and pilgrim offerings. In all these matters it was the school of Shammai which was less concerned with the problems of the poor and the school of Hillel which was deeply sensitive.

Since, as we have already noted, the halakha followed Hillel because he was liberal, the halakha in all these matters reflected the needs of the poor. The poor required the right to have even a "mini" *sukkah* which, as Hillel held, if only the person's body was in it and the table extended into the house, almost as if the diner were sitting under a "*hupah*" *sukkah,* it would suffice. Hillel permitted the shopkeepers to open their stores to supply the poor on Yom Tov who were unable to stock up before Yom Tov for lack of time or funds. Hillel insisted that the *hagigah,* the festival offering which was consumed by the worshipper, be the more expensive offering so that there would be more animal to be consumed, while the pilgrim offering, which was an *oleh,* entirely consumed by the altar fire, could be a less expensive one so that less of the poor's meager resources would go up in flames. All these are examples in their contexts of what was termed *mipnai kavodan shel anee'yim,* "out of respect for the poor." This formula also served as rationale for a whole array of burial practices modified by the Rabbis.[25]

According to the Talmud, originally the faces of deceased rich persons were exposed at the burial service, whereas the faces of the poor, who were emaciated from hunger, were covered. This was soon seen to be an injustice, and the practice to cover all persons was instituted. One might infer that in modern times, when funeral specialists arrange all deceased to look well, there would be no inherent prohibition to have a respectful viewing. The same reasoning, respect for the poor, was used to modify the garments of burial or the vessels in which a funeral repast could be delivered, prepared or eaten.[26]

Another significant principle by which the Rabbis governed themselves also had wide ramifications. This was the idea referred to previously that the sages should not enact a practice that the community would not observe. This was applied to matters of ritual, such as using the oil prepared by gentiles, or of civil law, such as permitting the raising of large cattle despite the ecological hazard it posed to the conservation of meadowland.[27] Since the Rabbis prohibited "destructiveness" and "waste," we would have expected them to prohibit all cattle-raising. But they did not, because they anticipated that this would be a prohibition that could never gain public acceptance. The Torah had enjoined the Jew from destroying the orchards of a besieged city so as not to diminish the food supply. The verse in which this was forbidden was taken to cover all wanton destructiveness in an expanded sense. It was cited as authority to forbid obstructing the flow of streams, or diverting them for no evident benefit, or destroying or wasting food, clothing, buildings or artifacts.[28] Nevertheless, although the Rabbis were concerned about natural resources, or the environment—in modern terms, the ecology—they restrained themselves from enacting environmental-protection legislation that would conflict with the psychology of their day. As a matter of fact, in our day, with popular clamor for the conservation of the environment being what it is, the Rabbis would have been in their element.

Another way of looking at the twin effort of leniency and sparing the community enactments which they could not absorb was the Rabbinic attitude toward prayer. The Rabbis varied in their sentiments, but they did not waver in recommending that prayer be meaningful and spiritually enhancing. The Rabbinic sages opposed perfunctory and vacuous worship.[29] Part of their effort at stabilizing meaningful worship was directed at a problem that is still very much with us: the tedium and boredom of certain worship services. Thus they advocated that the congregation ought not to be burdened in prayer. For this reason they abbreviated the daily service and omitted the reading of the Bilaam story.[30] Although we no longer have to concern ourselves with the straw man of the Bilaam story, we have still to be exercised over the tedium experienced in our various forms of worship. As the Rabbis eliminated the Ten Commandments for theological reasons and the Bilaam story for aesthetic reasons, there are portions of the service which we ought to seriously consider eliminating or modifying.

The Rabbis were concerned about the *general* welfare, but were not less concerned about the welfare of every individual. They thought that the preservation of life was the most significant contribution man could make to his environment. There is a wide realm of halakha related to the concept of *piku'ah nephesh,* the preservation of life, which is extremely illustrative for us. This, combined with the action of not destroying that which is of value, is a significant idea in our time, when the environment and our resources are in perpetual crisis. The preservation of life took precedence over the Sabbath and over practically everything else. We might today question the few exceptions to this rule, but in ancient times only idolatry, adultery, incest and murder were exempted from this rule. The underlying motive in Judaism was that man is created in the image of God and that therefore we have no right to take anyone else's life, as he has no right to take ours. The commandment to save life was quite comprehensive and superseded all other considerations. As a matter of fact, even if it was not certain that the violation would save life, it was imperative to try.[31] Although the Rabbis enunciated the three aforementioned exceptions, it has to be kept in mind that these were extraordinary. They constituted the basis of civilization: the sanctity of the human person, property and faith; and they suggested only one's volitional martyrdom and not the taking of another's life. Since the conservation of one's own life is a gesture in futility if civilization is nullified, civilization took precedence over these exceptions. But other than in these cases life took precedence. Thus the Sabbath was declared to have been given to man and not man to the Sabbath, and it was therefore better to save man at the expense of the Sabbath so as to be able to observe future Sabbaths. Human life was considered so inviolable that suicide was banned, and man was not even permitted to injure himself.[32]

As the body of man was to be preserved, so was his spirit—his soul, or his *dignity.* This is borne out in extensive halakhot ranging from the cogent statement that a man's dignity is more important than a Torahitic prohibition through the vast realm of interpersonal relationships. In employer-employee or master-slave relationships, the Rabbis repeatedly stressed their opposition to overwork, corporal punishment and degrading conditions, while they concomitantly stressed prompt and fair payment of salary, generous treatment of workers and a host of other rights, such as the right to strike and to rest from labor for fulfillment of religious duties and similar privileges. Man was not a beast of burden but an image of God. And for humane halakha the gentile was also included.[33]

The ethical concerns of the halakha are probably most lucidly epitomized in the expression "a mitzvah derived from an *averah* is an *averah":* a pious act performed through a transgression or violation of a religious standard is a sin and not a pious act. The halakha therefore established the concept that ends do not justify means. How we attain our objectives is as vital as that the objectives be noble.[34]

Chapter VI

HISTORICAL AND INTELLECTUAL FACTORS SHAPING RELIGIOUS PRACTICE

HISTORICAL FACTORS AS "REMEMBRANCE"

ALTHOUGH THE Religio-Humanitarian motivations were the most extensive ones in the fashioning of halakha, there were other significant considerations that came into play from biblical times on. We have already read of the Historical category in Scripture, where certain observances were designed as "remembrances." Israel was to remember the Exodus from Egypt, its wanderings in the wilderness and the perils of religious, ethnic or national hatred as exhibited by hostile or uncooperative nations who refused succor to the migrating Israelites. A host of biblical halakhot, both ritual and ethical, were tied to the Exodus or to the historical memory of bondage in Egypt, the overriding realities of ancient Israelite history.[1]

Certain practices in Jewish ritual arose as a consequence of historical incidents and were later retained although the reason had long before disappeared. Thus during the Hadrianic persecutions in Judea observance of ritual became very precarious, even endangering life. At that time the Jews began to recite the *Shema,* which was forbidden by Roman authorities, in an undertone so that a soldier-spy who stood guard at the place of worship would not hear it. The line *barookh shem k'vod,* "Praised is His Majesty," the response to *Shema Yisra'el,* "Hear O Israel," was also recited in an undertone. This line carried the potential of a charge of treason should it be misinterpreted as a secret code for

expressing loyalty to some sovereign other than the Roman emperor. It is further surmised that the inclusion of the Shema and
barookh shem into other portions of the liturgy, such as the
Kedusha in the *Amidah,* where the government spy would not
expect to hear them and would be off guard, dates from that
period as well. Similarly the reading of the Scroll of Esther was
moved from the morning of Purim to the evening before in the
hope, I presume, of outwitting the Romans. And courts introduced
the custom of tearing a *Get* (writ of divorce) right after it was
handed to the wife so as to destroy the evidence that they had
violated the Roman proscription of issuing such documents in
Jewish courts.[2]

Although the Hadrianic interdictions eventually were rescinded, all these precautionary changes that took place in Jewish
ritual remained intact. Thus the Shema is still repeated in several
places during the service, some Jews still recite *barookh shem* in
an undertone, and *Gittin* are still torn when delivered to the wife.
The natural conservatism of religious institutions had something
to do with this. But an even more important factor probably was
the intense awareness of history that always predominated in
Judaism. This was an attitude that could be explained on several
levels. In the first place, as was the case from the beginning, to
remember the Exodus, there always remained in Judaism the
same propensity: a rallying cry *to remember.* Once an observance
was introduced, if it had more than local and temporal interest
or significance, it remained an integral part of the halakha, albeit
time and circumstance might see much transmogification take
place. The Hadrianic persecutions struck at the very heart of
Judaism, as earlier those of Antiochus IV had done. If there had
been a Bar Kokhba victory in the second century of the Common
Era such as the Maccabean victory in the second century before
the Common Era, there undoubtedly would have emerged the
equivalent of Hanukkah. But in place of that, the fragmentary
rituals I described in the above paragraphs were retained as the
historic reminiscence of the peril through which Judaism had
come.

It is true that there once existed many presently unremembered semi-holidays upon which Jews were not to fast, and some upon which they were not to mourn. These were delineated in *Megillat Ta'anit,* a scroll of Tannaitic times. Most of the days therein were abolished in very early Talmudic times. This would appear to contradict what I have written about the retention of historic memories in the ritual. But I would venture that, on the contrary, it sustains what I have suggested, since all the days abolished were minor. The major ones—Hanukkah and Purim—were retained. The others, neither those that reminded of perils nor those that described triumphs, cut through to the heart of Judaism.[3]

Frequently, the exigencies of the milieu in which the Jews found themselves prompted halakhic changes of lesser or greater magnitude. There was a great need throughout the Middle Ages for self-protective communal solidarity as well as for preserving the juridical autonomy afforded the Jewish community by medieval feudal monarchs.

It would take us too far afield to explore the evolution of Jewish life in Spain, France and Germany, the three great centers of Western Europe, and to collate and analyze their similarities and differences and to document the mutually interacting influence of the halakha on life and of life on the halakha.[4] Furthermore, what became commonplace in Western Europe was later extended to Eastern Europe, and there too, for centuries, Jews lived by Jewish "law" in the sense of the civil law within their own semi-autonomous communities. Again, new directions had to be sought and adjustments and accommodations made to meet the needs of Poland and Russia. But to survey these would take us into historical considerations which are not germane to the essential purpose of this book.[5]

One scholar has indicated that there are perhaps over fifteen hundred books dealing with responsa; and the geographic and temporal spans of this literature are vast.[6] Spain, Germany, Algeria, Turkey, Poland, Hungary and Galicia were all centers out of which prolific responsa literature emanated from the tenth century through the nineteenth. It is self-evident how socio-economic and political conditions of the Jews would have varied remarkably. The halakha, to be viable and compassionate, had obviously to undergo many transformations to meet new forms of government, new patterns of local, regional and international commerce, and new technology.

These halakhic adjustments, albeit prompted by history, were not necessarily directed toward "remembering" an event. They were simply the responses to the stark realities of everyday Jewish life. For many centuries Jews lived by all the components of halakha, by that which in English is also termed "law"—the law of domestic relations, public law regulating communal life and taxation, and civil and criminal law. In our time, only the halakha of domestic relations and religious ritual is observed by even the most devout and traditionalist Jew. Nevertheless, the transformation of the halakha related to civil and public law during the Middle Ages is instructive to us in imparting the major thesis of this volume: that not only has halakha always changed, which is self-evident truth, but that contrary to any so-called Orthodox or traditionalist supposition, new halakha has not only "supplemented" old halakha, it has also contradicted it and therefore rescinded it.

An example may be cited at random. In 1089 Emperor Henry IV granted the Jews of Spires a charter of privileges. This charter enabled Jews to live by their own halakha and even regulated the law of the land in relation to Jews in accordance with Jewish halakhic prerogatives. But among its provisions was one which stated that if a Jew converted to Christianity, he would lose his inheritance rights. Since this would tend to discourage Jewish conversion, it is obvious that the Jews would request it of Henry IV. They were apparently successful in convincing him to grant it, although it was contrary to the interests of the missionizing church. The Jews undoubtedly were concerned about the rate of conversion and wanted to place this very real material obstacle in the path of one's spiritual uncertainties. But commendable as it may appear to some to deny an apostate his inheritance, it was contrary to Talmudic halakha. The previous halakha clearly did not deny his inheritance to one who changed his faith.[7]

HISTORICAL CONDITIONS STIMULATE
NEW CONCEPTS

The halakhists required basic precepts or premises on which to base modification, repeal or supplementation of older halakha. This is the essence of the halakhic structure—a combination of case law and precedent. The scholar exercised pragmatic examination of each situation and sought out precedents upon which to structure new approaches. A basic premise was needed which could serve the needs of communities everywhere through many centuries and allow the halakhists to adapt secular law to Jewish needs or infuse secular law with Jewish principles and then adapt the law of the land. The original formulation of such a premise was the Talmudic concept given in the name of the third-century Babylonian Samuel, *dinah d'malkhuta dinah,* usually translated "the law of the king is law," but which I believe is best translated "state law is binding." Eventually the term *malkhuta* signified whatever sovereign power governed.[8] The Talmud recorded a limited selection of examples in which this legal principle was applied. But we are not compelled to assume that the Talmud exhausted all cases. Even more significant, however, is the extensive use made of this principle throughout the Middle Ages.[9] It was in keeping with the Talmudic method itself for the medieval halakhists to extend the principle, for the Talmud had already extended it from the "law of the sovereign" to the law of his delegated emissaries with the principle *sheluha d'malka k'malka,* "the king's deputy is the king himself," or in a more contemporary translation, "the state's agent has state authority."[10] That meant that governors, tax collectors and others who were charged with the administration of geographic areas or of certain facets of urban or rural life were to have their ordinances obeyed though they ran counter to aspects of older Jewish civil law. This even affected the area of ritual halakha, although it is often stated that Samuel's principle does not apply to ritual.[11] Most significantly, for instance, medieval halakhists utilized the principle of "state law is binding" to permit the Jews of a town to "purchase" the town from the town's authority and thereby make it a private domain of the Jewish community to allow for the establishment of a Sabbath *eruv hatzerot,* a boundary that delineated private and public domains or included varying domains under one "ownership." This would permit the Jewish residents to carry objects out of and into their homes, into and from the thoroughfares, as if the entire town were one *hatzer,* one private courtyard.[12]

This instance where the principle of *dinah d'malkhuta* (the civil law is sovereign) was invoked to ease the Sabbath carrying restrictions is a self-evident example of where it had at least an indirect effect in the field of ritual halakha. That is to say, the Rabbis were not invoking a state law to compel the practice or the repeal of a ritual observance, but were invoking a principle of civil law to establish proprietorship over a district in order to affect ritual practice. It is of course true that the Talmud, so far as can be ascertained by the present state of research into the problem, apparently only refers to the concept in civil matters, such as legal instrumentalities, real-estate transactions, taxes and related affairs. But the apparent silence of the Talmud is not evidence, and the lack of a systematic scientific study of all the ramifications of invoking the principle further cautions us to refrain from radical conclusions.

On the side of affirming that the formulation may have validity beyond the civil law, we have the obvious case of *eruv* (the establishment of a fictional boundary by including disconnected properties into one ownership). Here the principle of *dinah d'malkhuta* is invoked in a ritually related facet of the halakha. In other words, it may be true that no state, no sovereign power, would be recognized within the context of halakha to nullify halakha; but that does not rule out accepting contemporary municipal, state or federal law as a basis of governing matters related to ritual. One example would be the area of marriage and divorce. Another example would be to accept civil holidays and recognize in them a source of religious enhancement in synagogue life by incorporating them into the Jewish religious calendar. In the place of constant Jewish objection to humane-slaughter legislation, such legislation could be applied to the killing of animals for kosher usage. There are, in addition, other facets of our religious life that could be considered in this light. For in the final analysis the dogmatic assertion that *dinah d'malkhuta* applied only to the civil law was quite fallible. As in the case of the *eruv,* there are other examples where the principle was invoked with a view to determining "ownership," but indirectly affecting ritual.

Another example of the use of *dinah d'malkhuta* with ritualistic consequences was the question of testimony regarding the death of a husband to allow the spouse to remarry. The Mishna had required that before a witness was eligible to testify to the death of a man for the purpose of freeing his spouse to remarry, he must have witnessed the actual death. The Mishna explicitly barred witnessing of a mere hanging as adequate for testimony and required that the witness actually be present at the expiration of life. In the face of this, some seventeenth- and eighteenth-century halakhic authorities accepted the testimony of a hanging as adequate, since it was *dinah d'malkhuta* to break the victim's neck, which in turn implied death.[13]

This is not only a case of accepting *dinah d'malkhuta* in an instance which has serious ritualistic ramifications that arise from remarriage, such as the legitimacy of children or the problem of possible adultery. It is a clear case of abandoning a standard set by the Mishna itself in the light of differing historical conditions. The same use was made of *dinah d'malkhuta* by the *Hatam Sofer* (R. Moses Sofer 1763-1839), who flourished in the Austro-Hungarian Empire. The imperial courts set twelve months as the terminal date for declaring a missing person dead, arguing that twelve months is sufficient time for a missing person to inform his next of kin that he is alive, through the postal services or printed media. (The age of wireless telephone and television makes even twelve months more than sufficient.) The Rabbis therefore began to accept this *dinah d'malkhuta* (civil law) for declaring a missing person dead as valid for halakha to allow the spouse to remarry. In our own society a person is not declared legally dead until he has been absent for seven years or other proofs of death are provided, or in accordance with the Federal Missing Persons Act. But again *dinah d'malkhuta* governs our considerations. To argue the subtlety that in such an instance the *dinah d'malkhuta* is influencing not remarriage but only the declaration of death is hardly convincing. For actually the purpose of such statutes is to exempt the spouse who remarries from the charge of bigamy. But even if it were arguable that the statutes affect only the status of the dead or missing person and that remarriage within Judaism is only an indirect consequence allowed by halakha, and not by *dinah d'malkhuta*, it is still the state law which validates the halakha and which prompts the mourners to say *kaddish* and observe *Yahrzeit* and the like.[14]

The nineteenth and twentieth centuries saw increased discussion of applying *dinah d'malkhuta,* especially in the ritual areas of marriage and divorce. What halakhists have done since the French Revolution is to accept civil law as binding, but only as supplementary to halakha. Thus marriage and divorce, except within the Reform group, functions in accordance with both the halakha and civil law, no marriages being performed that are not in conformity with the state law and no *Gittin* (ritual bills of divorce) being issued where there has not yet been compliance with the civil divorce laws and a writ of civil divorce issued. In 1837 Abraham Geiger suggested that a combination of three halakhic formulations allow for civil divorce to be adequate in Judaism. He suggested that two formulations related to Rabbinic marriage halakha—"Whoever contracts a marriage [*mekadesh*] does so in conformity with standards of Rabbinic approval" and "The Rabbis may annul the marriage [*afkinhu*]"—be combined with *dinah d'malkhuta,* that the state law is binding. Consequently when the state issued a writ of divorce, the Rabbis could declare the marriage null without the additional requirement of a *Get,* and in this way a civil divorce would be adequate to sever a Jewish marriage.[15]

HISTORY AS CONTINUITY

We have now seen how the desire to "remember" significant events, and the changing geographic and socio-economic conditions under which Jews lived, and the factor of changing governments, all affected the halakha.

But history includes more than the past or socio-economic conditions or geography. It also pertains to the present and the future. Thus communal solidarity and communal identity—in broader terms, the horizontal preservation of Jewish life in any given period, and the vertical continuation of a living Jewish history—played their roles in the halakha as well. For this purpose many *takkanot* (positive enactments) or *gezerot* (prohibitions) were again and again instituted to enhance ritual, to provide communal institutions, to allow for the training of the young in religious life, and to protect the interests of minors, or of others with handicaps, such as deaf-mutes or women. The Talmudic literature abounds with such *takkanot* and *gezerot,* and the principles behind them were generally, as indicated in the previous chapter, religio-humanitarian. But they were also of significant historical value in several ways. They helped to preserve the community in its own time and enabled the community to transmit the heritage to the next generation in a generally enhanced form.

Thus certain rituals were prompted by events and philosophy. We read that originally in the Jerusalem Temple the closing clauses of blessings included the words "praised is the Lord, God of Israel from everlasting." But this was later revised to read "from everlasting to everlasting." This revision was to emphasize the existence of two worlds, since the Sadducees cited the original version as evidence that there was only one world, this real world, and no *olam habah,* no future existence in an afterlife.[16]

By the same token, however, historical circumstances required other measures to preserve communities in new places and in new periods. At times, existing halakha was inimical to the welfare or the interests of communal preservation. And so we find that there were many relaxations of binding enactments. Thus the preference of the Rabbis for *halitza,* releasing a woman from levirate marriage, was the virtual repeal of a Torahitic practice, since levirate marriage became a rare practice and *halitzah* common.[17]

The court calendar influenced halakhic practice. The courts

sat on Thursday, and consequently there was a *takkanah,* an enactment, for a virgin to marry on a Wednesday in case her groom
desired to charge her before the court as having fraudulently
claimed virginity for a more advantageous marriage contract. But
this was suspended where courts did not adhere to this rigid
calendar.[18] Another example of historical circumstances significantly affecting halakha, even to the extent of violating the Torah,
is the decree by Rabbi Judah the Prince that Beth She'an should
be exempt from paying tithes, and a series of other localities from
the Sabbatical prohibitions. Rabbi Judah also sought, unsuccess-
fully, to abolish the fast day of the ninth of Av. In due time
the *gezerot*—prohibitions—against the use of heathen oil and
bread were abolished, undoubtedly in response to the growing
mobility and dispersal of Jewish communities.[19]

INTELLECTUAL FACTORS IN THE HALAKHA

The categories under which we can subsume the motivations
for or causes of modification of halakha through the centuries
often overlapped. This was evident in the Historical category. It
will also be seen now in what we may term the Intellectual factors
underlying the development of halakha in the form of both expansion and limitation or repeal of halakha. By Intellectual motivations or causes I have in mind principally ideas that presented
themselves to the scholars. The ideas and principles may have
been part of the religio-humanitarian concerns evident in the
previous chapter, or they may have been molded by changing
historical forces, technology and learning. There were "patterns
of piety" to preserve. But there was as well a desire not to impose
these upon others. Intellectually the scholars were often motivated
by a desire that the average man have a modicum of freedom
to express himself at his own level of piety. Science naturally
played a role in the halakha as new products were developed, new
substances composed the artifacts of civilization, and new modes
of transportation came into being. Some of these considerations
will naturally be seen to overlap with the Economic category.
Among all these factors in the halakha which I am here in-

corporating under the Intellectual category there stand out certain basic formulations that played a major role. These include such well-known Talmudic axioms as *kol mekadesh al datah d'rabbanan mekadesh,* "whoever consecrates a wife does so in compliance with Rabbinic standards." This implied that if a person willfully violated the Rabbinic standard, the Rabbis were empowered to take radical measures. The Rabbis, in other words, were quite prepared to annul such a marriage; and concerning this we read another halakhic formulation, *afkinhu rabbanan kiddushin mineh,* "the Rabbis may terminate the bond of marriage consecration."[20]

This approach was utilized in limited instances, so far as we can determine in Talmudic literature. But it was utilized in a variety of ways. For instance, it was invoked to prevent a man from nullifying a bill of divorce he had already dispatched to his wife. The case would be, let us say, where A, residing in New Jersey, had granted a divorce to B, residing in New York. While the bill of divorce was in transit, A relented and abolished it before another court. Meanwhile, before news of the abolition reached B, she received the bill of divorce and married C. We are, of course, speaking of an age when transportation between distant places was slow and often hazardous. Messages and messengers could be seriously delayed or lost en route. Complications could develop, and B might be guilty of adultery. Consequently the sages instituted a prohibition on the husband's abolishing the writ of divorce once he had dispatched it to his wife. Other sages questioned the propriety of so limiting a power unqualifiedly granted to the husband by the Torah. But the proponents of the new procedure argued that all marriage was on the grounds of compliance with Rabbinic intent and that this concept gave the Rabbis the power to declare this marriage null although Torahitically there has been no divorce, since the husband had canceled it. The Rabbis felt they were justified in what was essentially the abolition of a Torah right possessed by the husband in order to protect children from a status of illegitimacy and the woman from the cardinal sin of adultery. Furthermore, they would protect society in general from the complications in which such tragedies result. Perhaps there was also a little desire on the part of the Rabbis to concentrate the power of marriage and divorce in their own hands and consequently they were actually superseding the more limited strictures of Scripture and expanding protective devices for women, children and society not anticipated in the Torah's much earlier social setting.

This should not obfuscate the fact that the halakhic formulations here referred to in which the Rabbis claimed radical powers were opposed. The Mishna which dealt with the question of a husband's nullifying a divorce after he had dispatched the documet by messenger recorded a dispute between Rabbi Judah and Rabbi Simon b. Gamliel. R. Judah held that the declaration of nullity stood and that the wife was therefore not released. R. Simon b. Gamliel maintained that Rabbinic authority permitted them to discount the husband's cancellation on the basis of the concepts that a Jew married by virtue of Rabbinic authority and that it was in Rabbinic power to nullify the act of marriage. The medieval summary of marriage and divorce halakha, Joseph Karo's *Even ha'Ezer,* decided in favor of Rabbi Judah, that the husband's declaration had taken effect and the wife would not be free to remarry, notwithstanding these principles of Rabbinic power. But there was nevertheless a strong body of opinion that supported the position of R. Simon b. Gamliel, who stressed the logic of Rabbinic authority if anarchy was to be avoided. And there are clues in earlier commentaries, antedating Karo's *Even ha'Ezer,* that Karo's decision was not correct.[21]

Similarly a whole range of halakha in the field of civil law and monetary obligations was possible only because of the principle formulated by the sages, *hefkar bet din ha'yah hefkar,* "whatever the court declares ownerless and free for transfer according to their court processes, is so." This was the original premise upon which Hillel's famous *prozbul* was predicated. This allowed the court to collect those debts which were canceled by the arrival of the *shemitah* year when there was a general cancellation of debts. The logic was that in periods of tight money creditors would not lend their capital for fear of losing it to an ancient ritualistic procedure. Hillel therefore instituted this document whereby the court took the power of attorney to collect the debt, for the court was not enjoined by the Torah to allow the debt to lapse. In turn this power of the court to determine transfers of property ownership by arbitrary fiat was based on a verse in the Book of Ezra which they interpreted to mean that the court had virtually total control of the property of a community although there was no scriptural warrant for such powers.[22]

In matters of criminal law too the power of the sages to adjudge and execute penalties for which there was no scriptural warrant, such as meting out the death penalty for riding on the Sabbath during the period of Seleucid persecution, was explained as being "to meet the needs of the times," or "to constrict behavior" in a period of religious laxity. But lest the Rabbis be unfairly assessed as unduly harsh, it must be remembered that the halakhic authorities greatly improved upon the looser Torah halakha and made capital conviction and execution a very rare and difficult matter.[23] The point to be inferred here once again is simply that the Rabbis did not allow the Torah's halakha to stand in the way of their constant quest for a viable halakha. They consistently emphasized that human authority was the divine will by stressing that in the scriptural admonition to seek solutions to problems and follow the decisions of the authorities, there was found the phrase "the judge who will preside *at that time.*" This gave the Rabbis the courage of their conviction that *contemporary authority* had validity.[24]

THE ROLE OF SCIENCE

Technological advances and new discoveries also brought about a determined effort to have halakha keep pace. The extent of Rabbinic knowledge of the natural sciences has not yet been fully documented. But we clearly see that the Rabbis possessed expertise in a number of fields to the extent that scientific knowledge was available in their day. Botany, horticulture, agriculture and anatomy were fields the Rabbis were familiar with, as is attested to in the Talmud in the tractates dealing with agricultural and dietary matters. But the latter facet of halakha also required knowledge of physics, as the calendar required familiarity with astronomy and mathematics. And it is evident that the Rabbis moved about with ease in all these sciences. They gathered their data from both observation and experimentation and were probably also educated in the classical Greek writers.[25]

The Rabbinic use of science is cogently demonstrated in the expanded dietary regulations of Talmudic literature. It was a well-known scientific fact that salt extracted blood from meat, and this motivated a whole range of Rabbinic requirements in the preparation of meat for kosher use so far as the soaking, salting and rinsing of meat was concerned, although there was no warrant for any of this in Scripture. Subsequently the Gaonim decided that if meat had not been salted for three days after the animal was slaughtered, the blood had congealed within it and even the salt would not affect it. In such cases only roasting on an open fire would achieve the purpose and allow one to eat the meat. Flowing from this and from their understanding and the status of scientific data of the time, the Rabbis enacted a whole array of halakhot related to *kashrut*. These include many notions that may appear bizarre to the modern mind. They held, for example, that what had been pickled in a brine or fermented juice was to be ritually regarded as cooked. Therefore if a forbidden article of food was mixed into the brine with a permitted item, they were to be regarded as cooked together and both were forbidden. Thus they also held that when part of an iron vessel, such as the handle of a ladle or part of the spoon, had been heated, the whole of it was considered to have conducted the heat. Consequently if only part of a spoon used for milk had been dipped in a pot standing on a fire and containing boiled meat, it was as if the entire spoon had been inserted; and many complications arose as regards the spoon, the pot and the food in the pot.[26]

The dietary regulations contain dozens of provisions that can only be interpreted as the Rabbinic understanding of scientific data available in the various periods when certain practices arose. The Rabbis considered the penetration of vapors, the relation of heat to cold and the varying absorptive capacity of different metals and temperatures. They discussed and acted upon the differences involved when a vessel was in the first or second degree, that is, the vessel in which the food was cooked or the one in which it was served, respectively. They disputed whether fish served on a plate that had absorbed the taste or particles of meat might be eaten with milk. Rav and Samuel, third-century colleagues in Sura and Nehardea respectively, differed on this matter, but according to the fourth-century sage Hezkiah reporting in the name of his contemporary Abyeh, the halakha was decided in favor of Samuel, that it was permitted since the flavor of the meat dish entering the fish was only a second-degree penetration.[27]

In this particular case it deserves digression to comment on the interesting fact that the halakha was decided in favor of Samuel. Usually matters of ritual were decided in favor of Rav, whether he was lenient or strict, and monetary or civil matters were decided in favor of Samuel. Apparently it was here felt precisely that Samuel was more correct scientifically, that the supposed flavor that remained on a meat platter could not be taken seriously as a penetrating agent if fish were eaten with the sour-milk preserve.[28] Obviously the difference between them was a question of scientific judgment, and it further bears out the thesis being stressed in this chapter, that one of the elements of the halakhic profile was *science*; and science consequently should again play a greater role in governing our considerations than it presently does. This would hold true for both Sabbath and dietary halakha, where what we know today about sources of energy, the nature of work and leisure, chemistry and all the other facets of modern science that could be brought to bear upon Jewish religious observance would contribute to a far more pleasing and joyous halakha. Centuries ago the Rabbis studied the nature of food products, the action of salt or other preservatives upon food and blood, the nature of fat, the unique feature of liver and the action of heat upon, and the absorptive properties of, earthen, wooden or metallic vessels and implements and set the premises of an ever-expanded dietary halakha. Similarly in our time the study of chemical composition, the results of glazing processes, new knowledge concerning the production of utensils, our knowledge of the harmfulness of tobacco, and humane-slaughter and hygienic standards set by government should point in the direction of new halakha.

A very interesting Rabbinic reliance upon science was evident when the Rabbis modified the Torah's prohibition of marriage with a *patzuah dakkah,* "a person whose testicles have been crushed," by defining its limits and exceptions, indicating cases where procreation remained possible, considering modes of healing, and drawing a distinction between "acts of God" (natural causes) and injuries having come as a result of human action, the latter being more serious.[29] It would appear from this that new scientific information and more sophisticated attitudes might allow us to reconsider the whole question of lesbianism and homosexuality. There can be no question about the need to formulate a modern halakha in this area as well as in the area of premarital sex morality.

THE ROLE OF LOCAL USAGE (MINHAG)

In addition to the scientific and economic principles that played a role in the intellectual motivations of halakha, there was the concept of *minhag,*—current custom—and a wise approach to human nature and psychology.[30] The concept of *minhag*—the usage of the people—applied to economic halakha as well as to domestic relations and ritual. Thus the first paragraphs of chapters 7 and 9 of the Mishna Baba Metziah and of chapter 1 of Baba Batra depend entirely on custom. One scholar has gone so far as to assert that "if you search through the treatise of Baba Batra, which is larger than any other, you will not find any *halakhot* based on the written law or received by tradition from Sinai except in its eighth chapter . . . all the decisions and rulings discussed in it belong to the category of laws whose main grounds, as given by the Rabbis, were either common reasoning or the customs of the land. . . ."[31]

The characteristic phrase is *Makom shenahagoo,* "where the usage is such and such, one does similarly; where it is done otherwise one follows the other usage." The conclusive phrase is *hakol k'minhag ha'medinah*: one follows local usage. The term *medinah* in the Mishna did not mean a "state" in the modern sense of that word. It referred to any recognized regional unit, perhaps a tax area, a Roman province or other fiscal or governmental area. Therefore, when the Mishna stated that it was proper to follow the usage of the *medinah*, it simply meant the recognized local scene. This obviously must have made for much diversity and must have applied to ritual as well as to fiscal halakha. Yet this diversity did not shake them up, and was taken for granted. It is an important lesson for us in an age when we seem to be pressing for more and more uniformity and a reduction of individuality or even of local regional usage in halakha.

There can be no question that what I am here saying and using as grounds for promoting diversity has warrant. Without extending this into a tedious philological treatise, it should be observed that the term *medinah* is derived from the root *doon,* "to rule or to hold court," among other significations. This root gives *medinah* its meaning of a "jurisdiction"—any form of jurisdiction, whether fiscal or political, and only a given context would determine that. Sometimes the term was used in contrast to Jerusalem, the halakha being one way in Jerusalem, another in the *medinah,* which then signified the countryside, which was under a separate jurisdiction from the urban center. It was defined as a "province" in distinction to a "capital," and the term "province" simply meant any "administrative division." The nature or extent of a province naturally depended on the general political organization of a given empire. The point to be borne in mind here is that the scholars of the Mishna were perfectly content to allow diversity. And while in Baba Metziah and Baba Batra we see this in matters of economics, it is evident for ritual observances in the tractate Pesahim.[32] It is of interest to read that when we witness that an incorrect practice has become a *minhag* in a given locality in which we are visitors, we make no effort to change it. But this apparently is only when the area does not have scholars to teach the people differently.[33] Too often entrenched *minhag* is regarded as so sacrosanct that the pious will argue against changing it at all. But while we must recognize the role of *minhag* as a determinative force in the fashioning of halakha, we must never lose sight of the inherent balance of halakhic development. *Minhag* was important, but never at the expense of reason or religious values. Thus the principle that is too often cited with a view to preserving the latest restrictiveness of Eastern European ortho- doxy, "*minhag* nullifies halakha," with the implication that cur- rent emergent usage makes the prior halakha obsolete, should be properly evaluated. By the same token and for the same reasons new *minhag* in new areas and places may automatically supersede old *minhag*. In matters where *minhag* is faulty or unnecessarily restrictive in matters of ritual the halakha may be brought into play to correct the local usage or modify its severity.[34] This was clearly the opinion of medieval commentators, who could not be regarded as impious modernists. Thus, in commenting upon the custom of noisemaking at the mention of the name of Haman on Purim, Moses Isserles of the sixteenth century thought that al- though it was not in the best of taste and had no warrant in the halakha, it should be retained. One of the commentators, in his marginal notes to the text, reflected that Isserles himself had written in a responsum that when the circumstances that had given rise to a *minhag* had been altered by time, the *minhag* might be modified to meet current needs, and that in any case a *minhag* for which there was no ultimate hint in the Torah was an error of judgment. The same commentator then referred to the state- ment that *minhag* nullifies halakha, but specified only when it has logic and history in its favor. Furthermore, as another commenta- tor on the same passage related to the *megillah* noisemaking indi- cated, when a prohibitory *minhag* has not been accepted by and disseminated among a majority of Jews, it need not be observed.[35]

This noisemaking at the mention of Haman's name is clearly a matter of ritual, and it has given rise to interesting comments on the nature of *minhag*. *Minhag* can nullify halakha and in turn become halakha—the rule of guidance, the procedure, the prag- matic response to a religious question, the "how" to do that which in a concrete manner expresses one's religious values or yearnings. *Minhag* is the result of natural growth. It is born and grows and spreads among people, and for that reason the Rabbis, having grasped well the nature of man and his psychology, promoted local usage and accepted the inevitability of halakhic diversity. A perfectly cogent example is the one affecting the use of a sandal in the performance of *halitzah* (the removal of the shoe to free a widow from levirate marriage). There were certain technical qualifications related to the sandal, but we read in the Palestinian Talmud how a sage declared that even if Elijah the Prophet appeared and said it was wrong to use the sandal, we would not listen to him, since most people use a sandal and *minhag* nullifies halakha. Here we have, incidentally, a case where the usage of the people uprooted a prior halakha. The people used the artifacts at hand to express their halakha rather than abide by that which had been done for generations or centuries simply because it had been done.

An excellent example of a *minhag* abolished because it did not meet the intellectual standards of the time is given in the Talmud. There was a group of Levites called "wakers" who were accustomed to rise on the platform where the service was conducted in the ancient Jerusalem Temple and cry out, "Awake, O Lord, why do you slumber? Awake, abandon us not forever." This apparently harked back to an older period which had a more simplistic view of God. In the first century it was felt this was a contradiction to a loftier vision of God, and so the verse "The Keeper of Israel neither slumbers nor sleeps" was appealed to as authority to abolish the wakers.[36]

When the Rabbis exercised their prerogatives to abolish old customs and approve of new usages based on intellectual standards, socio-economic conditions or historical trends, they were also taking into consideration human feelings and human nature. Consequently psychological factors played a legitimate role. They observed man's nature and his habits and strove neither to expect too much nor to underestimate man's religious potential. We have seen how the Rabbis avoided setting standards the community could not accept. Even more did they avoid imposing upon all people that which certain pious exceptions thought to be appropriate. Thus Joshua b. Perahya, during the early Tannaitic period, prohibited Alexandrian wheat on the ground that it might have become impure during the course of its handling. Whether or not this was related to the question of economic competition, as Louis Ginzberg understood it, will not detain us here. The importance of Joshua's contemporaries' reaction to his opinion was not in whether they were less concerned for the Palestinian farmer but in that they were opposed to the imposition of his personal standard of piety upon others.[37]

In all the above ways the forces of history and of the intellectual gropings of man combined to influence the evolving halakha. But there were also other ingredients, to an extent overlapping, but to an extent entirely separate. Thus in addition to *ideas,* man's emotions as aroused by his senses had a significant effect on the halakha. And so too, despite the striving of religion toward achieving a spiritualized society, man remained an economic animal, still characterized by the need to earn his daily bread. The halakha was so structured as to consider these facets of human nature and society.

Chapter VII

AESTHETICS AND ECONOMICS AS FACTORS IN HALAKHA

DECORUM AND BEAUTY IN RITUAL— HIDUR MITZVAH

ON THE ONE HAND the Rabbis were conscious of human limitations in the pursuit of piety. But on the other hand they sought to excite the religious imagination and to stimulate religious yearning by improving rituals, introducing new practices and expanding old observances through the device of *hidur mitzvah.* This is the fourth category, the Aesthetic, under which I believe we can subsume the halakha.

The concept of *hidur mitzvah* played a great role in the evolution of many rituals in Judaism. Perhaps the oldest segment of Jewish religious rite is the sacrificial cult. This is a sacred pattern that takes us back to biblical days and theoretically should have seen the most conservative approaches, since it was believed to have been divinely revealed at Sinai. It was under the governance of a fundamentally conservative institution, the hereditary priesthood. Yet we find that the halakha consistently made room for modifications. And frequently these modifications were adaptations of non-Jewish practices. Apparently neither the fear of change nor an antagonism that one sometimes encounters even today toward adopting gentile patterns deflected the old halakha. Too often the verse "you shall not follow their usages" is appealed to as the authority to ban non-Jewish practices without qualification.[1]

The Rabbis wanted to distinguish the Jewish from the pagan cult, but at the same time they utilized environmental realities in the enhancement of Jewish rites. Sometimes they denied that parallel practices involved Jewish "borrowing" from pagan practices and saw them simply for what they were: parallel practices which either arose independently or were so remote in their origin that one could not tell who had borrowed from whom.[2]

The concept of *hidur mitzvah,* aesthetic enhancement, encompassed both the beautification of the ritual and its objects and the improvement of efficiency in performing the rite, since this in turn led to a greater aesthetic experience. There was no fear of being accused of an "edifice complex" in an age when a temple was built for the greater glory of the Deity whose "dwelling place" it was considered to be. This is, after all, the actual meaning of the term *temple,* just as the original Hebrew term for the Israelite sanctuary, *Mishkan,* signified the dwelling place of the Divine Presence, from which the epithet for the Deity, *Shekhinah* (Divine Presence), was derived. Religious objects and houses of worship were to have dignity, beauty and value in accordance with the standards of the time and the means of the people. Consequently improvements were always made in the Sanctuary; and although the original plan provided a wooden urn which had the lots used in the Yom Kippur ritual when the High Priest selected the scapegoat, Ben Gamala replaced it with gold and was commended for this by the sages of the Mishna. The priests had to wash their hands and feet before entering the Sanctuary or performing the service, and for the washing there were two spigots on a laver which was filled with fresh water carried in buckets from a well every day. The Rabbis commended Ben Katin for developing a labor-saving device, a machine that brought the fresh water from the well every day, and for replacing the two old spigots with twelve new ones. Gentile royalty of Adiabene supplied golden handles for all the vessels used on Yom Kippur and a new golden candlestick over the door of the inner sanctuary.

None of this is earth-shattering. But it cogently illustrates that the Mishnaic sages gave high priority to such embellishments. These changes, furthermore, not only were historical facts but were soon incorporated into the halakha as the mode which ought to prevail in the Temple. They were not fundamental rites, only instruments used in the cult, but were nevertheless treated with a high sense of decorum. That is the essential meaning of *hidur mitzvah,* providing for the aesthetic experience.[3]

The Rabbis took simple biblical rituals and embellished them in accordance with the standards of the color, drama and pageantry of the Greco-Roman Near East. Thus, while the Bible prescribes the bringing of the first fruits "to the place which the Lord your God has chosen," there is nothing in the primordial custom reminiscent of the elaborate public festival described in the Mishna, which mentions that the bull brought as a sacrifice— a post-biblical innovation—was crowned with a wreath of olive leaves and its horns were overlaid with gold. These were typical pagan modes used in classical Greece and Rome.[4]

The aesthetic sense was emphatically at work in the rule that the best of the flocks be used as sacrifices, the choicest produce in the *minha* offering and the best oils and wines on the altar.[5] This held true for the *lulav* and *etrog* used on Sukkot, and for other ritual instruments involved in religious ceremonial. The Rabbis interpreted the verse the Israelites sang after their redemption from Egypt, "This is my God and I will adorn Him," to mean that we will symbolically add to His glory and beauty through the manner in which we perform the mitzvot. Thus R. Ishmael is cited in the Mekhilta as saying, "Is it possible for a human being to add glory to his Creator? But rather, the verse signifies that we are to be beautiful in His Presence by using a beautiful *lulav,* building a handsome *Sukkah,* wearing an attractive *talit* [prayer shawl] and phylacteries." The Babylonian Talmud expands upon this, adding a beautiful shofar and a highly valued *Sefer Torah* with the finest of inks and parchments. Furthermore, in the performance of his ritual the Jew was not to be injured or to feel uncomfortable, for this too deprived him of aesthetic feelings. And so the *kufra,* or young spiked twigs of the palm, were not to be used for the *lulav* lest they injure him or even divert his mind from the ritual while he thought of the spikes. Similarly the *hirduph* branch was not to be used, because the *hirduph* was a tree (perhaps rhododaphne—oleander) with stinging leaves from which was extracted a lethal poison.

This reflected the consistent attitude of the Rabbis which im-

pelled them to an ongoing program of beautification, of adding
to the decorum and the interest of the ritual life. Nevertheless,
they took economic matters into consideration and did not expect
the Jew to undergo unnecessary and damaging expense to fulfill
the aesthetic desideratum. They characteristically qualified their
emphasis upon the aesthetic by limiting the amount of money a
person should expend beyond what he was planning to spend.
This limit was set at one-third of the cost of the object.[6]

In this way the Aesthetic category which motivated Rabbinic
halakha emerges like all other facets of the halakha, both balanced
and humane. It calls for man to exert himself in the observance
of his religious life. But it also places upon man the onus not to
overdo it in a manner which becomes pretentious or gaudy. The
poor man is not made to feel that he must sacrifice all his meager
resources. On the contrary, the later halakha was explicit in the
statement that even if one were to miss the mitzvah, one should
not spend exorbitant or inflationary funds to acquire the object
for use in a ritual. Obviously, what was exorbitant would have
to be left to one's individual conscience.

THE ROLE OF ECONOMICS IN HALAKHA

Throughout these chapters it has been evident that the categories which motivated Rabbinic decisions and recommendations
overlapped. This was true among the Religio-Humanitarian, Historical, Intellectual and Aesthetic. And in those four categories it
was apparent that the Economic was a consistent concern. We
have just now seen the economic factor operating within the
Aesthetic category. Rabbinic feeling for one's fellow man made
it inevitable that the rich would be advised toward modesty and
the poor would be given humane consideration so that wealth
or the lack of it should never be a negative factor in religion.
Economic considerations were therefore present in ritual matters
no less than in the civil law, and motivated changes in the
halakha of marriage and divorce to provide financial security for
the woman. The economic factor, therefore, permeated all branches
of the halakha. Consequently this "profile" of the halakha will now

be brought to its completion with a more specific survey of the role of economic motivations of the halakha.

In the previous chapter we discussed the operation of the principle *hefkar bet din hayah hefkar*, "whatever the court declares ownerless and for transfer according to their court processes, is so." This principle, enunciating in effect that a court had ultimate jurisdiction over the disposal of property in a society, was undoubtedly the primary economic instrument which enabled the Rabbis to institute their *takkanot* (enactments) and *gezerot* (prohibitory decrees) and to modify the halakha throughout the generations. The concept that allows a modern government to "condemn" property and transfer it to other use is a natural corollary. The Fourth Amendment to the American Constitution, which ensures the people against "unreasonable searches and seizures," did permit the seizures so long as it was done legally, in which case it became "warranted." The decision whether the search or seizure is warranted is a court decision, and in this sense the Fourth Amendment is progeny to *hefkar bet din hefkar*. Since the states are prohibited by the Fourteenth Amendment from depriving any person of his property without due process of law, and since every municipality functions only by virtue of state law, the citizen is protected from even the most localized attempt at seizure. But he is nevertheless subject to a court's writ which would allow a governmental body under "due process of law" to compel him to involuntarily sell or transfer his property. This is clearly *hefkar bet din hefkar*. And just as our Constitution requires the observance of "due process," so the halakha required that courts or sages must give consideration to the rights of private property, and most especially in relation to matters of ritual.[7] For this reason few Rabbis were so inconsiderate as to lightly render foods or articles unfit for usage. Instead they traditionally sought every means possible to spare a person's funds by finding wine handled by gentiles fit for Jewish use, to permit meat seemingly unkosher as kosher and to decide that certain foods suspected of leaven were not forbidden on Passover, or that certain vessels used in food preparation or serving, or articles used in rituals, were not contaminated or forbidden.

This was one way in which economic or property considerations affected halakha. To preserve or conserve property or assets, the Rabbis did not function as strict constructionists of the halakha. This concern goes back to the Torah, where a man of lesser means was permitted to offer two pigeons instead of a sheep or goat for an array of transgressions listed in chapter 5 of Leviticus. And a poor man who had no means at all could offer up a measure of flour. Similarly in all subsequent halakhic development there was concern for the poor man, consideration for the assets of all people, and a careful exercise of the power placed in the hands of courts to dispose of property.

But while we grant the widespread operation of economics in halakha, in addition to which there was the overall function of economic principles and the economic needs of the community, we should also take note of certain qualifications. There are times in the vast ocean of the Talmud that we may incorrectly pinpoint a halakha as having an economic motive or as having been caused by economic conditions. This is only natural in a literary corpus which is in total disarray in terms of how a legal manual ought to be organized, spans the experience of Jewish history over vast intercontinental spaces, and which reflects the thought, legislation and judicial conclusions of almost one thousand years. Certainly during the course of the past century during which modern scientific critical analysis has been applied to Rabbinical literature, there has been a reasonable amount of disputation over the role of economics in the development of the halakha. It is not the purpose of this chapter or this volume to join, defend or be critical of any particular school of thought on this subject. The writings of scholars of Rabbinic literature since Zechariah Frankel's discussion of the political-economic conditions of the Palestinian Jews in the period of the Amoraim—those of Louis Ginzberg, Louis Finkelstein, Saul Lieberman, Ellis Rivkin, George Foote Moore, Travers Herford, and Jacob Lauterbach, among a host of others who flourished in the nineteenth and twentieth centuries—are accessible.[8] These writings contain extensive discussions of the role of economics in the halakha, just as one can find in a host of volumes on the history of civilization extensive and comprehensive discussions with a wide variety of points of view on the role of economics in history.

The emergence of economic determinism in the analysis of history during the nineteenth century was bound to give rise to varying schools of thought and was destined inevitably to be carried over into other fields of cultural activity. This carryover into the field of halakha became evident in the nineteenth century and reached a peak in the twentieth. But I do not think that we have to be concerned with whether economics played a major or a minor role in the halakha, or whether in any given instance it was really an economic question or a question *allied* to economics, such as technology. What I have in mind here is that there were instances when the Rabbis modified or innovated halakha for reasons that are not explicit. Some scholars may surmise an economic motive. But it may also be that while indirectly economic conditions would be affected, or certain facets of the economy would be affected, some other reason might underlie the actual adjustment of the halakha.

We may have an instance of this in the matter of glassware. Here was a new product of advancing technology. It had to be related to the halakha governing purity and impurity as well as to the dietary provisions that governed the use of implements and containers. There were also questions affecting the right of import of glassware and how such imports would affect the local glassware and metalware industries. Some scholars have therefore taken the position that it was an economic concern that motivated the early Tannaim Yose b. Yoezer of Zeredah and Yose ben Yohanan of Jerusalem to decree that glassware could become impure like other vessels, although it is not mentioned in the Torah. This hypothesis may be correct. On the other hand, their action may have been an innocent extension of an old halakha to a new product, the recognition of new technology. Then again historical considerations might lead us to examine it from another angle. Before the flourishing glass industry arose in the area of Tiberius, Canaanite craftsmen in Tyre and Sidon were the major source of supply. They exported their wares to

Judea during the third century before the Common Era, when those two sages flourished. Since these products were not subject to the original biblical restrictions of impurity which applied only to metalware and earthenware, they became serious competition for the manufacturers of earthen and metal vessels or later for the growing local glass industry. This protective decree took away any advantage the imported glassware enjoyed over the local industry and that the local glass industry enjoyed over the makers of earthen and metal products. In either case, whether the extension to glassware of the susceptibility to defilement was economic in motive, the fact stands out that the Rabbis innovated changes to meet the challenge of new technology.[9]

Louis Ginzberg indicated that sometimes it was not only the personal liberalism of Hillelites which impelled them to differ with Shammaites but that the differences between their socioeconomic classes often gave rise to halakhic divergence. The Hillelites, for instance, decided in favor of the poor in all matters that affected measurements. For example, the Hillelites took the poor into consideration when deciding on the minimum size of a *sukkah,* reckoning with their scarcity of space and materials, and ruled that it was sufficient if only one's head and most of one's body was under the *sukkah* roof even if the table projected into the house. The Hillelites similarly reduced the minimum required for a festival pilgrim offering, since it was a whole burnt offering and the pilgrim had no share in it. Therefore, while the Shammaites ruled that a pilgrim's offering should be worth at least two pieces of silver and the festival offering one, the Hillelites decided the reverse in order to make the festival offering, in which the pilgrim did partake, larger, and less of a total loss to the poor man. While the Shammaites favored Arbor Day on the first of Shevat, the Hillelites insisted it not be observed until the fifteenth, a possible reason for the difference being that the poorer peasants considered by the Hillelites had a more unyielding and meager soil which took longer to produce its blossoms, while the Shammaite estate holders had better soil and better methods and their trees blossomed earlier.

In this last instance we also have a possible example of the type of situation I referred to earlier, where the economic or class motive for the halakha may or may not be the accurate one, or may be only one facet of the problem. For actually, since Hillel was from Babylonia, where produce ripened later and the spring season came later, it is possible he favored the fifteenth as a day that could be universally meaningful.

Other examples abound in the Talmudic literature. Many halakhot related to grief and mourning as we still know them today were instituted during the first century of the Common Era in response to the needs of the poor or out of sensitivity to their feelings. The Talmud phrases it *mipnai kevodan shel anee'yim,* "out of deference to the poor." Actually they were discovering that the poor were abandoning their dead because of the high cost of death; and perhaps social revolution against Rabbinic Judaism threatened unless affirmative and palliative action was taken. The liberal tendencies always present among the halakhic scholars asserted themselves and modified long-standing customs.[10]

Only a few examples of the attitudes that arose at that time will be given here. One was a negative attitude toward viewing the deceased. It was originally the custom to leave the faces of the rich open to view but to cover the faces of the poor. The reason for this was that the rich looked better in death, since they had always eaten more nutritiously and presumably had methods of skin care and the like. The poor appeared less attractive and were often emaciated, and the mourners were ashamed. It was therefore decreed that *all* should be covered. In deference to the less affluent, who were embarrassed at not being able to supply the ornamented bed upon which the dead were to be carried to their graves, it was instituted that a plain bier be used for rich and poor alike. This without doubt was the forerunner of the simple wooden coffin. Similarly, because the poor could not afford the more ornate and expensive death wardrobe, it was ruled that white linen shrouds be worn by all. No less a prestigious person than Rabbi Gamliel II of the end of the first century in Palestine set the example by directing that he be buried in ordinary linen shrouds. This became common practice in the Diaspora as well; Rabbi Papa, who lived during the middle and

latter half of the fourth century, was reported to have said that
"nowadays everyone follows the practice of burial in a very in-
expensive shroud."[11]

Whether precisely the same practices should still be compulsory for a tradition-loyal Jew in our time could stand some
scrutiny. What was deference to the poor in the early centuries
of the Common Era may no longer be so. The deceased is no
longer carried out on the open bier. The public no longer
sees what the deceased is wearing. The simple wooden coffin
which resembles an orange crate is not necessarily the best or
most beautiful way in modern times to satisfy our desire for
simplicity and egalitarianism in funerary procedures. Thus the
specific customs that arose in the first century in Palestine require
re-examination and should be relevantly applied in our time to
meet our aesthetic and economic standards.

There were many more fasts observed in Talmudic times.
Communities often fasted as a supplement to prayer in periods of
drought or other public calamities. Frequently the fasts were conducted in sequences of three days, although not in succession.
But the sages were quite practical in dealing with an otherwise
ritualistic piety. They regulated the fasting halakha so that one
of those ad hoc public fasts would not take place on Thursday
lest the inordinate demand for food on Thursday night and again
immediately on Friday in preparation for the Sabbath give shopkeepers an excuse to exorbitantly raise their prices. One need go
no further to find an excellent and cogent example of the ecoomic
humanitarianism that played a commanding role in the halakha.
In our own time, when prices are unnecessarily increased for
kosher food or for Passover food beyond a reasonable level, the
Rabbis, far from expressing opposition to the practice, merely
contend that if someone wishes to be faithful to his tradition a
little sacrifice is in order![12]

In these and countless other ways the sages acted in the
socio-economic interest of the people. Judaism was to be enjoyed, not resented; was to uplift life, not cast a pall upon it.
Economics is a seemingly unspiritual facet of human life. But it
originally merely signified "household management"; and a person

cannot be spiritually uplifted, at ease with his God, enjoying peace of mind and the blessings of religious faith, if that very religious faith requires him to sacrifice his personal economy in the fulfillment of unreasonable demands that cannot possibly add to his spiritual inspiration.

To apply this concept relevantly in modern times, we would feel a compulsion to re-examine and re-evaluate the "Passover label" practices. We are all aware that many products are sold on the market for which a higher price is asked at Passover, with the packaging supervision and labeling process given as an excuse. Yet we are equally aware that halakhically many of these products absolutely do not require a label and that the year-round products could be used just as well. The same re-examination and re-evaluation ought to be given to the whole area of *kashrut* and the availability of kosher meat in the supermarkets at supermarket prices. Arrangements could be made for the slaughtering of all meat in a given locale in a manner acceptable to Jewish practice. The dairy-meat separation as it affects glazed china, the cycling processes of automatic dishwashers, Passover-all-year dishes, all require re-examination with a view to developing a revised and updated household halakha.

In their day the halakhic sages, from the pre-Pharisaic teachers of the third century before the Common Era through the Tannaim, Amoraim and Gaonim, saw this periodic requirement of revision quite clearly. For them, the economic motive in halakhic interpretation was not materialistic but was profoundly religious and highly humanitarian. And so it must become once more for us.

Chapter VIII

LOOKING FORWARD
IN HALAKHA

SOME TEN YEARS ago Rabbi Boaz Cohen, of blessed memory, had a collection of his essays published.[1] At the time, I wrote a review article on it (*Reconstructionist* of January 22, 1960). This chapter is based on that article, omitting its critical elements and confining itself to the objective halakhic material, as well as expanding and updating its content.

Rabbi Cohen was an erudite scholar who was able impressively to marshal data on any question in Rabbinic literature. I wrote then that Cohen could amass "an awesome amount of information and references that in some instances stagger even the initiated." As in the case of Professor Saul Lieberman, Boaz Cohen provided a large body of material that helps us find guidance for a future halakha, even if he was too reticent to draw his own conclusions.

Rabbi Cohen enabled us to see how the Rabbis bypassed the literal meaning of the scriptural text even when their interpretation might have resulted in the opposite of what the Torah intended. He taught us to see the Rabbis of the Talmud as "skilled jurists" who "employed all the art and artifices at their command to make the Bible a living law in their day," and he lauded them "for their exhibition of a remarkable ingenuity and resourcefulness in making the Scriptures a living source of inspiration for Jewish law and ritual, for manners and morals."[2]

The only justification the Rabbis could have had for bypassing Scripture—and in effect abrogating scriptural law—was that they regarded the *spirit* of the law as more significant than the letter of the law. This is well illustrated, as Boaz Cohen noted, in an interesting passage in the Talmud.[3] R. Yohanan quotes R. Ishmael on instances where the limitations of the scriptural verse were extended by halakha. This is not the place to enter into an exposition of that passage, but one example will be offered. The Torah indicated that if a man stopped being pleased with his wife, he might write a bill of divorce. The scriptural term used is *sefer keritoot*, and implies a formal court document, just as elsewhere the term *sefer* signifies a formal "bill of sale" or a "deed." It may even imply that there existed a technical format. But the halakha permitted the severance passage to be written on anything, even on a fig leaf or a scrap of clay. It was sufficient for some sages, among them Rabbi Ishmael, if the *intent* or the *spirit* of the law was fulfilled even if the precise technical details were bypassed. Rabbi Ishmael went further in this emphasis on the spirit of halakha when he pointed out that the *lex talionis*, the famous "eye for an eye" injunction, did not mean that at all but meant monetary compensation. And he supported his opinion by an even wider deviation from the text when he interpreted the punishment to be meted out to one who assaulted a man as monetary damages, although the verse clearly states *yumat*, "he shall be put to death."[4]

The Jews of the Talmudic period lived in a watershed of history. The destruction of Jerusalem ushered in a new world. The socio-cultural underpinnings of Jewish society were gone. Palestine was prostrate and Jerusalem destroyed, and a whole cultic system was uprooted. It is therefore no wonder that the Rabbis responded to the profound needs of the time with alacrity. They were distressed at having to bypass the Torah but were conscious of the need to do so. Thus, despite the opinion that no new mitzvah should be innovated, other opinions were repeatedly expressed to indicate that they were totally conscious of innovation![5]

Similarly in our age, the style of Judaism in Eastern Europe was swept away by the consequences of the Emancipation and the Haskalah, the nineteenth-century Enlightenment. These historic forces reached their culmination in the evolution of American Judaism. A transformation has taken place in our thinking.

Consequently a transformation ought to take place in Judaism similar in potency and sweep to that of the Talmudic age.

Boaz Cohen clearly enunciated this as the challenge of our time. He wrote, "It is imperative now more than ever, to recapture the spirit and significance of the Talmud with its uncanny insights and previous intuitions, its homespun philosophy, as well as the courage, independence and resourcefulness of its teachers. Let us be awakened and instructed by their intelligence and live in the new dimensions created by them."[6] What this calls for is resourceful men who seek new directions in the path of halakha and new vistas in our faith. Thomas Jefferson once wrote, "To lose our country by a scrupulous adherence to written law, would be to lose the law itself, with life, liberty and property . . . thus absurdly sacrificing the end to the means. . . ." And this was precisely what Rabbi Yohanan in the Talmud meant when he taught that the destruction of the Temple and the exile from the holy land was the fault of the overscrupulousness of R. Zechariah b. Avkulos. The latter refused permission for an animal donated by the Roman emperor to be offered to the altar because although it was not disqualified from the pagan altar, it was from the Jewish altar. Other sages present at the time favored offering the gift upon the altar, since it was a pagan gift, which was permitted, and since it was qualified according to Roman cult practices. But R. Zechariah b. Avkulos protested that it would be unseemly to offer on the Jewish altar that which possessed a disqualification under Jewish law even if it was a pagan gift. This refusal was interpreted as treason according to that story and was a decisive factor in the siege and destruction of Jerusalem. Here was a case where the Essence, the very existence of Judaism, was subordinated to the Forms, the halakha of sacrifices. Too often we are so scrupulous about detailed minutiae intended to preserve Judaism that we become indirectly responsible for the very spiritual disasters we fear.[7]

This is well borne out in the matter of *shevut,* an occupation or activity considered by the Talmudic Rabbis to be out of harmony with the nature of the Sabbath. The Rabbis regarded such an activity as a Rabbinic prohibition. Considered *shevut* by the

Rabbis were such activities as swimming and dancing. Nevertheless, dancing has been permitted for centuries.[8] And in more recent times both activities have been permitted to varying degrees in both Orthodox and Conservative circles. Hasidim have always overlooked the prohibition; and in Camps Ramah of the Conservative movement, while swimming on the Sabbath is not a general and scheduled activity, it is a permissible one. These lapses, as one might term them, are allowed despite the many stringent statements made in the Talmud concerning the violation of Rabbinic law.[9] Setting aside *terumah* (dedicated contributions of various sorts) or tithes was also prohibited on the Sabbath as *shevut*. Although we no longer set aside *terumah* or tithes, there appears to be little objection, even in presumably halakha-oriented synagogues, to Sabbath and holy-day appeals for UJA and other charitable causes, as well as for strictly capitalist investment enterprise as represented in the purchase of Israeli Bonds.

We continue to live in a strange halakhic universe of discourse when we are in favor of the preservation of a category of halakha such as *shevut*. Our ancient sages were certainly more consistent. From Sifra we learn that *shevitat mitzvah* and *shevitat reshut* were equally prohibited. This meant that it made no difference whether the activity was related to the performance of a religious obligation or merely an act for a secular purpose. But in our day we draw arbitrary lines within that which we consider part of the mitzvah of *Oneg Shabbat,* such as "Israeli dancing." This we apparently do not consider a *shevut,* and we permit it. And we categorize other dancing, such as popular ballroom steps, as not being in the spirit of the Sabbath and hence prohibited as a *shevut*. Yet this approach is wholly without warrant in Tannaitic literature. I am not objecting to Israeli or Hasidic dancing on the Sabbath. I am merely initiating a call to redefine the whole concept of *shevut* so that we will have an opportunity to approach Sabbath observance in a far more rational manner. The Rabbis prohibited an activity which they considered out of keeping with the spirit of the Sabbath, a *shevut,* even if it was in the nature of a mitzvah, such as setting aside tithes. What our generation requires is a restatement of the concept of *shevut* so that we consider as *shevut* only that which detracts from the enjoyment of the Sabbath in the home or the synagogue and in whatever recreational activities a person may engage. Thus I would find it perfectly consistent with halakha to permit several people to travel to a tennis court to play a friendly game on the Sabbath. But I would advocate the prohibition of *shevut* to discourage participation in a tennis tournament, which I would consider not in the spirit of the Sabbath because spectators pay admission to a game which is shot through with aggressive competition. The Sabbath should be a day of integration of man's faculties—the intellectual, the physical, the psychological and the emotional. Aggressive, organized, competitive sports would not be in the spirit of that objective.

This is merely one example, and a highly relevant one, in our recreation- and sports-minded society, vital as guidance for Jewish centers and country clubs as well as synagogue youth groups, not to speak of those individuals who would still like to feel they have not deserted the Sabbath although they are unable to observe it in a highly traditional manner.

Consistency is not necessarily a desirable objective in halakha. But neither is it desirable to make a fetish of inconsistency. Therefore the approach we take to *shevut* would involve us in greater consistency than that of the present traditionalists, who have been utterly inconsistent. On the one hand, they have disregarded the Tannaitic position in which no distinction was drawn between mitzvah (a religious act) and *reshut* (a secular act). And on the other hand they cling tenaciously to those acts of *shevut* which they have permitted but which are in violent opposition to other acts of *shevut* which may be of even greater moment for the future of Judaism. This frozen inconsistency is even more damaging than consistency, although neither position is desirable in a halakha which demands flux and adjustment.

The *Mekhilta de R. Shimon* is cited by Boaz Cohen as a source for prohibitions within the category of *shevut*.[10] Random examples can be quite rewarding in teaching us how to apply the concept to our own time. During the Middle Ages there was a uniform practice of interrupting religious services to allow petitioners to bring accusations against their fellow townsmen. Yet, as Cohen pointed out, "the making of pleas and the bringing of accusations" was a *shevut,* although it was not labor. This had been prohibited in the Mekhilta, but the prohibition was ignored. It therefore appears that certain compelling reasons often exist to sweep away or ignore Rabbinic prohibitions. This is undoubtedly the justification for charitable appeals and the sale of bonds during a religious service. It would undoubtedly be argued that the cause is of such overriding importance that the *shevut* may be disregarded. It is perhaps also likely that because of the overriding importance of restoring respect for the halakha and making conscientious and intellectually honest observance of some form of Sabbath possible in the year 2000 that the category of *shevut* should immediately undergo a complete re-examination. It is conceivable that permitting a youth group to have rock-and-roll sessions on a Friday night might be as compelling a reason to ignore a *shevut* as the right of a medieval Jew to present his planned litigations before the community.

The other side of the coin of *shevut* is *menuha,* "restfulness." In other words, certain activities, although they were not "labor" or creative acts that could be embraced within the primary or secondary categories of the thirty-nine *melakhot,* the interdicted activities, were nevertheless prohibited so as to make *menuhah,* a quiescent restfulness, possible. But it is not questioning the sincerity or the brilliance of the ancient sages to point out that in different periods of history and under varying circumstances of the material civilization in which human beings live, "restfulness" is bound to have varying interpretations. For one person, sleeping all Saturday afternoon may provide reinvigoration for the coming week. For another a drive in the country with his family may serve the same purpose and be far more enriching spiritually and emotionally. The person who endures a week-long bout with the difficulties of urban transportation and crowds and noise and pollution might find the Sabbath surcease more rewarding amidst the beauties and quiet of field and stream. To deny him this possibility because of unwarranted travel restrictions is not to provide him with *menuha,* the objective of the Talmudic sages; it is to deprive him of it.

The Mishna prohibited such activities as plucking hair or applying cosmetics on the Sabbath. Yet our pious forebears always plucked their beards as they sat over the Talmud on Sabbath afternoon, and we do not refrain from applying cosmetics. Few outside the ranks of intense fundamentalist orthodoxy would refrain from carrying on the Sabbath, an activity which is of the thirty-nine interdicted categories of *melakha*. Boaz Cohen pointed out that "the mere literal fulfillment of the Biblical precept proscribing work left many loop-holes for the desecration of the Sabbath." The Karaites took that sentiment to its logical conclusion and went far beyond the Rabbinic insistence upon closing loop-holes with *shevut*. They sought to prevent all possible violations, instituting a system of "hedges" which they hoped would be foolproof by prohibiting one from leaving his home at all, requiring him to sit in the dark and consume cold food.

There is no question about the reality of history. In their time the Rabbis of the Talmud built the bricks of the edifice of *shevut* with a noble purpose. The aim of the Tannaim who began the process, and of the Amoraim who followed, was the development of a quiescent Sabbath. They sought to produce a day of complete physical restfulness, psychological peace and emotional tranquillity. Men were not to speak or even think of weekday activities. The earliest Tannaim interpreted the words *Shabbat Shabbaton,* a complete rest, as requiring that any act which was incompatible with complete rest be prohibited. Other Tannaim used the biblical verse *et Shabtotai tishmoroo,* and similar phrases derived from *shamor* instructing the Jew to "observe" the Sabbath, as implying to "guard" it by refraining from many activities which were not at all physical activities. The idea behind this was that all possible precaution be taken not to violate the Sabbath. Here in the matter of *shevut* on the Sabbath we have, perhaps to a greater degree than in any other area of the halakha, the negative, restrictive idea of building a "fence" taken to its furthest reaches.[11]

These early Tannaim, of first- and second-century Palestine, seeking perhaps some form of "nirvana" in their hectic Greco-Roman civilization with its noisy and crowded cities, its constant turmoil and its severe drudgery of life, were pursuing a noble idea.

Perhaps our society offers parallel conditions casting shadows upon our minds and jarring our nerves. Some would therefore argue that we can benefit from the excessive quiescence of a traditional Sabbath. But we are simply not constructed that way. Some of the Tannaim voiced their deep but for us impossible piety by prohibiting even the *thought* of activity, although later Talmudic authorities did not accept this. The *Mekhilta de R. Ishmael* quite firmly said that one must rest even from "the thought of work," and in that instance used the term *avodah,* which does not have the same technical relationship to the term *melakha* used for the thirty-nine interdicted categories.[12] As a matter of fact, because the word does not have a technical limitation it can refer to almost any form of manual labor or service and it obviously taxes our psychological powers to their utmost. To attempt to fulfill this form of Sabbath is somehow to contradict all the emphasis upon the enjoyment of the Sabbath, for to erase from our lives all conversation and from our minds all thought of weekday affairs, events and plans is to require not an injection of ancient-vintage piety but a very modern tranquilizer drug. We would be so neurotically preoccupied with the rigors of restraint and the fear of petty violation that this concept of total Sabbath rest would set up an obligation which could only lead a modern person to despair of ever fulfilling the will of God. So impossible was this standard suggested in the school of R. Ishmael that the later Tannaim and the Amoraim who followed them no longer accepted it.

There is an interesting passage in Babylonian Shabbat which is of great value in this discussion.[13] The sages evidently were troubled by the Tannaitic stringency, and they sought relief. They found relief by interpreting a suggestion by Isaiah that Jews ought not to discuss business on the Sabbath, or in accordance with a translation of Professor H. L. Ginsberg which I have adopted, ought not to "arrange matters." The later Tannaim who lived in the latter half of the second century, after the end of "the time of troubles," having survived Bar Kokhba's war and Hadrian's persecutions, seem to have taken a more relaxed attitude toward the Sabbath. Thus Rabbi Joshua ben Korha indicated that one might think about business on the Sabbath and even contribute by indirection to another person's giving thought to it. This point was apparently well taken, since Rabbi Yohanan, a giant of the third century, decided the halakha in Rabbi Joshua's favor and this was approvingly cited by Rabbah bar bar Hana of the fourth century. It is further recorded in the same passage and accepted as halakha by Maimonides and Karo that it is permissible to "arrange matters" or discuss those activities which can be classed as mitzvah, or in the words of the Talmud, *heftzai sha'mayim,* "divine matters."[14]

We would not want to distort Rabbinic opinion to the extent of claiming that this proved that an open Sabbath, modern-style, virtually an unobserved Sabbath, would be the logical inference to make from Rabbinic leniency. But what it does prove is that when standards were set too high, a way out had to be found. When early Tannaim seemed to feel the need to retreat into a Sabbath shell and advocated almost a Quaker-like silence, they were simply misconstruing human nature. Such a Sabbath may be a possibility for individuals or for small sects living an isolated existence, but most certainly not for a real people living in a real world and carrying on the usual inevitable social intercourse with their fellow men. Later scholars tried to alleviate this monastic-like Sabbath by returning to the individual his free conscience and the right to the privacy of his thoughts. But they went even further and permitted discussion and "arranging matters," contrary to Isaiah's advice, as long as they felt that these matters fell under the purview of mitzvah.

There is a degree of guidance in this for us, if we are intensely concerned with saving the Sabbath as a vital core of Jewish life and handing it on to our successors. It will be our task to discover new avenues of amelioration, such as R. Joshua ben Korha did in his day and as the later Amoraim did in theirs. As always we can turn to Hillel for inspiration, for in the case of Hillel we have a very early Tanna. When the question of calculating and designating charity for the poor or even a sum of money as a dowry for an orphan on the Sabbath arose, Bet Shammai prohibited it, while Bet Hillel permitted it.[15] Bet Hillel was our perennial progressive school whose members apparently instinct-tively understood that one cannot hold a community to impossible pietistic standards. It was natural to discuss and arrange such human and communal matters on a day when one was free from the weekday drudgery of making a living. Furthermore, the Rab-bis understood, as we see from references discussed in other chapters of this book, that Jews required recreation on the Sab-bath. They permitted the use of the hot baths of Tiberias, as one example, to which reference has already been made.[16] That the concept of recreation and leisure was far different from the one we of today entertain is apparent from the fact that as late as the time of Maimonides there is not evident a specific discussion of a child or an adolescent playing ball on the Sabbath. Although there are dozens of references to throwing and carrying objects from one domain to another or within the same domain, or throwing objects to the top of a pole (in basketball style) or onto a ledge (as in certain forms of handball), there appears to be no actual discussion of the playing of games of ball, whether in teams or individually as purely recreational fun. The references one en-counters are largely not applicable to our own day and hardly serve as guidance for us. Thus Maimonides codified that women may not play games on the ground with walnuts on the Sabbath lest they level off ridges in the ground. I assume the meaning here is: lest they perform the labor of leveling the ground so that the walnuts will roll better; leveling a groove is considered prohibited as a derivative of ploughing. Similarly he decided one cannot play dice on the Sabbath, because it "resembles buying and selling."[17] There seems to be no awareness of one of our major problems, the question of opening Jewish centers to recreational activity or the playing of games such as golf, tennis, basketball and handball on the Sabbath in the outdoors. To say that we should not open a Pandora's box by permitting that which is already done anyhow is merely to express despair of ever restoring a healthy attitude toward our halakha. The question is not whether many people are doing it; the question is, what is the Rabbi's answer if some-one asks whether he may? Swimming also has always constituted a problem. Here too the question is not whether it is a *shevut* ignored by all. The real problem is, may one swim or not? It is apparent that the ancients did swim on the Sabbath. Maimonides informs us that one may swim in a pool inside a courtyard where there is an embankment preventing the water from spilling over. Similarly, if one bathes in the sea on the Sabbath he must dry himself immediately as he emerges from the water. In both cases the only reason is so as not to be guilty of carrying, splashing, throwing or transporting an object, water, from one domain into another or for more than four cubits within a public domain.[18]

It is an elementary deduction, therefore, to say that swimming per se, or having fun as such, is not to be frowned upon. The problem is whether we would give recognition in modern times to the whole question of *shevut* in its aspect of moving an object from one domain to another or within a public or semi-public area, especially when the activity is related to recreational pleasure and the enjoyment of leisure time. Again, the overwhelming majority of Jews today condone swimming and playing ball on the Sabbath. But that is not the issue. The issue is whether individual Rabbis and other halakha-oriented loyalists will allow themselves the luxury of permitting it in their synagogues, in communal centers, for their youth groups and for their own families. The real problem is, what will the public posture be? Shall we continue to pay lip service to an obsolete and stultifying concept or shall we re-examine it radically?

It is clear that later alleviation of the earlier stringencies was in the area of mitzvah. This means that we will have to reconsider what the area of mitzvah shall encompass. For example, if we give greater weight to the criterion of personal spiritual enhancement, it will be valid to explore whether participation in private recreation in a noncommercial setting and without the aggressive competitive facet connected with it might not be a perfectly permissible activity for individuals and groups, and especially within the confines of Jewish communal facilities. It is true that vigorous exercise is forbidden on the Sabbath, including, according to Maimonides, walking until one perspires because perspiring has curative value. It is not the exercise apparently which is the prohibited activity but the fact that one is applying a curative treatment on the Sabbath. Moreover, it is interesting to note that to perform a mitzvah, such as attending synagogue or such as studying, one may even run on the Sabbath.[19]

Again, the challenge that confronts us is the definition of mitzvah in our time. Furthermore, it is highly questionable whether we conscientiously object to medical treatment on the Sabbath, or to the application of even minor medication. We no longer allow people to languish until after the Sabbath even if it is not a life-and-death matter. We use dentrifices, cosmetics, dietary cuisine and most certainly aspirin without really questioning whether they are prohibited as curative agents. Exercise would be no different. The problem, then, once again, at the risk of redundancy, is the willingness to re-examine categories of work, definitions of terms and criteria of halakha within the context of contemporary thought and the current life-style.

The consolation offered by the traditional halakha when one violated a *shevut* was that he would not receive societal or corporal punishment, such as lashes, capital punishment or excommunication. His punishment was between himself and God, similar to that which he would receive for violating a positive commandment in the Torah. In other words, *shevut* was a law without teeth. Its effectiveness depended on voluntary acquiescence and the degree of one's piety. It is well to reflect upon this, for while the nature of our piety is *different* from that of our Palestinian and Babylonian precursors of almost two thousand years ago, and may be no greater, it may also not be lesser. It may simply be *different;* and it is entirely conceivable that we could restore respect for halakha if we, like the sages of that day, concentrated upon creating a halakha for today rather than fight a constant rear-guard action to preserve the halakha of yesterday.

After the Tannaim set up their system of *shevut* prohibitions, aside from certain reconstructions they placed upon some categories, as we have seen, the Amoraim proceeded to compound the restrictions tenfold. The Sabbath was hedged in by countless minutiae that would almost compel one to stay at home like a Sadducee for spiritual safety. That the Jew did not ultimately develop what has inaccurately been styled a "Puritan blue Saturday"—which the Puritans never really developed either—was probably due to their sense of humor. They simply never listened too attentively to their Rabbis, and as time proceeded, exemptions, adjustments and reinterpretations made the Sabbath a day of joy and festivity. For one thing, the Rabbis themselves made a very significant exception. They became so entangled in restrictions that even religious services could not be conducted. And so they devised the theory of *ain shevut bamikdash,* "the rules of *shevut* do not apply in the Sanctuary." Naturally this was a very broad principle and had in turn to admit exceptions, just as post-Talmudic authorities found other inconsistencies. But it is a formulation of vast consequence. It is one of those brilliant Rabbinic manipulations of the halakha that ought to encourage and inspire every generation. Not only were all the activities otherwise regarded as *shevut* that were needed for conducting the worship service permitted, but even such remote activities as allowing the High Priest, who had to be a married man, to betroth a woman on Yom Kippur should his wife have died on that day.[20]

The question of *shevut* will be pursued in a future volume both as it pertains to our approach to the Sabbath and as it might manifest itself in its nonapplication to the Sanctuary. Here it will have to suffice to sum up the problem and make a tentative suggestion. It is my considered belief that while it is proper for religion to include the idea of restraint *(shevut),* undue restraint should not apply to the conduct of religious life. The challenge is to determine where restraint from given activities is desirable and how to extend the principle of *ain shevut bamikdash* from its literal meaning to a more symbolic application in keeping with current need. Post-Talmudic halakhists expanded the field of *shevut* restrictions, always with a view to further constricting the lives, activities and thoughts of Jews on the Sabbath. Nobody gainsays their piety and sublime motivation. What must come under critical scrutiny, however, is the wisdom of using the results of their piety to attempt to regenerate ours. What must be clearly recognized is that the scholars of the present should not merely serve as phonograph records reproducing the structures of the past or as stereophonic amplifiers of the medieval codes. They must become laser beams that cut through to the core of the sources and restructure the historic edifice.

Many revisions of halakha have been made in the past. These revisions were required in their day, as other revisions are required in our day. Medieval authorities, not generally credited with adjusting halakha, did a great deal of it. They set aside a *shevut,* asking a gentile to perform a prohibited act on the Sabbath, when it was for the purpose of fulfilling a mitzvah. Rabbi Hai Gaon permitted the violation of the *shevut* prohibiting dancing, when dancing was for a mitzvah. This was despite the fact that, as noted previously, the Tannaim had made no distinction between a *shevut* for a mitzvah and one that was not related to a mitzvah. For kindling a *Yahrzeit* lamp, Rabbi Solomon Luria ignored the *shevut* of asking a gentile to kindle a light on the Sabbath because he considered kindling the *Yahrzeit* lamp a *tzorekh gadol,* "an urgent or highly essential need." In ignoring or setting aside a *shevut,* these authorities were not only violating the Rabbinical restriction, they were ignoring Rabbi Joseph's dictum that one does not set aside a *shevut* to permit a prohibited activity.[21]

But it is therein that the greatness of halakha truly rests—in the fact that halakhists always changed, set aside, expanded and abrogated the laws of the past. Some all too often employed casuistry to harden the fast lines already drawn. But others arose to ride into the fray like a courageous St. George to slay the dragon of puritanical excess. It was indeed a misfortune for modern Judaism that it found itself in twentieth-century Western society encumbered with a sixteenth-century code and several generations of Orthodox scholars and Rabbis who were reluctant to employ the inherent flexibility of the halakha.

Thus even so erudite a scholar as the late Professor Boaz Cohen, who made available a vast treasure of possibilities for our halakha, was himself reluctant to cross the *tehum shabbat* (Sabbath boundary), so to speak. In effect, therefore, he wrote a "Prolegomena" to a reconstruction of halakha, and it is the function of this book to attempt to carry that work further.[22] The premise advocated here is that certain ages call forth restrictive retreat into a halakhic system that protects the Jew from the outside world. Certain other periods of history demand a movement outward that liberates the spirit and enables the Jew to integrate into his society while yet preserving the nature and function of a viable and meaningful halakha.

The Italian Renaissance produced what Cecil Roth has termed "an efflorescence of genius, of vitality and of versatility, coupled with a universality of aesthetic appreciation" during the fourteenth to sixteenth centuries. As always before in dynamic societies such as the Hellenistic, Jews were prominent participants interacting with this Italian Renaissance. There were flourishing Jewish communities in that part of the Italian peninsula most affected by the Renaissance. Jews became Italianized in language, manners and morals. They became card players and sportsmen. They especially became tennis players because tennis was an Italian folk sport played by everyone and was always on the program at popular festive occasions. In 1560 the question whether tennis might be played on the Sabbath was submitted to Rabbi Moses Provenzal of Mantua. His responsum is an interesting illustration for us of how we can attempt to distinguish permissible and prohibited facets within the same activity and permit an activity which is inherently not a violation of the Sabbath and yet restrict the manner and setting in which it may be conducted.[23]

The problems of tennis on the Sabbath in 1560 were no different from many of the problems related to recreation in our own time. Players and spectators placed bets on the results, and the owner of the court received a percentage of the betting pool. Jews expressed their bets in food, since they did not handle money on the Sabbath, but the winnings were later converted to cash. All too frequently young men played tennis during the afternoon Sabbath lecture period which had been customary since Talmudic times and which gained in importance throughout the Middle Ages.[24] Thus there were a number of severe objections to playing tennis on the Sabbath, in addition to which there was the problem of carrying or repairing a "scoop," their form of the racket, and perhaps traveling on the Sabbath. Rabbi Provenzal nevertheless arrived at an affirmative response, requesting they play with their hand—which was another popular form of tennis at the time—

lest the players be tempted to repair a broken string of the racket.

This was a decision which said in effect that the playing of tennis—and there is no reason why this would not be extended to all analogous sports—was not in itself an occupation or activity prohibited on the Sabbath. Those features of the game which were un-Sabbath-like in nature were to be avoided. Presumably when rackets were so plentiful in a tennis court that one need not repair a broken one, this restriction too could be removed in accordance with the halakhic position that when the reason for a practice disappears the practice may be removed.[25] Actually we do find that Isserles, at around that same time in Poland, was lenient toward the playing of ball on the Sabbath, although in the unfortunate process of cumulative restrictiveness later scholars called it an "evil custom," but even these permitted it for children.[26] The commentators were rightly concerned about certain categories of prohibited Sabbath activity, such as *tiltul,* carrying on the Sabbath, and *muktzah,* handling an object which is not necessary on the Sabbath. But whether such concerns should encumber modern man is the real question of our time. For us the real problem is to discover the will of God, and the first task is to dig through the encrustations of centuries of the human attempt to interpret that will. We must not become embroiled in polemics but must take a clear position that there is a difference between theological doctrine and the moral imperative on the one hand and between the forms of expression and acting out these doctrines and imperatives on the other hand. We should not confuse the premises of our faith with the forms. We should not confuse phases of man's relations with God with phases of man's relations with his fellow man. The crucial point is that outside the moral sphere the bulk of our operative halakha is in the field of ritual and domestic relations. The "way" (as some would translate halakha) to observe such forms as are related to the Sabbath, the liturgy, dietary laws—virtually the whole complex of our practices related to God, Jewish history and the personal life-cycle—is not "revealed religion" in the same sense as we might refer to other statements in the Torah as "revelation." An extremely large proportion of these forms of observance are not in the Torah and are basically not reflected in prophetic literature. The bulk of ritual practice reflected in the Torah is related to the sacrificial cult which the Lord himself abrogated in the flames of the last Temple. Even in that segment of Pentateuchal law which we might call divine, the civil and criminal law, we have for centuries recognized *dina d'malkhuta,* the law of the land. Certainly, therefore, there is little reason not to modify this unrevealed, humanly evolved corpus into closer conformity with our cultural concepts and technological realities.

The Sabbath, to which considerable attention has been given in this chapter, must be one of the priorities of our halakhic activity in coming years. For that reason a future volume will devote to that subject one or more extensive chapters. If we are to make "looking forward in halakha" a profoundly conscientious objective, we must study the means to reconstitute a meaningful Sabbath experience in Jewish life which will not only enhance the spiritual life of the individual but also enrich the environment of the Jewish and general community through contributing to the development of better and more-integrated personalities.

Chapter IX

THE FUTURE
OF RELIGIOUS DIVORCE[1]

IT WAS NOTED in the last chapter that the preponderant segment of halakha still practiced by Jews is related to the area of ritual. Included are the rituals of the life cycle—birth, marriage and death. The halakha of marriage, or of domestic relations, is subsumed under the general rubric *hilkhot ishut,* and this sphere of halakha contains the practices connected with both marriage and divorce, as well as with all the related facets of remarriage, levirate marriage and so forth.

The overall sphere of *ishut* is beyond the concern of this chapter. Here we will concentrate upon *Gittin,* religious divorce, an aspect of domestic-relations practices still extremely important in our time. It is important because divorced persons often seek to remarry, and thus valid divorce is related to that most intimate facet of human existence: marriage. People are overwhelmingly concerned lest their marriage be tainted in any form. Perhaps in addition to loyalty to tradition there is also an element of superstition. But wherever there is superstition, rather than denounce it we should seek ways to channel it into meaningful spiritual patterns. This is what Professor Lieberman has indicated the ancient sages did.[2]

The question of religious divorce is one that frequently agitates lay and Rabbinic religious groups. The cumbersome machinery involved in securing a *Get* (bill of divorce) leads to great reluctance on the part of many Jews to subject themselves to the complex arrangements. This in turn has led to widespread disregard of what is basically a very worthwhile institution. How much psychological damage is done to partners who remarry without benefit of a *Get* will never be known. How many women have been condemned to a single state for long years because they were unable to procure a *Get* will similarly never be known.[3]

For those of Reform Jewish persuasion there is no problem. The Reform movement officially recognizes the validity of a civil divorce decree for remarriage within the Temple. But although this is so, many a Jew affiliated with a Reform temple, or Reform by intellectual convictions, may nevertheless seek remarriage with a Jew who finds an emotional need, if not an intellectual one, for the valid religious severance of a previous marriage already dissolved by a civil court. Yet, too frequently the process and obstacles are so numerous and frustrating that those who would rather remarry with a *Get* dispense with it altogether and abandon their respect for and loyalty to halakha.

What has been lacking in the discussion of religious divorce for over a century, since the Reform movement undertook the modification of the institution, is a profound reconsideration of the question from its roots. To abolish the *Get* is not to give it radical halakhic reconsideration. To change the rules, procedures and requirements radically is to reconstruct halakha in a modern mode. *Gittin* is a plant which is in the process of decay. What is required is to examine the soil in which it was first planted and later nurtured. It is necessary to survey the evolution of the cumbersome machinery of *Gittin* and arrive at fresh conclusions.

The ancient right of the husband to divorce his wife at will was the keystone of biblical divorce. Although the harshness of the right has been ameliorated over the centuries and was effectively abolished in the eleventh century by the *Takkanah* of Rabbenu Gershom, one insurmountable obstacle to a rational modern form of *Gittin* has remained: the exclusive right of the *male* to issue the divorce. For whatever reason, the Rabbis throughout the long evolution of halakha have not seen fit to abolish this male right. Its effectiveness has been reduced in certain circumstances, but it nevertheless remains an unjust and obsolete disability upon the wife. Basically a man can no longer divorce his wife at pleasure or at his convenience. But neither can a suffering wife divorce her husband in the extremity of distress. Prior to the eleventh century the husband's initiative was circumscribed in certain unusual cases. He was penalized with loss of liberty to divorce his wife if he falsely accused her of unchastity; furthermore, if he seduced a young lady he was compelled to take her as wife and deprived of the right of divorce. To these restrictions on his power the Rabbis added others. He was prevented from divorcing his wife during her insanity or while she was captive in war or while she was yet a minor. Similarly, if the husband was insane, he was barred from executing a bill of divorce except in his lucid periods. If he was in a state of delirium or intoxication he was barred from divorcing his wife.[4] In effect the Rabbis were conceding the Torah's law that a woman may be divorced without her consent, but allowed for certain limitations upon the husband's powers. Nevertheless, though the husband's initiative was restricted, the wife was dependent on his willingness to order the writing of a *Get,* and was and still is dependent on his will even in the unusual cases where she may sue for divorce.

Grounds for divorce in Judaism were never as restricted as they still are under church influence. Either the wife or the husband was entitled to ask for freedom where there was a physical incapacity to conduct normal sexual relations or a refusal to do so. In cases of apostasy the apostate spouse could be divorced involuntarily. The wife could apply to the *Bet Din,* the Rabbinical court, for a divorce if her husband contracted what was considered an incurable and loathsome disease, such as leprosy, or if he insisted on continuing a disgusting occupation which caused his person to emit a permanent odor. There were many other particular instances in which husband or wife or both or the courts could sue for divorce. But it must be remembered that not even the courts were able to "issue" a divorce. Only the husband had, and according to the present application of the halakha by traditionalists, exclusively still has, the power to execute and cause its delivery. The court could punish him for refusing, but this would not free the wife![5]

The foregoing has simply attempted to indicate that there is liberality and reasonableness in the halakha of *Gittin* with one historic shortcoming consistently persevering. This shortcoming is the husband's sole power to order the execution and delivery of the *Get,* and the absence of a power vested in the wife to do so, or in the courts to do so when they find that a divorce is warranted and the parties are recalcitrant. But it is the very liberality and evident growth of the halakha which should invest us with the inspiration to carry it forward.

It is apparent from the cited sources that the institution of divorce in biblical and post-biblical Judaism was not frowned upon. On the contrary, when a man was deprived of his right to divorce, this was considered a penalty. Divorce was a respectable socio-religious institution. A priest was forbidden to marry a divorcee, but this indicates not a low opinion of divorce but merely a higher standard for the priesthood in which all possible alliance between a priest and a married woman was discouraged by preventing him from ever being allowed to marry her should she be cast out by her resentful husband. For a similar reason of high standards in domestic life the priest was forbidden to marry a prostitute or a daughter of a priest who had become disqualified through incorrect action. It is also obvious that in the biblical period a divorcee was regarded for a number of social practices as similar to a widow. Like a widow she had no male "superior," and she was herself responsible for her pledges or vows. All this merely signifies that the institution of divorce was a respectable one and sanctioned within the halakha, and the person who practiced it was not looked down upon. The negative attitude toward divorce and divorced people was one that emerged with the New Testament and the early Christian abandonment of halakha.[6]

The biblical law, therefore, not only presupposed the respectability of divorce, it encouraged a moral outlook which included divorce within its domain. A man might divorce his wife. She might then remarry. But once she had remarried he was no longer free to marry her again should she be divorced by her second husband or widowed. The reason for this is understandable in the light of the fact that the halakha always pursued higher moral objectives. Thus to be deprived of the right to remarry his wife at some future date under given circumstances would deter a man from easily sending her away. It would encourage him to give serious and profound consideration to saving his marriage. This law in Deuteronomy was evidently part of the growing process in which divorce was within the moral framework of social custom and in which concern for the women was expanding. Earlier, in the days of the early monarchy, David was given Michal as his wife by her father, King Saul, and just as simply taken from him and given to another. When David had the power he retrieved his wife. It was this kind of easy exchange related to the disputes of men that the later halakha prevented, as well as providing husbands with the need to ponder mightily the ramifications of divorce.[7]

In any case, there is no specific statement in the Torah which explicitly ordains the right of divorce or legislates its procedures. All we can surmise from the Torah is that a man was able to divorce his wife for sufficient reason, and that if he did so they were both free to remarry. We can also see that when a man divorced his wife he had to present her with some form of *Sefer Keritoot,* a "severance document," the term *keritoot* in this context probably having the same force as the Latin *divortere,* "to separate from," whence we derive our English term "divorce."[8]

There is not a shred of information to teach us what the severance document contained, how it was written, what procedures were followed in executing or delivering it or whether there was any religious ceremonial involved or not. We have no hint of any method used to safeguard against falsification. There is no mention of the husband's involvement with elders or judges, witnesses, priest or sage. Although it is only with some reluctance that we ought to make any inference from silence on a subject, it would appear that the silence of the Torah on all these matters in rather eloquent. It might follow that the institution of divorce was ancient and respectable but was a mere technicality in which any form of written proof was given the woman by the husband, even in private, for her protection. This written document alone gave her the right to remarry, and saved her from being cast adrift in the world. The severance document was the first step in the long process of emancipation which women underwent. It was simply seen as inhuman to allow a man to summarily dismiss his wife at his arbitrary whim by word of mouth in a moment of impulsive anger. The very need to collect himself and execute a formal document, as well as to ponder that should she remarry he would never again regain this woman who was the love of his youth, would afford both partners the necessary cooling-off period to recapture their reason and restore moderation to their relationship. It was therefore perhaps even more than protection of the woman against the highhanded tyranny of a dominating male in an ancient patriarchal society. It also had a strong psychological force that could serve to save a family. Furthermore, it forever prevented a despotic or vengeful husband from playing with the emotions and security of his helpless spouse. If she had no written evidence of the divorce and planned to remarry, he might claim that he had never really divorced her and that she was still bound to him. Finally, it was indirectly protection for the male against himself as well. A moment of temporary or compulsive anger might have deprived him of a good mate, while the period involved in executing a formal writ might provide him with the opportunity to restore balance to his thinking.

Nevertheless, it is unquestionable that the law of divorce was primarily for the protection of the woman. This is evident from the manner in which at first the rights of the husband were restricted and later the rights of the wife were extended. When a husband falsely accused his bride of unchastity and stood exposed to the public as a fabricator of lies, he was forbidden to divorce his wife thereafter. On the other hand, as we learn from Philo of Alexandria, although the Torah does not say so, the Oral Law in this instance was that she might leave him.[9] In other words, after he had tarnished her reputation, her potential in the marriage market would have fallen despite her exoneration. We are familiar with the way the rumor and suspicion of scandal cling to their victims long after the contrary facts have been determined. Consequently, the Torah required the husband to retain the woman as wife and to maintain her economically and provide her with the respectability that the marital status afforded one in the community. His separation from her would only confound the appearance of guilt on her part. On the other hand, after having been publicly excoriated by her husband and made into a communal mockery, if she willingly decided to leave him because she was confident of achieving her own respectability and security she was not to be regarded as a captive bound to him forever.

Along similar lines, when a man raped a woman he was compelled to marry her and was deprived of his right to divorce.[10] The reasoning would be similar. This ruling compensated the woman against the tarnished reputation which affected her desirability as a wife and reduced her opportunity for economic security and communal respectability. The Torah halakha was always on the side of human right and welfare. It strove to protect the underpriviledged and those exposed to the social, economic or political power of the wealthy and influential. Conversely, when necessary, it promoted the defense of the upper classes against the possible envy and quest for vengeance of the weak or the poor. In either case, the halakha of the Torah was concerned for the welfare of man. The sages used this concern as a fundamental basis of halakha in their own deliberations and termed it *mipnai darkai shalom,* "for the sake of the ways of peace." In this context the term *Shalom* may be properly understood in its comprehensive sense of "human welfare" and not restricted to its narrower meaning of peace. What the sages intended in their halakha, as did the Torah, was to legislate for the promotion of social welfare as it affected both society collectively and the human person individually.[11]

With this in mind we can understand the Pharisaic-Talmudic halakha of marriage and divorce as endeavoring to mitigate inequalities suffered by women at that time. For this reason the *Ketuvah,* the marriage contract, was introduced. This provided the wife with economic security in the event her husband suddenly and arbitrarily sent her away, or in the event he died. Similarly the extension of the halakha of divorce was intended to reduce the wife's legal disabilities. The emerging halakha further restricted the husband's arbitrary powers and expanded the wife's rights. The halakha may have reached a peak in pre-modern times when Rabbi Gershom of the tenth and eleventh centuries engineered the edict that no divorce might be issued without the consent of the wife. In the Middle Ages, despite the supposed insulation of the ghetto, the husband learned from his gentile counterpart that a regular beating might induce his wife to obedience. But the Rabbis were repulsed by the idea, and they compelled the inveterate wife beater to divorce his wife. Such provisions, along with the ban on polygamy, were all directed toward one objective: the curbing of the husband's arbitrary power and the extension of the wife's right.[12]

As will be more extensively discussed later, this tendency reached what might be considered a dead end in modern times when those who were responsible for decision-making in halakha were reluctant to take creative and innovative steps. Yet to judge the overall philosophy or tendency of the halakha by certain inexcusable problems that arose to plague the modern Jewish woman who desired to remain loyal to halakha would be unfair. It was not the halakha but the decision-makers—in current parlance the "Establishment"—who were at fault. For in previous generations, whether to divorce or not to be able to divorce, to free the wife or to curb the husband, the halakha was directed toward human welfare and was not bogged down in technicalities. All the restrictions, refinements and extensions of the halakha of divorce which evolved over the centuries connected with the right to issue a *Get,* the manner of writing and delivering it and the restriction upon issuing a *Get* were in reality a "liberalization" of the halakha. All the minutiae which served as a "hedge about the Torah" were safeguards for the rights and security of the woman. This in effect serves further to elucidate the conception I have expounded that the injunction to make a hedge about the Torah was a positive one, an injunction to create greater possibilities of affirmation in Judaism and not exclusively an admonition to crawl into a shell of restriction.[13]

George Foote Moore has pointed out that the legal status of woman under Jewish law "represents a development of Biblical legislation consistently favorable to woman."[14] Moore has helped greatly in dispelling the palpably untrue idea derived from New Testament polemics that the ancient Rabbis were hardhearted legalists more concerned with the meticulous technicalities of the law than with human relations. The tragedy of modern times when there developed a vast multiplication of *agunot,* women who were "chained" to husbands who had left them, deserted them, divorced them civilly and remarried, while they remained unable to remarry within the procedures of the halakha, was not the result of Talmudic-medieval halakha but the reluctance of modern decision-makers to deal with the problem realistically. The ancient Rabbis overdid the technicalities of halakha only in the interest of preserving righteousness and harmony among men. They conceived of the Torah as having the objective of elevating life. Our problem has been that we have not acted on enough occasions and in enough cases of halakhic obsolescence with this philosophy uppermost. Instead we have too often chosen as our incentive merely the need to preserve tradition. Our energies are expended in the struggle to conserve *forms,* often forms empty of true religious significance, hallowed as the forms may have been by age. Frequently we are preserving vessels emptied of their contents, although it is the contents and not the vessels which are really significant.

The Rabbis did not recognize a *Get* executed in a non-Jewish court. The reason for this was not obstinate antipathy to a civil decree as we understand it, for the Rabbis recognized other documentary attestations and decisions entered by gentile judges in civil cases as fully valid. What the Rabbis were laboring under was their apparent uncertainty whether the gentiles possessed any form of divorce document and consequently whether they possessed proper and precise judicial proceedings and expertise that would measure up to the needs of halakha. The Palestinian Talmud reflects this uncertainty when the query was posed, Do the gentiles have divorce proceedings? The reply given by R. Yohanan reflected their uncertainty; he said, "Either they do not have divorce proceedings or husband and wife may divorce one another." Obviously they had in mind the contrasting attitudes current in their day. The emerging Christian sect prohibited all divorce, while the Greco-Roman pagan culture allowed for either party to dissolve the marriage. For the halakha, therefore, the validity of a writ of divorce issued in a gentile court was brought into serious question. When the question arose, therefore, about the validity of a *Get* executed in a gentile court, there was a difference of opinion. According to R. Simon, those who disqualified a *Get* executed in a non-Jewish court did so only if the *Get* was executed and issued by laymen *(hedyotot)* who were not judges. Later, in the Talmud's observations on this line in the Mishna the stress is placed on the idea that gentiles are not subject to the Jewish marital halakha and therefore cannot serve as functionaries in cases pertaining to those matters.[15]

It is evident that the scholars were not clear on this question of divorce proceedings among gentiles, but they had a firm realization that it was not mandatory. It therefore appears that their greatest concern was that there were ambiguities in a gentile-executed divorce which the Rabbis hoped to avoid by banning it. Thus, although divorce may have been a civil matter before Christianity turned it into a religious one, because the Rabbis did not recognize the civil transaction for the reason already stated, *Gittin* never came under the Rabbinic category of *dinah d'malk-hootah dinah,* "state law is binding." Therefore civil divorce law never superseded the Jewish halakha of *Gittin.* It is a moot point whether in our time, when, for the most part, divorce is again a civil matter and is a required court procedure governed by state legislation, the Rabbis would have taken the same position. Furthermore, in our time it is probably a safe guess that no Rabbi will issue a *Get* before a civil decree has been executed. By the same token no Rabbi will refuse to execute a *Get* if the husband desires to issue one after a civil decree has been executed. This is a tacit admission that we regard the civil decree, not the *Get,* as taking priority *because of the law of the land* and that we accept the subordination of the marriage status to the law of the land. It is the state license that permits the union of two people and the civil decree alone that severs the bond. The *Get* permits remarriage according to the halakha, and only when the *husband* absolutely refuses the *Get* is there an obstacle in the way of remarriage. Now that Rabbis have decided creatively within *halakhic procedure* to remove this impediment—as has been done in the Rabbinical Assembly (Conservative)—the tacit admission that the *civil law* takes priority and that the *civil law* makes and severs marriages is even stronger.[16]

Finally, the ancient concept of the "non-Jewish courts" categorized in the Mishna is no longer valid in modern society. In the courts of many countries there sit Jewish judges, and judges of all faiths or no faith. Most especially in Western democratic society, where the problem concerns us, the courts are *our* courts. They are neither "Jewish" nor "non-Jewish." They are domestic, civil, criminal or appeals courts. All things that pertain to the judiciary, the legislature and the executive on a federal, state or municipal level are neither Jewish nor non-Jewish. The old Mishnaic category simply no longer applies, and we have to consider whether *our* civil courts would be considered adequate for the purposes of *Gittin,* that when a marriage is severed in a civil court both parties are free to remarry within the halakha. In modern society generally, where church and state are separate, divorce is a civil matter, and consequently, since Judaism recognizes the civil courts in all civil matters because of the principle of *dinah d'malkhutah,* the civil divorce would be adequate. This would mitigate any further need to "liberalize" the halakha of *Gittin.* In fact, this is the opinion chosen by the Reform movement during recent generations. But it is not the option I would choose. A state license is required for a marriage, yet we offer a religious ceremony and *ketuvah;* so too, although a state divorce may be executed, it remains a matter of religious relevance to have a religious severance of the marriage. Marriage is a sacrament and should not be undone by a mere secular act. People should be required to end their sacred relationship in the dignity and the spirit of reconciliation offered by a religious rite. The hatred and venom often generated by divorce might thereby be dissipated, and the children and other innocent bystanders might be better for it. What is needed in our time is not the abolition of *Gittin* but a new approach to the process.

There are many built-in opportunities for modifying the halakha of *Gittin* within the framework of tradition. There is that aspect of divorce as noted previously that may allow it to be considered a civil matter. But to transform the institution of *Gittin*

from a religious concern to a secular legal matter requires far
more study and consideration; and even after that is accorded
the subject, it may be a matter of "the gain being dissipated in
the loss," as Pirke Avot put it.[17] Such drastic surgery is neither
required nor desirable. There are other possible avenues of approach. The Mishna teaches that a *Get* may be written on any
material and with any substances that leave a permanent mark.[18]
In the light of this it would appear that simplification alone in the
process of producing a *Get* would alleviate some of the incon-
venience, annoyance and expense involved in its execution. A
Get could be printed with good type on good vellum or bond.
The traditional need for parchment, a quill and specially con-
cocted ink, with a scribe seated for several hours copying an exact
form of block lettering, beginning over again each time he com-
mits a minor error, should not be mandatory. Essentially the *Get*
is as legally meaningless a document as a *Ketuvah*. It is basically
a superfluous document serving no real part other than a symbolic
one in severing the already broken marriage bond. The purpose
it serves is to evoke a religious sanction for the eventual remarriage of the severed parties to others. The *Ketuvah* has far
more significant symbolic value as a certificate attesting to the
religious sanction of the union of two people created in God's
image entering into a life devoted to mutual love and companion-
ship. Yet the *Ketuvah* can be bought by the dozen or the hundred
in all styles and forms. The *Ketuvah* marks hope and promise,
yet is a haphazardly executed event often concluded in two separate hotel rooms or in caterer's cubicles amidst jolly jesting. The
Get which marks the failure of human courage and love, the *Get*
which attests to the impatience and inadequacy of the partners and
to the defacement of God's image, has been given a prominence
it hardly deserves in Jewish religious life. Reconsideration of the
manner of execution, therefore, should take top priority in the
future halakha of *Gittin*.

There can be no question that the bill of divorce as a formal
document is of high antiquity, although it is evident that its nature was not yet determined in the seventh century before the
Common Era. The prophet Deutero-Isaiah used the same term

as Deuteronomy, perhaps a century later. But like so many other biblical institutions, the *Sefer Keritoot* (severance document) mentioned in Deut. 24:1-4 depends on the oral halakha for elucidation. The ultimate evolution of its rules and form, like that of all legal documents, was designed to reduce uncertainty and to maximize exactitude in determining the mutual financial obligations and rights of the severed couple. But here again the *Get* in modern times is merely symbolic. It settles no property rights and establishes no obligations. The necessity for a complex procedure which can be executed only by an expert is drastically reduced.

Under the halakhic procedure concluded in Talmudic times the husband had just to issue the order for the writing of the *Get* and the person who wrote it was not authorized to deliver it to the wife unless the husband specifically authorized him to do so. This is understandable under the laws of "agency" in which an agent, a *sheliah* or "deputy," is not permitted to exceed the precise assignment given him. If a husband died between the writing of the *Get* and its delivery, when he had not yet authorized his agent to deliver it, we do not assume that he meant to divorce his wife! She would therefore be considered a widow and subject to levirate marriage or to the *halitza* ceremony which would free her to marry someone other than her brother-in-law.[19]

Obviously these considerations are of little significance in modern times after a civil decree has been issued. It is evident from the fact that a civil decree has been issued, whether secured by the wife or the husband, whether contested or uncontested, whether the husband intended and desired to divorce his wife or not, that marriage of the man and his wife has been dissolved. It may be argued that as long as he has not issued the *Get,* the man evidences a possible intent to rejoin his wife should he be able to persuade her to this. But certainly once his wife intends to remarry another, she is giving her reunion with the first husband no further thought and should be able to regard the dissolution of her marriage as complete. In such an event, it should not be impossible for her to appear before the Rabbi by whom she seeks her remarriage to be blessed and to receive from him an appropriate document severing the religious bond of *kiddushin* (marriage) and declaring her previous relationship as null in the eyes of God and the halakha.

The fact is that a specialist was not actually required for the writing of the *Get*. Anyone could write it as long as a *bar dat* (a person who was a major in age and had all his faculties) supervised it. It was the witnessing of the document which was crucial.[20] Another crucial aspect in the halakha, which will be discussed more extensively later because of its importance today, was the absolute requirement that the *husband* alone direct the scribe to write the *Get,* and if he established an agent the agent could not delegate this authority to another. Not even the authority of Rabbi Hanina, who claimed he brought the halakha from Rabbi Akiva, who was then in prison, sufficed to allow a *Bet Din,* a court of three who received the instructions from the husband to give his wife a *Get,* to appoint a fourth person to write it. Rabbi Meier apparently agreed with Akiva and is so quoted in the Mishna, but Rabbi Yosi's opposition to this was accepted by the codifiers as halakha.[21]

Nevertheless, as always, our sages intrigue us with the manner in which they were able to reverse their halakha in their time when they decided it was in the best interests of human beings and of the viability of the halakha. Thus, originally the Tannaites insisted on the husband's paying the fee of the scribe, but later the Babylonian Amoraim decided the wife must pay the fee. This change was intended for the further protection of the wife, for they must have discovered that husbands balked at the fee and held up delivery of the *Get,* or they may have encountered cases of desertion in which the husband refused to bother with a *Get* owing to its expense. In such instances the wife would become an *agunah,* unable to remarry. It would therefore be a small price to pay if the scribe's fee was all that stood between her and a *Get.* Women would be prepared to pay an even higher price for their marital freedom in such instances, and it behooves us in modern times to reverse other regulations for the enhancement of the woman's position.

In making the change the Rabbis used an interesting phrase; they said, "But nowadays, when we no longer do this," namely, when the husband no longer writes the *Get* himself and delivers it on the spot to his wife, as simply prescribed in Deuteronomy. In "modern times," in other words, the Amoraim were saying that the whole process had become quite complex, and along the way there were many opportunities for the husband to relent or to procrastinate, and by excusing him from the fee they were reducing somewhat the likelihood of his reneging. On the passage in the Talmud which indicates this change of halakha, Rabbenu Gershom added an interesting observation. He attributed it to the institution of the *Ketuvah.* In other words, since one Rabbi had already ameliorated some of the wife's difficulties, recalcitrant husbands were thinking up new ones. They would procrastinate, Rabbenu Gershom supposed, to avoid having to pay the property right of the *Ketuvah.* The Rabbis therefore arranged for the wife to pay the scribe and receive the *Get* from him.[22]

It was a matter of fanciful exegesis which eliminated the practice of having available blank forms of the *Get* for use whenever needed. This definitive objection came about in the third century of the Common Era. The Mishna reflects a time when forms of *Gittin—tofsai Gittin*—were in vogue, as were blank forms of other documents. But the halakha followed Rabbi Elazer, who allowed blank forms for all documents except *Gittin.* The reason for the exclusion of *Gittin* alone was an imaginative interpretation offered for Deut. 24:1, where the Torah refers to a husband who "wrote her a severance document." Rabbi Elazer took this in a most literal manner, emphasizing the word *her,* and insisting that a man must write for *her,* ruled that he must write the entire document, and not only the relevant information of names, place, and date, specifically for his wife. He claimed that the Torah's intent was that each *Get* must be freshly executed for the specific woman to be divorced.[23]

Earlier the signatures of witnesses to a *Get* could be written in any language. Later there arose insistence on a precise Hebrew form in printed block letters. The custom of tearing the *Get,* with which we are still today unnecessarily concerned, never had religious significance. It originated at a time of pub'ic danger when all religious and quasi-religious documents were forbidden by

Roman decree. The *Get* was torn in the presence of witnesses after delivery and was disposed of so that the Romans would not detect the evidence of the violation of their decree. In modern times, though this ancient reason no longer applies and the procedure serves no valid purpose, it is often insisted upon.[24] As regards matters of delivery, Maimonides indicated that witnesses to the delivery were not essential. The Mishna earlier reflected an arrangement in which the *Bet Din* appointed messengers who did not have to repeat the customary formula "Before me was it written and subscribed." In modern times, however, we still require a *Bet Din* to name messengers to deliver a bill of divorce in a place distant from where it was written, with its delivery attested to by witnesses.[25]

All these facets of the traditional halakha of divorce exhibit opportunities, as was suggested earlier in this chapter, for modifying the halakha within the framework of tradition. What is obviously called for is a return to a simpler procedure which would have the sanction of earlier halakha. A modern text for a bill of divorce could be devised with the necessary blanks for the crucial information as in the *Ketuvah*. It could be a printed form, executed by any Rabbi, and handed to the woman as any legal document is executed in a lawyer's office or in a court of law. If the woman is not present, there is no reason why it cannot be sent by registered mail with a postal receipt returned to the sender.

It is quite interesting that Rabbi Solomon Kluger, a foremost nineteenth-century authority, wrote responsa regarding the use of mail facilities for the transmission of a bill of divorce. In one of these he advocated the use of the postal service by the prospective divorcee in a distant place to send a letter appointing an agent to receive the *Get* for her in the city where it was written. Kluger's point was that the gentile mail carrier was not acting as an agent in a religious matter. He was not handling the *Get*. He was merely carrying a letter of appointment of agency, fulfilling a mechanical delivery task that cast no reflection upon the proper execution and delivery of the *Get*.[26]

In modern times there is much opposition to a similar procedure. More than a century after Kluger we still labor under the anomaly that when a *Get* is written in Philadelphia for a woman in Los Angeles, a *Bet Din* must be set up in Los Angeles to summon the woman to receive her *Get* or to arrange for its delivery. Thus, a century after Kluger opened new frontiers for us to explore in the use of mail facilities and non-Jewish subagents, we are still doing business at the old pushcart.

There is little in the halakha to prevent us from going well beyond our present procedures and the intent of Kluger. There should be no objection to our taking a properly executed *Get* and mailing it special delivery and registered directly to a woman in a distant place. The post office and the mail carrier merely serve in the mechanical role of transporting an article. As an agency of the United States government they are neither Jewish nor non-Jewish, and as a "transporter" the post office is not the sender. The sender is the Rabbi, and because the document is registered and he receives a receipt, it is as if he delivered it by hand. The direct "receiver" is the woman who signs for it.

This chapter does not purport to be a study of the history of the halakha of *Gittin,* and is not designed to be a full-scale responsum on how to approach the specific questions of *Gittin* in modern times. It is designed only to adumbrate a few of the facets of *Gittin* which require modification and could be modified with relative ease even within the general framework of tradition. The procedure simply requires reorganization and reformulation. The *Even ha'ezer* lists one hundred and one items in the procedure of *Gittin,* from the reminder that divorce proceedings customarily are not conducted on Friday to the caution that if we are not careful in such matters we may bastardize children. Between these opening and closing items we have a potpourri of such matters as the scribe's being required to furnish the materials which the husband then acquires from him so that the scribe is actually using the husband's materials and not his own. Some of the items listed are repetitious. Many are unnecessary in the age of the printing press, departments of vital statistics, civil divorce courts, marriage licenses with detailed information, and other amenities of the twentieth century. Some items are rather gratuitous, such as Isserles' admonition that the witnesses should "review their lives and repent any sin that they may have committed."[27]

It would require a separate treatise to examine, analyze and evaluate all these one hundred and one items. But without our becoming involved in such an enterprise, it is valid to suggest that we develop a modernized form of *Gittin* rather than witness *Gittin* fall into desuetude for lack of public respect or agree to its abolition. There are many places in the world where Jews will continue to practice a form of religious divorce regardless of what the American community decides. In a mobile world such as the twentieth century is proving to be and the twenty-first will most certainly be, it would be advisable for Jewish women to possess proof of a *Get* when they have been divorced and travel to other lands. Even if a civil divorce became universally acceptable in America, it may never be for religious remarriage in Israel, in South America or elsewhere. A Jewish woman may find a *Get* a mandatory requirement in a non-American community when she presents herself for remarriage. The same holds true for her spouse.

For this practical reason, aside from the spiritual considerations discussed earlier in the chapter, I do not advocate the abolition of *Gittin*. Yet if *Gittin* is retained as a significant and functioning institution in Jewish life, there may be certain situations in modern times in which it can be waived. If a woman has already remarried without a *Get* and thereby become unavailable under the civil law to her erstwhile husband, he should not be required to go to the trouble and expense of issuing her a *Get* when he desires to remarry. For it would be in effect a "Mock *Get*." A *Get* "frees" her to remarry, an act she has already committed. This is even more the case when she has remarried out of the faith and has thereby already expressed her disdain of the traditional Jewish procedures. In such instances the *Get* loses any iota of significance it could possibly claim under normal conditions.

These are instances in which a woman has indicated that she does not desire the protection or the rights which the synagogue has offered her in the form of a *Get*. There are also instances in which the husband is utterly opposed to issuing a *Get*, whether because he lacks the necessary humanitarian instinct or because he is genuinely irreligious or indifferent and negative to any ritualistic requirement. In such cases it is also a Mock *Get* to subject him to whatever blandishments may be possible to procure a *Get* from him. It can only leave a great distaste for Judaism among moderns and damage other facets of Judaism. This is more the case when husbands are subjected to black-market divorce mills. Whatever purpose is being served by preserving the minutiae of traditional *Gittin* is lost in the mockery involved. It is a case of *Yotzo s'khoro b'hephasaido,* "the gain is dissipated in the loss," as our Rabbis phrased it.[28]

Ultimately consideration has to be given to the wife's right to execute the bill of divorce. In ancient times a man was permitted to indulge in polygamy. If he desired another woman he had no need of a paramour; he was free to take her as a wife to enjoy her company. His first wife might have suffered from this but was not entitled to a *Get*. In modern times if he wishes to legally indulge his desire for another woman, the husband secures a civil decree and marries his new love. She may even be non-Jewish. He defies all facets of halakha, but his wife remains ritualistically incapable of remarriage as long as he is spiteful and recalcitrant and refuses to execute a *Get*. Mindful of the advances made by the Conservative Rabbinate in such cases, we should also consider her right in such an instance, among others, to initiate and execute a divorce. In this age of the equality of all individuals in the rights to be enjoyed under law, it is inconsistent with the spirit of Judaism and the historic liberalism of the halakha to limit the power of *Gittin* to the husband.[29] For this consideration we also possess halakhic warrant. The Talmudic Rabbis were perfectly amenable to the equality of the sexes in wide areas of the halakha, and there is little reason to suppose that had they been alive and functioning in the twentieth century they would not long ago have extended this equality of the woman to the area of divorce. The Rabbis said, "Scripture has equalized the woman to the man regarding all the laws of the Torah," but unfortunately in their time permitted women only to sue for divorce and not to execute divorce. It is difficult to ascertain why, aside from their exegesis based on Deuteronomy 24. Perhaps because the emancipated woman of the Greco-Roman world was simply "too equal," and the Rabbis were inclined to grant Jewish women wide resources for protection but at the same time remind them that a stable family life must ultimately rest upon respect for the male's authority. Another explanation may be semantic. The term used in that statement regarding equality under the law is *din*, which traditionally has been limited to civil law. But while this may explain the text, it does not establish the motive. Nor is it clear that there is any real warrant to limiting the term to civil law.[30]

There are many principles in the halakha which can be evoked. It is true that these were used warily and rarely in Talmudic times and under the most extreme of exigencies. But the fact is that they were used, they do exist, and they could be applied in equally extraordinary circumstances in modern times. There is the "power of annulment," which is phrased in the Talmud as *afkee'inhu rabbanan l'kidushin minai*. There was the notion that the Rabbis possessed the power *l'akor davar min ha'Torah*, "to abrogate a Torah law." But even more to the point on the modern scene is the principle in the Talmud *kol d'm'kadesh adatah d'rabbanan mekadesh*, "when a person consecrates a wife it is on the basis of Rabbinic authority." Boaz Cohen has pointed out that this was so bold a principle that the Rabbis never applied it. The only modification we may allow ourselves is that its application is not recorded in a specific case in our extant literature. These principles require extensive thought and research with a view to applying them to our present needs.[31] It is not becoming to merely adopt American law and call it halakha. But it is apparent to all who wish to inquire that our classical texts contain adequate material for a reconstruction of a viable halakha that can serve our present needs. The Rabbi who will take a humane and compassionate approach, opening doors rather than close them in the face of people who have already deeply suffered, when they present themselves for remarriage, is closer to the spirit of tradition. When people present themselves to remarry, they are in a state when they once again enjoy faith and hope for the future, and a little spiritual understanding at that hour might go a far way to win friends and influence people for Judaism. We possess the power to act in the halakha but too often lack the courage, initiative and imaginative creativity. What we need is a philosophic prompting such as propelled the Pharisees, a faith that God's word was meant to bring about human righteousness and welfare. We must come to realize that our task is not merely to preserve relics but to expand our spiritual horizons.

Chapter X

REJOICE ON YOUR FESTIVALS[1]

IN FEBRUARY of 1969 a responsum of which I was a co-author was discussed and voted upon in the Rabbinical Assembly Committee on Jewish Law and Standards. In effect, the Rabbis who associated themselves with this responsum offered for the first time to Jews outside the Reform Movement a halakhic option to cease observing the second day of Sukkot, Passover and Shavuot, the eighth day of Passover and the second day of Shemini Atzeret (Simhat Torah). In the light of this it might seem unnecessary at this time to further expand upon or appear to rationalize and justify the option. It might be considered in the nature of beating a dead horse. But I think otherwise. There is still a great deal of reluctance to accept and implement this responsum; and worse, there is a great deal of confusion regarding its halakhic legitimacy. The American Jewish community is bombarded from all sides with misleading information about the "abolition" of the second day and with emotional appeals to save the second day for the sake of those who need it. It seems, therefore, advisable and prudent to provide a comprehensive discussion of the subject in the context of a work which traces the historic growth of halakha, outlines the future challenges to halakha and proposes at least in outline form certain solutions to vexing problems as we approach the twenty-first century. The mode of observance of our sacred festivals and whether to observe the scriptural or the Talmudic calendar are still very much of a vexing problem.

Aside from the halakha concerning the emergent Passover festival observed while Israel was yet in Egypt, the first biblical statement concerning the observance of festivals requires that three "pilgrimage" occasions be celebrated each year. These are Passover, the spring harvest and the fall harvest. On these occasions the males were to be seen at the Sanctuary with the gifts of their first agricultural yields. What is called in one source "the feast of the harvest" following Passover is called *hag shavuot,* "the feast of weeks," in other sources.[2]

The fullest treatment of the festivals is given in chapter 23 of Leviticus. There they are called "holy convocations," a term not mentioned in Exodus, and they are given more specific dates. It is apparent that the halakha regarding the festivals in Leviticus is of a later time and provided for them in a more specific manner. It is in this passage that the prohibition of work is introduced and the days are proclaimed "holy." They have left the mere naturalistic realm of agricultural thanksgiving and have become holy days, on which the Jew is to devote his time and his mind to things spiritual. The first and seventh days of Passover, the first day of Sukkot and the eighth day, that is, the day after Sukkot, are set aside as "sacred," as is the fiftieth day after the first day of Passover. We therefore find ourselves in a far more spiritual halakha. The first day of the seventh month is mentioned for the first time as a day of "holy convocation" with no work to be done, called by a name which is hardly translatable into English as a mere name, *zikhron teru'ah,* "a blowing memorial" or as elsewhere, "a day of blowing." The Day of Atonement is now introduced as well, when the Jew is to humble or afflict himself, or both, depending on how one reads the Hebrew, although the precise form in which he is to do so is not here expressed. Other new elements in Leviticus are the commandment to dwell in *sukkot* (booths) for the seven days of that festival, the ritual of the *lulav* (palm branch with myrtle and willow twigs) and *etrog* (citron), as well as the introduction of the interesting commandment to *rejoice* on this festival. The historic element is here injected as a complement to the agricultural, for Sukkot.[3]

Once again the festivals are catalogued in Deuteronomy. The seventh day of Passover, like Shavuot, and like the day that follows Sukkot, is called *Atzeret,* which signifies a religious gathering, a parallel term to the *mikra kodesh,* the holy assembly. Once again the element of *rejoicing* is added to Sukkot, but here no mention of "holy convocations" is made as in Leviticus; but the thrice-yearly pilgrimage is once again repeated.[4]

Since this chapter does not purport to discuss the ramifications of biblical text criticism, it will suffice to merely indicate that the differences in biblical sources and omissions or additions in one text over another can naturally be seen as reflections of different editions of the halakha current in biblical times. It may be taken for granted, on the basis of the new Jewish biblical scholarship exemplified by Yehezkiel Kaufman and H. L. Ginsberg, that Leviticus is early, and not late, in biblical literature, perhaps from the time of the early monarchy. Its more highly developed ritualism and ceremonialism does not necessarily point to a later dating, because all the ancient peoples preceding Israel had very detailed ceremonial books.[5]

For the modern Jew, then, the Bible delineates stated calendar occasions which he ought to observe as "holy convocations" with his fellow Jews, restraining himself from his normal occupation, as on the Sabbath, worshipping God in the current manner and *rejoicing* in this. The Mishna and the Talmud reflect how in the course of time customs evolved that became accepted halakha. These have played a significant role in providing avenues of rejoicing, a technique, as it were, whereby the Jew was able to fulfill the mitzvah in great *simha,* in profound gladness. The Jewish tradition developed a "refinement" in the festivals—the necessary additions to the halakha to stress one's dress and one's food, adapting normal psychological wisdom to halakha. The material trappings necessarily influence our mood. Joyousness was more likely under conditions of improved food and drink, singing and dancing, and lengthier worship services with embellished characteristics.

But the greatest stumbling block to the observance of the festivals in modern times has been the need to undergo severe economic hardship and even dislocation, owing to the multiplication of these days since Talmudic times. What would have happened during the nineteenth century if the Diaspora second day of the festival had not existed is an unknown factor of history. The fact is that it did exist and that a great need was felt to dispense with it. As a result the Reform movement did remove it from the calendar. But the bulk of Jews did not turn to Reform and continued to give lip service to both days of the festivals. They were universally observed in the synagogue outside the Reform movement. While every Jewish community was infused with the atmosphere of the theoretic holiness of the days, most Jews were slowly but steadily abandoning *both* days. The reality of life collided with religious theory. Whether the reality of life would not have collided with religious obligation had there been only one day cannot ever be known. But perhaps had there only been one day of each festival, Jews would have observed something of it. The burden of two days with the consequent guilt feelings attached to such intensive sin was a remarkable fulfillment of the Talmudic *tafasta merubah lo tefasta,* "if you try for too much you will achieve nothing."

The economic burden and socially oppressive nature of the Diaspora second day was a prime motivation for change in the nineteenth century. During the Rabbinical Conference at Breslau in 1846, Salomon Herxheimer presented a definitive essay for the abolition of the day. Aside from the expected halakhic arguments, he presented the problems of the viability of the festival status quo under the conditions of modern life. He said, "It is precisely the strictness in the celebration of our important festivals which makes them economically oppressive to the business man, the merchant, and the artisan, for competition is pressing and demands made upon them seem to be growing steadily. The observant Jew feels this pressure strongly and is so disadvantaged that only the most unusual person will have the strength to make such a religious sacrifice." He pointed out that they finally fall prey to "religious indifferentism."[6] We are all aware of the popular argument "all or nothing," which in effect says that if the person cannot observe his religion "correctly," he might as well drop it and not be open to charges of "hypocrisy." This attitude, perhaps more than any other, has led to the debacle of observance in modern Jewish history. The Herxheimer argument of 1846 was no less true in 1969, when I collaborated on a responsum to make the Diaspora second day optional for Jews outside the Reform movement as well. In our times, to the economic question has been added the very serious one related to college and high-school students who are unable to take so many absences and who find themselves at serious disadvantage in the matter of examinations. But what Herxheimer said in 1846 was perhaps even more true in 1969, that even for the observant Jew the "pious enthusiasm" with which festivals were begun was transmuted into "loafing and painful boredom." This may not be the case for all, but there are so few who today observe the restrictions of travel or writing that it appears there is a tacit admission that one need be either "orthodox" or "sinful." It is this impossible alternative which must be eliminated from all facets of halakha and religious life. The halakha must be flexible enough to accommodate a variety of levels of observance.

A great deal is said from time to time about bringing halakha up to date. Rabbis and laymen call for examining our ritual with a view toward making accommodations appropriate to present-day thought and current conditions. It is apparent by now that regardless of what some people may say about religion being basically unchangeable because it is "the word of God," it remains a historical truism that religion *must* change or perish. It is also a historical fact that every religion *does* change.

Judaism most certainly has often undergone mutations and transformations, as became clear in previous chapters. Despite the evolution traceable from pre-Talmudic Judaism to post-Talmudic Judaism, the Judaism of the tenth century of the Common Era had undergone a virtual metamorphosis from that of the fifth century before the Common Era. Similarly, if Judaism is to survive, that of the twenty-first century will have to undergo a radical transmogrification from the Eastern European Judaism of the nineteenth century, which is still basically the Judaism we observe and with which we are struggling. We have inherited a weltanschauung which is Eastern European in origin, and we are hampered by all the obstacles it places in our path. We are suffering under what Professor Walt Whitman Rostow called "neurotic fixations of history." He was referring to nations which are confronted by a whole set of radically new situations and yet cling to old concepts divorced from all reality.

New conceptions of society and a new way of life create a new intellectual trend and a new mentality. Many old ideas taken for granted, and old forms easily accepted, as meaningful and rational by an earlier generation may not be understood or accepted by a new generation. In the case of the Jew of this latter third of the twentieth century the new generation is so mentally divorced from the previous one in matters of religious thought and observance that it is virtually as if several centuries had intervened. In a very real sense, of course, considering the university training and the socio-political environment of the present American generation, numerous centuries *have* intruded between it and the Eastern European Talmudic thought-world of the pre-World War I era, which still constitutes too great a proportion of the conceptual framework of contemporary Judaism.

An example of a religious practice which has literally become a "neurotic fixation of history" in Jewish religious terms is the second day of the festivals observed outside the Holy Land. There was a time without doubt when it served a significant function. It was the Jew's opportunity to dress, rejoice, eat better and rest from a week or a season of drudgery. In the bleak ghetto conditions of poverty and social ostracism every precious day of Yom Tov was a welcome respite and a significant factor in humanizing and civilizing the Jew whom his tormentors sought to brutalize. But in modern times the festival no longer serves that function. The average Jew in the affluent societies of the Western democracies and in South America lives so well and enjoys so much leisure, good food, entertainment and good dress every day, as well as luxury vacations and travel, that he can no longer truly find a Yom Tov as serving that socio-cultural function for him. As a matter of reality, if he cannot rediscover it as a time of meditation and spiritual renewal, he can only find its traditional restrictions bothersome.

On the other hand, modern man must receive his spiritual renewal in shorter spans. He will experience it either in a rela-

tively brief period or not at all. Enforced idleness at home, two
days of lengthy three-hour repetitious services, including Torah
readings which last over half an hour, only tend to turn off the
modern Jew rather than renew him. There was a time when the
average Jew could spend two such long days at home and in the
synagogue, and three if Sabbath and Yom Tov were consecutive.
He was able to enjoy alternately swaying over his religious tomes,
sleeping, discoursing and drinking with his cronies at the corner
"shule." But life is no longer like that. And it would be fan-
tastically unrealistic to expect anything like that to be restored.

There is certainly no evidence in the biblical codes that so
much spirituality was expected of the ancient Jew. He was asked
to cease from his normal occupation and to join in public worship.[7] There is no evidence that he was under a complex web of
interrelated restrictions such as were evolved in Talmudic times
and expanded during the medieval period for legitimate historical
reasons. All the biblical "holy convocations" were commemora-
tions except Yom Kippur, which was unique. The precise day of
their observance, however, depended on the appearance of the
new moon, and this in turn had to be formally proclaimed by
the *Rosh Bet Din,* the president of the Sanhedrin or *Bet Din.*[8]
At first it was the Great Court in Jerusalem which proclaimed
Rosh Hodesh (the first day of the new month), which then determined when a festival fell. This Sanhedrin vigorously guarded
its right to be the sole authority for the proclamation of a new
month. After 70 c.e. this function was transferred to the Sanhedrin which met in Yavneh under Rabbi Yohanan b. Zakkai,
and later to the Sanhedrin at Usha, and wherever else it sat.[9]
For many centuries the prerogative to proclaim the new month
and to fix the calendar was zealously preserved as a Palestinian
prerogative. There was strong opposition to intercalating the
calendar even in Galilee, and although the need to allow it in
Galilee eventually determined the question, an intercalation declared entirely outside Palestine was invalid except in unusually
extraordinary circumstances. After use of the title Nasi ceased,
certain of the functions of the office, such as fixing the calendar,
fell to those sages who took the Nasi's place under varying titles,

such as *resh pirka, rosh metivta* and *rosh ha-sanhedrin.* This function continued down to the twelfth century despite the fact that Hillel II issued a permanent calendar in 359 or 345.[10]

It was a regular procedure for the *Nesi'im,* the "presidents," to send forth what were often termed in the Roman literature of the time "apostles" or "messengers"—men who traveled abroad for the Nasi and acted under his authority to carry learning to the Diaspora and bring back information to Palestine. One of their major functions was to proclaim the new moon, traveling as far away as a thirteen-day journey from wherever the *Bet Din* sat. These messengers crossed the Palestine-Syria border twice a year to notify the communities of the coming Passover and Sukkot.[11]

But before such messengers were dispatched for this purpose, there was a different procedure. Witnesses who saw the new moon came to testify before the Sanhedrin. When the Sanhedrin was satisfied that these witnesses were accurate, *Rosh Hodesh* was proclaimed. Bonfires were then kindled so that all the communities of the Holy Land became aware that the new moon had been seen and a new month had begun. The Mishna informs us that at a certain point cantankerous Samaritans began lighting bonfires to confuse the Jews. Consequently the Sanhedrin dispatched messengers to bring the news of the new month to the communities. Since the arrival of these messengers on the same day in distant communities, or even their arrival in distant places to tell them the accurate day for Passover or Sukkot, was not ensured, people began to observe two days to ensure the proper fulfillment of the Torah observance. Those who lived abroad were forced to rely on their own observations of the sky. Such individual calculations could be unreliable, and people were in fear of not celebrating the holy day at its proper time. Consequently, to satisfy the requirements of piety and to be sure that they would not transgress the true biblical ordinance, a second holy day for each festival was observed. What did this accomplish? It meant that if a certain day was the accurate *Rosh Hodesh,* the fifteenth day therefrom would be Pesah. But should the next day be the true *Rosh Hodesh,* fifteen days therefrom would be an ordinary day and the sixteenth day would be the true festival. By observing the sixteenth as well, consequently, they would not neglect the sanctity of the holy convocation as ordained by the Bible.[12]

After the calendar was permanently fixed in accordance with precise mathematical and astronomical calculations, there could have been no such error. But this second day of the festival was retained as a permanent observance. It has been retained for over fifteen hundred years outside Palestine and outside the ranks of the Reform movement.

The merit of preserving the second day of the festivals has become a subject of serious discussion in recent years, and not too long ago an option not to observe it became a legitimate point of view within the Conservative movement. The significance of the question, however, like that of divorce, or of many other questions, extends beyond the specific issue. It is intricately bound up with our whole present-day approach to halakha and becomes a test of a creative approach to halakha. For creativity in halakha signifies not only creating new modes and forms but pruning dead branches to beautify the garden of halakha so that it is not overgrown with weeds that cause disrespect and disregard. It may well be that the future of Judaism depends on what we do about halakha, and this is as true in the matter of the *Yom Tov Sheni Shel Galuyot,* the Diaspora second day, as in the matter of *Gittin,* divorce.

The positive Jew today can accept a Yom Tov which consists of certain basic home observances bound up with the festival meal, a synagogue worship order of reasonable length and some social visiting. He sees nothing amiss in spending the afternoon at gardening or some other form of recreation. People like to travel, they like to feel that after the *hetzyah la'shem,* after the half of one's Yom Tov which belongs to the Lord has been taken care of, they are free to enjoy the half which is theirs in whatever way their fancy dictates. Thus not only has the traditional observance of the *first* day so far as its restrictive aspects are concerned become relatively meaningless for the twentieth-century Western Jew—or even the Israeli—but to be asked to repeat the restraints on travel, leisure and one's occupation for yet a second day has no appeal at all to the overwhelming number of people. The result has been almost universal neglect of all the festivals except Rosh ha Shanah and Yom Kippur, and a minor obeisance to the Passover Seder. The problem that confronts us is one of a massive conversion of Jews to an observance of the festivals once again, and an understanding of the underlying theology of Creation, Redemption and Revelation that they express. But no return at all can be anticipated as long as the "legitimate opinion," if such it be termed, or better perhaps, the "Establishment," requires what is basically the outmoded, obsolete institution of *Yom Tov Sheni,* and the excessive restrictions of the halakha which take the joy out of joyous festivals as that emotion is understood in modern times.

This chapter, however, is not dealing with the specifics of the traditional restrictions, because I believe that such an exploration of change must be preceded by a study of the whole question of *melekhet avodah,* usually translated as "servile labor," as that term is employed in relation to the festivals. A serious desideratum, as noted in chapter 8, is a full-scale study of the terms *melakha* and *avodah,* and an exploration of how to redefine these concepts for the modern era.[13]

To return to the biblical observance of a one-day festival is adequately sanctioned in halakha itself. In a discussion concerning the use of an egg laid on Yom Tov, Rabbi Judah and Rabbi Assi disagree on whether, if the egg was laid on the first day of Yom Tov, it may be used on the second day.[14] This is obviously a realm of discourse foreign to the modern mind. The modern man is not concerned with the problems of *mukzah,* articles not to be handled on the Sabbath or festivals, nor can he intelligently relate the laying of eggs to the problems exacerbated by two successive days of festivals occurring so close to each other, as at Sukkot and again at Passover, when within an eight-day span there can be four restrictive days, not to speak of the Sabbath.

But the Talmudic discussion is of interest today because it demonstrates the willingness of the Rabbis to see more than one side to the question; and although in their time they concluded that the second day of the Diaspora should be retained, had they been living today, they would have been as imaginative and rational as they were in their own day.

The question in the Talmud was whether the second day was truly as holy as the first. It appears that Rabbi Assi, who recited the *havdalah* after the first day, did not regard it as possessing equal holiness. Yet he did not permit the use of the egg on the second day. Why? Evidently he did not enjoy absolute certainty on the question in his own mind. This discussion of the egg, therefore, serves to give us a basic premise: there was confusion from the outset regarding the sanctity of the second day. Abyeh supported the thesis that the second day was *not* as sacred. He argued that if the Samaritans had stopped lighting bonfires, we would all be observing one day of Yom Tov. He added that even in the days when Samaritans caused mischief, wherever the messengers came on time only one day of Yom Tov was observed. What emerges from this is that the second day was not regarded as a permanent, irreversible enactment. The ancients were aware that the Samaritans were no longer bothersome once the calendar was fixed, and so the question arose, sent by Alexandrians as well as Babylonians, whether the second day remained in force. The reply given by the Palestinian authorities was that "although we have written to you the Order of the Festivals, do not change the *minhag* [custom] of your fathers."[15] We should note well the use of the term *minhag*. The Babylonians and Alexandrians, regarded as somewhat second-class Jews, were told to preserve a mark of their subordination to the authority of Palestine. Just as it was always the office of the Nasi that promulgated the dates of the festivals, and those who lived in the Diaspora had to observe two days out of uncertainty concerning the accurate dates, so they would now continue to do so, reminiscent of the time when they were dependent on the Nasi's promulgation.

Rabbi Solomon b. Isaac of Troyes (*Rashi*) noted in the eleventh century that the second day of Yom Tov was observed only by those communities in the Diaspora which were so distant from the seat of the *Bet Din* that messengers were unable to reach them and inform them when the new month began. He added that when they saw bonfires "in olden times," they observed only one day *in the Diaspora,* and that later, after the messenger-relay system was introduced, they continued to observe one day wherever the messengers arrived, and two days only where the messengers had not arrived.

Rashi teaches us two things. He teaches us that the second day of Yom Tov was a *practical* measure enacted by quick-thinking, rational and pious Rabbis to deal with an emergency; and he further informs us that *in the Diaspora* some Jews observed one day and others observed two days. This has tremendous implications for the modern age, when people are so concerned about *diversity* in Jewish ritualistic observances. Conformity is too much with us, and the eleventh-century sage certainly offers us an analogy for modern times.

During the twelfth century Maimonides asserted the Rabbinic status of the second day. This point of view was almost universal. A dissenting voice was that of Saadiah Gaon in the tenth century, who expressed the belief that the calendar was divinely revealed to Moses and that God commanded Moses to establish *Yom Tov Sheni* in the Diaspora. This may have been anti-Karaite polemics; but regardless of whether it was polemical rhetoric or determined opinion, Saadiah's view was rejected by succeeding authorities, such as Hai Gaon and Maimonides. As Salo Baron has put it, Saadiah's dogmatic predilections disturbed his historical judgment. This incorrect historical judgment naturally influenced his halakhic position as well.[16]

During the twelfth century Maimonides clearly established the Rabbinic status of the second Diaspora day in a number of references. This was supported in the thirteenth century by Nahmanides.[17]

The sixteenth-century commentator Rabbi Meier of Lublin (*Maharam*) noted on the same text that there was no fixed custom in ancient times concerning the second day of Yom Tov. He too indicated that when messengers arrived on time, a community observed one day, and when messengers failed to arrive on time to confirm local calculations for the observance of Yom Tov, they observed two days. His concluding remark was straightforward: "The matter was not a fixed one, and this is easy to understand."

This attitude, that the matter was "not a fixed one," was already foreshadowed when Rashi interpreted the phrase *shtai kedushot,* two separate sacred entities. The Talmud had weighed the problem whether the two days of a Diaspora festival were as one sacred day or were two separate entities. *Rashi* explained the importance of defining this because if it were one sacred entity, the two days being like one long day, the enactment would be permanent, there being uncertainty about which was the correct day. But if the second day was merely added as a supplemental protective day, it would not possess any holiness once the calendrical confusion no longer existed. This definition of the two days as consisting of two separate "holinesses" was adopted by Maimonides for all days except Rosh ha'Shanah, which he considered "one long holy day." On the other hand, Nahmanides considered even Rosh ha'Shanah two separate entities.[18]

The nineteenth-century German scholar Rabbi Zakharias Frankel, considered a precursor of what today goes by the name of the Conservative movement in Judaism, once wrote, "At such times as an earlier religious ordinance was not accepted by the entire community of Israel it was given up . . . when the people allow certain practices to fall into disuse, then the practices cease to exist. There is in such cases no danger for faith."[19] The obvious implication here is that if the second Diaspora festival is not technically abolished, at least we ought to have no responsibility to promote its observance. It is certainly something few people regard with enthusiasm. If we allowed it to die gracefully and gradually, there would be no danger to Judaism. Rabbi Frankel went on to clarify: "Only those practices from which it [the Jewish community] is entirely estranged and which yield it no satisfaction will be abandoned, and will thus die of themselves." Actually the problem of our time is that Rabbis do not allow it to die. They strive to preserve it by teaching it to unwilling and skeptical children in religious schools, urging positive or creative programs to save it, and continuing to cajole enough Jews to attend for a proper worship service on a morning when everyone is at work. This condition may change now that a respectable non-Reform religious body has issued a *hetar,* a permissive option, for Jews to cease observing the second day of the festivals. But it will naturally take a long time and will have to be accompanied by a two-sided program. There will have to be constant reminders, and a defense, of the option, while Rabbis begin to exert every effort for better observance of the first day.

The Shulhan Arukh provides the gist of the argument when it refers to the fact that in the Diaspora two days of Yom Tov were observed "out of doubt."[20] This is essentially the problem. There has now been no doubt about the precise day of Yom Tov since the publication of the calendar in the fourth century. This was a work of genius on the part of the ancient sages, and it was an act of political courage by Hillel II when he promulgated it in 359 or in 345, depending on which authority we rely upon.[21]

Rosh ha'Shanah presents an individual problem. It was already a two-day festival as far back as Talmudic times. We know from our sources that *Kiddush* was said welcoming the sacred day upon the conclusion of the twenty-ninth day of Elul in case the moon was seen that night. That was understandable at a time when Elul might have been twenty-nine or thirty days. For us, however, Elul has been fixed at twenty-nine days, and no error would be likely about the arrival of Rosh ha'Shanah. We are informed, as a matter of fact, that since the time of Ezra, Elul was never intercalated to thirty days.[22] Following the normal line of halakhic reasoning and by analogy to the other festivals, Rosh ha'Shanah might legitimately be restored to a one-day observance. But we do not follow this reasoning, because there are other pertinent considerations, and before a halakha is modified all facets of the matter should be cautiously considered. In the first place, one of the objectives of some segments of our people for restoring the one-day Diaspora festival was to accommodate the liturgical calendars of Israel and the Diaspora. Israel observes the two-day Rosh ha'Shanah custom. Secondly, one of the cogent arguments for removing the second Diaspora day was its total neglect and the hardship it placed on the observant Jew who would prefer to observe the one day and truly rejoice thereon.

This does not hold true for Rosh ha'Shanah. Not only the observant Jew finds the two days of Rosh ha'Shanah perfectly acceptable, and even psychologically mandatory, but even the nonobservant accept the two-day Rosh ha'Shanah. Large masses attend worship and find in it a large degree of solace and spiritual satisfaction.

It is clear that social, economic and historical forces, as well as the interests of public policy and the sentiment of the contemporary community, must all play their roles in the formation of halakha. We must conclude, therefore, that it is advisable to retain the two-day observance of Rosh ha'Shanah despite the fact that halakhic reasoning could legitimize its cessation as it did that of the three pilgrim festivals. In other words, when modifying or innovating in halakha, factors other than midrash (interpretation of the existing sources) must enter into our calculations. And sometimes these factors must outweigh the logic of the halakha. On the other hand, even if these forces lead us to conclude that we must make an innovation, we must first be certain that the halakhic sources and methodology will sustain such change. Thus in this matter of the second Diaspora day, the halakha sustained the option to cease the observance of the second day. On the other hand, although the halakha would sustain the same conclusion for Rosh ha'Shanah, there are decisive socio-historical reasons not to invoke this halakhic permission.

The basic reality which one must accept on an emotional level perhaps is that the second day need not be considered to possess the holiness the Torah attributed to the first day. This attitude is already evident in the Talmud. There is an interesting anecdote concerning Rabbi Safra, who considered himself a specialist in calendar computation. He asked his colleagues whether he might work in an uninhabited area on the second day of Yom Tov where nobody would observe him. His meaning was clear: in such an event he would offend nobody's doctrine or sensitivities. Rabbi Ami replied that it was permissible to do so, and Rabbi Ami's reply was cited as halakha.[23]

The obvious inference is that the second day does not possess an *inherent* holiness. Thus our approach must take into concern local needs, local custom and local sensitivity. As a matter of fact, Maimonides wrote explicitly that one does not allow the people of a locality whose custom it is to work to think it is forbidden, for one should not deviate from local custom.[24] This would entitle us to conclude that if no Rabbinic body was ever inspired to offer this option to non-Reform Jews, each congregation would be entitled to deal with it as it views the problem and establish its local custom. One might question the right to deviate from the existing practice to establish new local custom. This, however, is not the place to enter into a discussion of this matter. In a future volume I will take up the utilization of *takkanat hakahal,* the institution known to medieval halakha in which a communal enactment was made to overcome dead ends in the halakha, and its application to contemporary challenges.

Another anecdote in the Talmud relates of a trip taken by R. Nathan B. Asia of Biram to Pumbedita on the second day of Yom Tov. We know from the Talmud that Biram was not in Palestine, for it was identified with Bet Baltin on the west bank of the Euphrates.[25] This gives an example of a Diaspora community which observed only one day of the festivals. This again underscores that the second Diaspora day did not possess *inherent* holiness, that sometimes Diaspora communities observed only one day, and that diversity in ritual did not disturb the Talmudic generation. In modern times, calendrical certainty and the will of the people should suffice to lift the restriction.

The anecdote concerning R. Nathan is of special interest to those who are fascinated by the history of halakha. R. Joseph, who placed R. Nathan under a ban for traveling to Pumbedita on the second day of Shavuot, died in 333 and was the head of Pumbedita for only three years. This means that the incident took place around 330, before the calendar was promulgated. This strengthens the view that although Hillel II did a great service to posterity with his calendar, it was its promulgation that froze the second Diaspora day into halakha. Previously, like Rabbi Safra, who was knowledgeable in calendar computation, men who were certain of the true day of Yom Tov were not convinced of the necessity, *even in the Diaspora,* of observing the second day. Naturally, as in all eras and places, power, in this case R. Joseph's power as head of Pumbedita, outweighed R. Nathan's halakhic convictions. It was apparent that there was a long-standing attempt to enforce conformity in the observance of the second Diaspora day and that it had not been happily accepted by all. Otherwise there would have been no need for the ban. As a matter of further interest, medieval commentators understood that violation of *Yom Tov Sheni* was more severely punished than other violations because it was "essentially" a Rabbinic ordinance, as the author of *Korban Netanel* indicated.[26] The implication is that because such a novel series of additions to the Torah's sacred festivals was introduced without the requisite sources to bolster midrash (interpretation), the sages had to fall back on the institution of *gezerah,* an enactment, to ensure the observance of the correct day. Since this enactment entailed considerable hardship for many small businessmen, artisans and farmers, there may have been something less than general enthusiasm for it. In such an event it would probably have been more appropriately renewed twice each year when the Sanhedrin announced the new moon for Tishri and Nisan, or at most a third time at Sivan, and allowed to lapse once the calendar was computed.

The Rabbis, however, chose not to do so. They allowed *Yom Tov Sheni* to stand as a permanent enactment for the Diaspora and saw in it a symbol of Palestinian authority. Undoubtedly, in part this was because they envisioned an ultimate restoration of the old order in Jerusalem, at least to the extent of a Sanhedrin and its juridical functions. But in part it was also the reaction of a community in evident decline attempting to salvage some last remnant of its old glory. In any case, the question of Jerusalem's authority is no longer a live issue for us. The Jewish community in the Diaspora would not accept the authority of Israel's "Chief Rabbinate" in our time. The idea of depending on visual testimony for the appearance of the moon and its proclamation in Jerusalem is no longer a tenable proposition in an age when mathematical computation is recognized to be more exact than an eye gazing into a cloudy sky. Furthermore, even if it be argued that the human eye can be relied upon better than astronomical computations, instant electronic communication today makes it possible for all Jews everywhere to hear the proclamation simultaneously with those in Jerusalem.

The question of "authority" was an aggravating one for centuries. There was clear rivalry between the Patriarchate in Palestine and the Exilarchate in Babylonia, which can be reviewed in any good work on Jewish history. Babylonian hegemony was established during the early Gaonic period but suffered a decline in the eleventh century. Saadiah Gaon, although a new arrival from Egypt, won the right to fix the calendar in Babylonia in 922 after this right had always been reserved to Palestine. It appears that the Exilarch Daniel ben Hisdai declared in 1161 that nobody any longer had any right whatever to intercalate the calendar. This would most certainly appear to sustain our present viewpoint that the astronomically computed calendar with which we function will not be, and halakhically need not be, replaced by a return to visual determination.[27]

Ultimately hegemony was vested in halakha and not in "geographic centers." As once before, religious centripetal forces took the cult out of Jerusalem and universalized it, so again halakhic authority was universalized, passing to the halakhists and their documented work wherever they were. The *mora d'atra,* the contemporary local authority, served his time and his community and wherever his writ ran. This essay is obviously not a historical thesis on the question of the changing nature of religious authority in Judaism or the shifting centers of hegemony. But it is essential to indicate for our time and posterity that there is nothing that requires the centralization of halakhic authority in Jerusalem. There is nothing that mandates control of the calendar in Jerusalem. That age and that climate of opinion are behind us. History and the will of God have brought about astonishing transformations which must be seen in all their significance.

In an address to the Rabbinical Assembly in 1927, Rabbi Louis Finkelstein wrote: "It was revolutionary for the Babylonian Amoraim to set themselves up as judges and rabbis without the traditional Palestinian *semikha* [ordination]; it was revolutionary for Rabbenu Gershom to gather a synod for the purpose of making new enactments; it was revolutionary to write down the prayers and codify the law. All of these changes, of which the least is far more radical than any proposed among us, were justified by the fact that they helped to save Judaism in crucial periods. . . ."[28]

When Rabbi Finkelstein wrote, "They helped to save Judaism," he was making a historical evaluation. He was, of course, completely correct. For seen in the perspective of history, had these definitive and revolutionary changes not been effected it is quite possible that Judaism could not have survived. Naturally historical evaluations can be made only generations later, and this is the advantage of being spared the need to suggest the revolutionary changes and being blessed with the opportunity centuries later to acclaim those who had the courage to make them. Obviously, although the light of history will allow others to pass judgment on any innovations we propose in our time, such innovations must be risked to enable halakha to function as a viable instrument of Jewish life.

The offering of an option to cease observing the second Diaspora day in our time provides our generation and those who follow with a number of positive advantages. It encourages the observance of festivals by making them more manageable and less repetitious and tedious and by removing a major source of negativism. It eliminates the need to teach increasingly sophisticated youngsters the indefensible calendar reasons for the second day. It cannot be gainsaid that the overwhelming number of them, even the religiously positive-oriented teenagers, resent the extra burden placed on them by what was obviously originally only a problem of communication and transportation experienced by Jews two thousand years ago. Furthermore, the communication problem existed only because of a religio-political situation in which the Palestinians sought to preserve their hegemony in the area of calender computation, proclamation and intercalation. The option to cease observing the second day, therefore, reduces the area of exacerbating conflict between the home and the religious school. It makes our demand for children to stay out of public school more reasonable and palatable. It makes it more practical for synagogues to offer a substitute program to keep the children out of school, a plan which is more feasible on a one-day basis. It allows, through its candid rejection of a questionable set of propositions, for a vastly improved respect for the halakha and consequently for the relevance of Jewish religion.

These positive values in the option are naturally not designed as predictions for its success. But there is no doubt in my mind that the second Diaspora day has long, albeit unwittingly, contributed to the disintegration of festival observance, respect for halakha and reverence for religious practice. Its absence from Scripture, its lack of *inherent* sanctity evident from Talmudic literature, its role as a political pawn in the assertion of Palestinian authority, and its total disregard in modern Jewish life and the disadvantages it poses even for the observant are all adequate considerations to motivate the withdrawal of this old enactment.

A great issue that always arises when innovations are proposed in modern times is the question of who can change halakha. But that subject is dealt with in appropriate chapters in this work. Certainly some still seriously argue that only a Sanhedrin sitting in Jerusalem can modify the halakha, that one group of scholars (the equivalent of a *Bet Din*) cannot nullify the enactments of an earlier group. They quote the statement "What one Bet Din enacts another cannot nullify unless it is greater in numbers and wisdom." Professor Solomon Schechter, however, long ago approved of the theory that this dictum was merely an administrative measure and referred only to another contemporary group of sages. He denied that this Mishnaic statement was designed to forever stifle halakhic change.[29] In view of the fact that the institution of the second Diaspora day was merely *minhag* and not a "voted *takkanah*" of a *Bet Din,* this statement could hardly apply to it. Furthermore, it is instructive to peruse the words of *Ikar Tosaphot Yom Tov* on the Mishna. There he noted that where a decision rested on midrash, the traditional form of interpretation through a process of reasoning, a successor *Bet Din* to whom "another explanation appeared to dispute the first, it may dispute the rule in accordance with its own reasoning," and he cited that key scriptural passage, Deut. 17:9-10, which universalized halakhic authority.

Surely we have here a case where all logic has evaporated and many compelling reasons now appear to use the halakhic procedures available to us in reference to *Yom Tov Sheni*. Moses Isserles was quite clear on this during the sixteenth century; he wrote that when a reason for an enactment is no longer operative the enactment itself becomes nullified.[30] The sources further negate any argument that earlier authority cannot be overridden unless it is "greater." Tosephta teaches that "whoever has been appointed *parnas* over the community, though he be among the least of lesser men he is regarded as a giant among giants." This is based on Deuteronomy 17:9 and is supplemented with a citation from the author of Ecclesiastes, who wrote, "Say not previous ages were superior to the present." This is not the place to discuss these verses from a critical standpoint as to whether they may be taken out of context and applied in the manner they have been applied in the Tosephta. But this has always been the Rabbinic method, and what counts here is the fact that the ancient sages legitimized their activity in *halakha* with these and other similar scriptural statements. What they legitimized for their day has been legitimized permanently and applies in our time.

The term *parnas* used by Tosephta is to be taken in its Mishnaic sense of "manager, administrator, leader of a community or chief." In various contexts it has reference to a religious leader, and regardless of what it came to mean later, at the time of the Tosephta it possessed that significance. Thus, from the standpoint of Rabbinic literature a *parnas*—head of the congregation, and in modern parlance, Rabbi—should not have his authority slighted on grounds that he is of lesser breed than earlier authorities. Considering the role and function of the modern Rabbi, it undoubtedly can apply to him. But even if it be pressed that the term must be applied only to the leader who possesses "constitutional" authority, which is today vested in the lay leadership, it would merely mean that after proper halakhic consultation the properly constituted *parnas* of a congregation, the board of directors, would be able to act as the local authority. This essentially would mean that every congregation, by nature and tradition autonomous, was allowed to deal with halakhic modification as an independent body. Central Rabbinic authority, such as a Committee on Jewish Law, or *Bet Din,* or whatever appellation may be applied, would only serve in a consultative capacity to offer guidance or to provide a relatively certain consensus of Rabbinic opinion.[31]

Naturally, during these years when the option to cease observing the second Diaspora day is first becoming a reality among non-Reform Jews many questions will arise and will have to be solved. It can be anticipated that Jews will want to know what provision will be made for those who wish to continue observing the second Diaspora day; how the saying of Yizkor on the eighth day of Passover and the second day of Shavuot will be handled. Questions will be asked concerning Simhat Torah, which is in effect the second day of Shemini Atzeret. Each congregation should seek to solve these and other problems in a manner which best answers local needs.

A few guidelines and alternatives may be offered here. It might be convenient to have an informal service on the second day for those who still wish to attend a festival service for two days. Yizkor could be said on the seventh day of Pesah. Yizkor might be eliminated on Shavuot, since it is, after all, a relatively recent practice for the other festivals and was once customary only on Yom Kippur. Shavuot comes so soon after Pesah that many people do not attend Yizkor on Shavuot. Furthermore, many synagogues celebrate Shavuot with much pomp because confirmation services are held that day. For those synagogues that do not observe confirmation on Shavuot another service might be initiated, such as a beginners'-class consecration. Others may choose to observe Yizkor on the first day. It is impossible to lay down a compulsory guideline formulation. Congregations are autonomous and will strive to respond to problems in keeping with the collective outlook of their memberships. Thus some will observe Simhat Torah on Shemini Atzeret Eve, as has been done in Hasidic congregations for generations, and others may switch Yizkor to the evening to accommodate adults and observe the festive Simhat

Torah processionals and joyousness on Simhat Torah morning to accommodate the religious-school population and young people. Some congregations may also elect to drop Yizkor altogether, since it has been said as recently as less than two weeks earlier on Yom Kippur.

Thus some congregations may decide to have Yizkor twice a year, on Yom Kippur and Pesah. Others may choose to move the Yizkor of Shavuot and Shemini Atzeret to the evening ushering in the festival. Some congregations may continue to have a second Diaspora day, and to accommodate traditionalists will present a Yizkor service on both occasions. To observe Yizkor on Shavuot morning while ceasing the observance of the second Diaspora day, some congregations may move confirmation to Shavuot Eve. These and other suggestions cannot meet the needs of all congregations.

One Passover Seder or two will be observed as each family decides for itself. There would be nothing amiss in observing a second Seder on a night which will be considered only semi-sacred, as part of the intermediate days of Passover. Some people who still strictly observe the prohibitions of leaven and will feel uneasy about eating *hametz* on the eighth day of Passover will naturally continue to discipline themselves. Others will naturally conclude that if we return to the biblical festival, the prohibition is only a seven-day prohibition and will conduct themselves accordingly.

This chapter is not taking up the question of Rosh ha'Shanah, because this is a question of an entirely different nature. First of all, I place some notable stress on what the public relates to, and two days of Rosh ha'Shanah still certainly have widespread public acceptance. Secondly, as is well known, two days of Rosh ha'-Shanah have been observed in the Holy Land as well since the early Middle Ages.[32] It is still a two-day observance there. The objective of this chapter is merely to indicate the propriety of observing all the other festivals for one day only, and not to return to the biblical Rosh ha'Shanah. That a return to a one-day Rosh ha'Shanah would be fully justified halakhically there can be no doubt. All the halakhic reasons for ceasing the observance of the second Diaspora day of the other festivals, with one major exception, could apply to Rosh ha'Shanah as well. But the one major exception justifies retaining the second day of Rosh ha'-Shanah. That major exception has already been mentioned: the public attitude. So far as I am concerned, a major motivation for re-examining the second Diaspora day is that it has become a *davar she'ain hatzibur yakhol la'a'mod bah:* a matter which the public can no longer abide. This motivation is not present in the case of Rosh ha'Shanah, since the second day is widely observed, respected and accepted. It is imperative that we recapture such acceptance for the first day of the other festivals so that Jews everywhere will fulfill the biblical mitzvah of "rejoice in your festivals."

Chapter XI

OVERCOMING THE CRISIS IN HALAKHA [1]

EVERYONE RECOGNIZES that halakha is currently in crisis. This crisis is the result of multifarious factors related to historical developments within Judaism as well as the socio-economic environment in which Jews and Judaism must function. These external and internal factors have produced a situation in which we find a growing ignorance of the traditional halakha and consequently an intensifying apathy toward it. Our period is characterized by increasing confusion about the nature and the sources of halakhic authority. When these facets of the problem are added to the conviction that certain new philosophical premises in our era are in fundamental conflict with halakhic postulates, the crisis is exacerbated. It is further aggravated by the apparent obsolescence of so many areas of the halakha. In secular legislation there are always old laws on the books which are no longer practiced; but the citizenry is not considered in some form of rebellion or a state of treason for the neglect of obsolete legislation. On the other hand, in religion, when old practices are neglected because they are obsolete, the pious will upbraid those who neglect these practices, will attempt to imbue them with a guilt complex or win them back to the practice of discarded custom. This is certainly evident in Judaism when so many people defend themselves in most apologetic terms for the neglect of halakha while simultaneously professing religious interest. Indeed, they may be very religious, and their neglect of observance may be the direct result, not of impiety but of the crisis in halakha.

From all this it becomes obvious that a new and creative approach is not only a desideratum but long overdue. Halakha was not a cultural phenomenon *sui generis*. While it became the special characteristic of Judaism, it did not spring out of a vacuum. As a matter of fact, the term itself was distinct from the term *ma'aseh,* which designated case law. Halakha more nearly expressed the principle of jurisprudence, the broad premises which underlay a more detailed regimen. Part of our task today will be to rediscover the halakha in its broadest sense so as to be able to respond to the needs of a new age with a new set of *ma'a'sim,* particular practice.

The development of halakha was normal in the ancient world. The Samaritans also possessed a *hillukh,* a guide to conduct which supplemented their Torah.[2] This application of new knowledge and new experience was a method common to all ancient peoples, and remained true throughout medieval and modern history.

The Roman church supplemented Scripture with canon law. Every "Torah" requires interpretation, and interpretation results in supplementation. A constitution is the equivalent of Torah, and every modern society supplements its constitution with a whole body of legislation and court decisions. As a matter of historical misfortune, the term Torah was construed as *nomos* in the Hellenistic period, and this was translated as "law" in English. This forever distorted the problem of halakha because people began to see Judaism as a legal system and emphasized the need for "certainty," as law carries with it certainty. This led to an unwarranted "orthodoxy" which is one of the major causes of the contemporary crisis. They failed to see Judaism as a *spiritual expression,* governed not by "law" but by halakha, an ongoing evolutionary pattern of conduct which contained options and flexibility.[3] The tragedy is that even when the word *nomos* was used in the Greek it was used only for the Torah and did not mean to convey the idea that Judaism is a legal system; it merely aimed at conveying an understanding to Greek-speaking audiences that for the Jew the Torah is equivalent to a Greek city's "constitution." This does not necessarily imply that it is a legal system rather than a religion. It merely signifies that like a constitution for a *polis* (city), the Torah is the source of all that is believed and practiced by the Jew. The corollary seems to have been lost on everyone, that just as a constitution can be amended or supplemented, the Torah too was subject to the interpretation of the scribes and priests of that time. It was the difference, however, that appears to have been missed: that while every citizen of a *polis* obeyed the same law, every Jew did not have to practice the same halakha.

Like the Jews, the Samaritans too adjusted their *hillukh* to make it viable under changing conditions. This was normal in all societies. The "period of adjustment" was really continuous, and for this reason the halakha as it affected ritual and certain elements of ethical and moral practices was never monolithic, enjoying absolute uniformity. For this reason all religious groups gave rise to sectarian offshoots. Not all such diversity resulted in schism. It was far more than mere diversity in ritual practice that brought about the schism between normative Judaism and Samaritan Judaism or between Judaism and Christianity.

The term halakha must be more clearly defined if we are to recapture its proper spirit. But definition is not a simple matter. Professor Saul Lieberman has speculated that the tax term *halakh* mentioned in Ezra 4:13 is to be identified with the Babylonian word for tax, *ilku,* a term already found in the Code of Hammurabi. In other ancient Aramaic documents, land tax is called *hilkha.* Professor Lieberman's effort was therefore directed to connecting the term halakha with the idea of the fixed land tax. On the other hand, he also indicated that the term is connected with the idea of boundary. This approach to the term is undoubtedly imaginative and even exotic. But although it may not be as cogent as the more common understanding of it as derived from the verb "to walk," it may nevertheless be combined with the concept of halakha as signifying a "way," or a "pattern of conduct."[4]

Briefly stated, halakha is Jewish religious practice. At one time the operative halakha encompassed all areas of life and law: business, civil and criminal law, personal and cultic ritual, the law of domestic relations, and ethics. History has consistently altered this, and large areas of the halakha have become inoperative from time to time. At this juncture of Jewish history the operative halakha encompasses mainly the sphere of personal, family and communal (synagogal) ritual, a large portion of domestic-relations procedures, and certain limited areas of the ethical or moral code. It contains none at all of that sphere that one would term "law" in a modern society. In that sphere Jews, like all others, are governed by the law of the government under whose jurisdiction they reside. This in itself is a halakhic injunction: that the sovereign law of the land is to be obeyed.[5]

In Judaism the beginnings of halakha are to be traced to *Midrash Torah,* that is, the exposition of Torah found in *Mekhilta, Sifra* and *Sifre,* among other commentaries on Exodus, Leviticus and Deuteronomy. During the Second Commonwealth (roughly from the time of the first return from Babylonia in 539 B.C.E. to the destruction of Jerusalem in 70 C.E.) it was deemed important to adduce scriptural sanction to validate customs and traditions that had evolved through the generations. The halakhic midrash, a commentary on the Pentateuch, served this purpose. When the sage Hezkiah defined the highest academic personage, the *Talmid hakham,* as one who studied "halakhot in addition to Torah," he was in effect indicating that the evolutionary process is the inevitable one. In the same passage R. Yosi goes further and declares that "in our day the study of halakhot without Torah" is also sufficient.[6] The distinction R. Yosi makes between "in former times" and "in our day" as to the necessary curriculum of a scholar is pedagogically instructive. But more important, he was willing to accept the study of halakhot alone, although this would involve basing life on the *latest* developments of the halakha and leading to the practice of the most recent traditions. Here we have a cogent recognition of an evolutionary concept.

The Torah was the only recognized authority in Judaism since the covenant entered into between the Jew and his God as described in the Bible. Ezra brought before the people the "book of the Torah of Moses which God had commanded for Israel," and they accepted it as their standard of practice. They determined *la'lekhet,* "to walk," according to the Torah of God which had been transmitted through Moses, and "to observe and perform all the mitzvot of the Eternal our Lord, His ordinances and statutes."[7] But it was even then that Ezra and his school began to "explain" the Torah to the people, and through midrash halakha they attempted to connect all post-Torahitic traditions with the Torah.

According to Jacob Lauterbach, Mishna was the first literary form to teach halakhot independently of Torah.[8] We can surmise that this was a revolutionary break with the past. Implied in this was the acceptance of the idea that non-Torahitic halakha can be authoritative. This is also the key to understanding the ensuing division between the Pharisees and the Sadducees. The former accepted this radical innovation in principle and the latter did not. It is true, of course, that many a Rabbinic reference expresses the idea that Mishna was old, and was even revealed to Moses at Sinai. But all those references are *agada* (homiletical). One cannot arbitrarily take such agadot at face value and reject such as the one that Methuselah studied nine hundred orders of the Mishna. Another old source tells that Ezra was commanded to withhold seventy books from the people, and it has been suggested by Louis Ginzberg that this is a reference to the old halakhic literature, which consisted of fifty-eight Mishnaic treatises, among others. Ginzberg pointed out that in Rabbinic literature, in contrast to the Torah, which was revealed for all mankind, the Mishna was considered a *mysterion,* a "mystery." I take this to imply that the Mishna was regarded as the Jew's special "way," just as all cults had a "mystery" into which one had to be initiated. It is clear in the Palestinian Talmud that from one point of view the unwritten halakha was what distinguished the Jew.[9]

What is to be emphasized here is the conviction of the antiquity of the process of interpretation, the antiquity of the human development of halakha. That Rabbinic literature did not give us a clear and documented history of the halakha is not to its discredit. The Rabbis were not historians, and the literary remains of the fourth century, perhaps a key century in the chain of tradition, were apparently not available to them any more than they are to us. But it is explicit that they were aware of broad and significant changes.

Lauterbach has shown in his essay "Midrash and Mishna" that there is a Talmudic tradition that from the time of Moses to the time of Yose b. Yo'ezer of Zeredah all teachers studied the

Torah as Moses did but that after the time of Yose a new form of study arose.[10] Lauterbach assumes this to mean that the *Midrash Torah* system gave way to the Mishna form. He therefore concludes that the origin of Mishna is to be traced to the Maccabean period, around 165 B.C.E., at the beginning of which era Yose died. This was a revolutionary age and a crucial period in Jewish history. As on previous occasions of crisis drastic solutions were required for the problems of the time. Throughout history Judaism has been confronted by such radical challenges to its survival in watersheds of history. Only courageous innovation and radical response have enabled it to respond to the challenge and to flourish in ever greater measure. In a sense, what Ezra did during the fifth century for the reconstituted Judean community and what Rabban Yohanan b. Zakkai was later to do for Judaism at Yavneh after 70 C.E., Yose b. Yo'ezer was attempting to achieve during the Maccabean crisis.[11]

The Maccabean watershed was one phenomenon in a radically transformed world. The great Hellenistic age inaugurated by the incredible achievements of Alexander the Great 160 years earlier brought vast new changes to the Middle East in technology, politics, economics, culture and religion. The Hellenistic flowering caused no less a dramatic transformation of mankind and history than the many-hued tapestry we call the Renaissance, the great Industrial Revolution, the contemporary nuclear age or the on-rushing cybernetic era.

The life of the Jew and the Jewish community from a spiritual-cultural standpoint during the long Persian period was relatively quiet and undisturbed. It was perhaps analogous to the isolation of the Eastern European Jew in his ghetto. The rushing currents of the environment hardly touched him. There were no socio-economic upheavals that caused a confrontation with his tradition. Then Greece shattered the silence as the Macedonian titan marched across the steppes and plains of Asia Minor and conquered from Egypt to India, introducing the first "ecumenical" idea, the first concept of a universal human system known to the history of civilization. This intrusion was traumatic in Judea.

As external change was slow and imperceptible under Per-

sian rule, inner change in the life of the Jewish community was
also minor and extremely placid. New religious customs undoubtedly arose but were easily expounded from scriptural verses. They were easily absorbed into the body of authoritative
practice. But with the cultural transmogrification of the Hellenistic Near East new conditions arose for which there was simply
no precedent in the halakha, not unlike such modern unprecedented
problems as the use of a camera on the Sabbath. Similarly, new
religious needs became apparent for which there were no previous
ceremonial or cultic practices, not unlike the modern motivations
that gave rise to such innovations as confirmation.

Authority in Jewish life, previously centered in the High
Priest, broke down. The high priesthood was discredited during
the Hellenistic period. The lay scholars among the Hasidim, the
party to which Yose b. Yo'ezer belonged, popularized the study
of Torah and promoted the democratization of the academic community. This is the significance of Yose b. Yo'ezer's statement
"Let your house be a gathering-place for sages."[12]

The new age with its subsequent new approach is well attested
to in the Mishna, when Yose b. Yo'ezer declared permissible
three items that had been previously prohibited. He ruled that a
certain species of locust was permitted for food, the liquids of
the place where sacrifices were slaughtered were to be considered
ritually clean, and only that which came into direct contact with
a dead body became ritually unclean.[13] The Mishna reports that
his colleagues called him *sharya,* "the permitter," but did not
overrule his opinions; nor did later Talmudists abolish his innovations. His statements registered a point of view contrary to
traditional custom. Nevertheless, they became and remained accepted halakha. And this is most significant when we consider
that one of his opinions, that liquids of the slaughtering place at
the altar were to be considered clean and not to impart impurity,
was not a restatement or adaptation of an old halakha but was
first stated by Yose.[14]

This is significantly relevant to our own period. Although Yose
formulated new halakha contrary to tradition and was given the
epithet of "liberal," the Judaism of his day absorbed the shock.

It is too often thought that the evolution of Talmudic halakha was always in the direction of the expansion of restrictions. But this was never the case. There was really a tendency toward leniency.

One of the characteristics of Pharisaism was that it recognized the authoritative nature of the extrascriptural tradition. The Oral Law became a "twin Torah." Not everything in the new halakha of Mishna and Talmud could be supported by direct reference to Scripture. Consequently a variety of methods were devised to connect the tradition with Scripture through ingenious exegesis. This too is relevant to our present crisis. We should not expect that everything we do today in modifying the old or creating the new will have *direct* sanction in the codes. We too will have to seek methods and establish criteria by which we devise the exegetical connection between our halakha and that of the past.

We are living in a time that is as fluid and uncertain as the Hellenistic period. The Jewish community of that time had an inherited authority in the form of Scripture which had only recently been canonized. At the dawn of our age the Jewish community also possessed an inherited authority, the *Shulhan Arukh,* the code of halakha which had been widely accepted as the final word during the seventeenth century. Proto-Pharisaic activity in ancient times probed the need to deal with a new age in a new way. And this is basically the need we face today. Many practices are without direct precedent in the historic codes, Talmud or Scripture. Yet they have been accepted and are being universally practiced. Confirmation is an outstanding example. But there is also a great need for the creation of new rituals along similar lines. Furthermore, there are also widely practiced observances which are militantly opposed by large segments of the Rabbinate as being contrary to the halakha. One of these is the use of flowers at a funeral or at a grave. It is questionable whether this has non-Jewish origins, for we know from the Talmud that myrtle branches were placed on a coffin in ancient times.[15] The use of flowers may certainly be seen as *kavod hamet,* the honoring of the deceased, a halakhic formula which is of utmost significance. Furthermore, even if customs to which we become attracted in any given geographic environment originated in non-Jewish circles, Saul Lieberman gave us cause to consider how to apply them to our needs. He wrote, "In matters of external decorum the Jews might imitate the gentiles without any feeling that they are breaking the law; after all it was commendable 'to adorn a religious act' [*hidur mitzvah*]."[16] Lieberman wrote this in reference to the sacrificial cult and pointed out that Jews could not relinquish rites merely because non-Jews practiced them. It may be argued that introducing new rites is different from preserving old ones, that while they did not relinquish old ones which coincided with gentile practices, we ought not to introduce new ones that are similar to non-Jewish observances. But Lieberman indicated that they also introduced new elements in the Temple design and that the sacred vessels were improved so as to conform to a general pattern in the ancient world. Such formulations as *kavod hamet* and *hidur mitzvah* might be of inestimable value in the rehabilitation and updating of halakha.[17]

Dr. Lieberman gave us more to think about when he discussed the challenge of superstition. He referred to the historic context of Hellenism and the fact that Jews, gentiles and Christians lived in close proximity in the great metropolitan centers of the Near East. As in modern times, it was inevitable that the Jew, like his fellow residents, would be dazzled by the externals of his society. It would be naive to imagine that Jews remained untouched by that brilliant Hellenistic civilization. Lieberman indicated that the Rabbis of the time encountered the challenge and met it well. He pointed out that they resisted that which was a menace to Jewish religion. "On the other hand," he wrote, "they tried to legalize strange customs which could be tolerated without endangering the vital principles of Judaism." Lieberman went on to state that in cases where they were unable to eliminate what appeared to be less than a desirable practice, "they succeeded in endowing it with Jewish character."[18]

There are a number of instances in our time of customs related to birth, marriage and death, to synagogue or home ritual, or to public functions, where conflicts frequently arise between private taste and tradition, or between contemporary public norms of decorum and traditional forms. The subject would require a separate comparative catalogue of traditional rites and customs of the Jewish life cycle and current taste and practice. On the basis of such a comparative study we would be able to compile a list of rituals which would be meaningful in contemporary terms with a view to strengthening observance and a sense of identity with God, religion and the synagogue. A great effort, for instance, is exerted to compel Jews to have a kosher dinner at a wedding. It would be more to the spiritual point if the same energy was expended in insisting that Jewish wedding ceremonies ought to be at home or in the synagogue, as most Christian weddings are at home or in a church, urging Jews not to succumb to the temptation of the convenience of having the wedding ceremony where the reception is to take place, even to the point of having it under objectionable commercial circumstances. On the other side of the ledger, considering the question of circumcision and the large number of young people who no longer have an appropriate ritual at the time of the surgery, it would without doubt be spiritually enhancing to allow for a regular boy-naming rite at the Torah as we conduct it for girls. These are merely two examples of a host of rites and customs which should be taken under scrutiny and to which we might apply old Rabbinic method with a view toward "legalizing strange customs" or endowing non-Jewish customs with Jewish character. In Lieberman's words, the objective would be "to Judaize foreign elements, to exploit the false religious feelings of the ignorant populace and turn them to the channels of true religion. . . ."[19]

In naming a boy in the synagogue, it would not even be a question of "Judaizing foreign elements," since naming a boy at his circumcision is not a mandatory halakha. It is nowhere mentioned in the Mishna or in the Talmud, and is therefore a later medieval development, a *minhag,* a custom which at some point during the Middle Ages came to be taken for granted. There is mention of naming a boy at his circumcision in Joseph Karo's *Yoreh Dayah,* but that is in reference to naming a dead child who is circumcised at the grave "that he may arise at the resurrection." The name is given to him that he may have an identity in "the world to come," but this is hardly to be employed as evidence that it is mandatory to name a child at circumcision or conversely that he must not be named in the synagogue.[20] As a matter of fact, the opposite may be true. If it were a universal practice to name a boy at his circumcision, it should not be necessary to specify the giving of a name to a dead child, as the naming would be provided for in the ritual observed at the grave. But if it were also customary to name a child *after* his circumcision, it would be understandable that Karo would remind his reader that a dead child, though dead, should now be named, since there would be no other opportunity to provide him with his identity in the era of resurrection. David Avudraham, the Spanish scholar whose work on liturgy dates to about 1340, refers to the prayer asking God to sustain this child, and his name is then declared. On the other hand, Maimonides does not refer to this passage at all in his outline of the circumcision ritual.[21] This would indicate that it was not necessarily customary to name the boy at circumcision, at least among Sephardim, as late as the twelfth century, although it had become so by the fourteenth. Admittedly, a custom some six hundred years old is halakha and in the normal course of events should be maintained. But by the same token, since it is not an *integral part* of circumcision but a custom probably introduced for the sake of parental convenience, to simplify procedures with boys and consolidate two joyous events into one celebration, perhaps for economic reasons, we might consider some flexibility in relation to the ritual. In the case of marriages taking place in a synagogue or at home rather than in catering establishments, we admittedly confront a difficult social problem. It would appear to be an unnecessary hardening of halakha in a liberal age. But, to me at least, it would also appear to be a significant forward thrust in the direction of spiritualizing Jewish life, which has increasingly become secularized.

The two examples projected here are merely symptomatic of what we are discussing. Halakha should not necessarily be labeled lenient or restrictive. It should be reinvigorated to deal with current conditions and to become a viable pattern. At times this might require leniency. At times it might demand a stricter attitude toward our social patterns. But in each case we should regard the halakha as potentially viable and move toward making it not merely relevant but *contemporary.*

In his *Law and Tradition in Judaism,* Dr. Boaz Cohen reminded us that Rabbi Yohanan charged the destruction of the Temple and the subsequent exile of the Jews to the overscrupulousness of Rabbi Zekhariah ben Avukolos.[22] The problem was discussed in the Talmud and involved nothing basic to Judaism. A sacrifice was to be offered in honor of the emperor. Rabbi Zekharia forbade it because it could not meet Jewish standards of the sacrificial cult although it met Roman standards and was acceptable on those grounds to other sages. Dr. Cohen cited the reference in a footnote, but it is far more than a mere footnote to history. It illuminates a central reason for the crisis in halakha. Overdevotion to minutiae can be detrimental to the high purpose for which the original halakha was intended. Sometimes obedience to obsolete details causes more damage than would the modification of these details. The second day of Yom Tov and certain scrupulous attention to detail in *Gittin,* for instance, as discussed in previous chapters, undoubtedly make for greater breaches in these institutions and in the fabric of Judaism than would progressive modification. These breaches overshadow whatever value it is believed is garnered by fostering the survival of obsolete minutiae.[23]

We would come closer to devising techniques for overcoming the crisis in halakha if we understood, as Boaz Cohen clarified, that the *Shulhan Arukh,* and every other great code that preceded it for that matter, was meant to be "utilitarian and not authoritarian."[24] This means that the codes were not conceived to be final, not really intended to be "law," which has certainty and fixity to it. The codes were not meant to convey the idea that the letter of the text was immutable. Rather the codes were halakha, a process of guidance, and were merely intended as handbooks of reference. The process of constant reinterpretation which had taken place since the days of Ezra was still a perfectly legitimate activity. This was the process originated in *Midrash Torah:* to attempt to determine the meaning of the text and apply it to a particular situation. This was the process of Talmudic exegesis and the process by which halakha always evolved. There are no grounds for aborting this process in our time.

It is a moot point, and here perhaps there is cause for wide divergence of opinion, whether some of this "interpretation" was not, after all, in effect, a subtle and indirect form of abrogation. We perhaps become involved here in semantics. The text was never abrogated, but certainly its effect often was abrogated. The institution of *hetar iska,* permitting a partner to profit from the transactions that resulted from a loan, was an innovative way to overcome the prohibition on usury which tended to frustrate or reduce commercial activity.[25]

In the *iska* arrangement—the word *iska* being Aramaic for "business"—there was a limited partnership in which one partner supplied the capital and the other the services. To define the arrangement as a partnership it was necessary for the partners jointly to own the assets, and therefore the Rabbis considered that the partner who supplied the capital offered part of that capital to the other person as a loan. But if the working partner received no payment for his services other than his share in the profits, and the supplier of capital received his profits on the transaction, the Rabbis were of the opinion that half the services he rendered contained an element of usury. To overcome this problem the medieval sages issued permission for joint ventures, the *hetar iska* embodied in a document called *shtar iska,* under whose terms it was permitted to pay and receive such sums as otherwise appeared to be "interest" forbidden by the Torah. In the provisions of a *shtar iska* the working partner, in return for the capital lent by the money supplier, would guarantee the investment and a return on it, but to mitigate the "appearance of interest," the working partner stated in the document that he had been paid for his services and that he agreed to share the losses. This was based on the opinion of R. Judah b. Illai, who held that even such nominal payment as a dry fig by the investor to the working partner exempted this form of monetary gain from the prohibition of interest.

It is evident from this and from other examples that although the Torah's prohibition of usury or interest was never abrogated, the scholars faced the challenges of more complex economic conditions or changing technology by reinterpreting, expanding or limiting the original halakha. In effect, however, the process of interpretation is a subtle form of abrogation. Despite the very severe censure suggested by several Talmudic sages for those who violated the canons of usury, which were in turn embedded in the halakha, the halakha provided exemptions, such as the right to use the estate of a minor orphan to accumulate more funds through interest or to save life.[26] There is some degree of disagreement on the question of saving life, and it appears to me that a word about it may be in order because it illuminates this whole question of a crisis in halakha. Joseph Karo had concluded that "it is permitted to borrow money on interest in order to save life." It was suggested that his source was a statement in Tosaphot regarding the biblical Obadiah, the steward of King Ahab. It was related of him that he fed the Prophets who fled from Jezebel. The midrash picked this up as a great credit to his benevolence but also embroidered the biblical narrative by adding that he borrowed funds at interest from Yehoram, the son of Ahab. Tosaphot was puzzled that a righteous man like Obadiah would pay interest to even a rebellious sinner like Yehoram, for although he had the choice of not lending at interest the borrower was not allowed to contribute to the sin of the lender by paying the interest. Nevertheless, Tosaphot concluded that this was an exceptional case, since it was to save lives and was therefore a mitzvah. Karo apparently governed his selection of the halakha by this statement. However, the sixteenth-century commentator Rabbi David b. Samuel ha'Levi (whose commentary goes by the name of *Turai Zahav* or *Taz*) took issue with him. He argued that Karo should not have included this as a halakha, since it was clear that the lender must never do so, and that the borrower might do so only when the *only source* of funds was a wicked Jew who refused to lend without exacting interest. In the light of Karo's statement, however, the *Taz* argued, it appeared that it was simply permitted to borrow at interest to save life.[27]

We can infer from this exchange of opinion that there was a

wide discrepancy in medieval attitudes toward the question of interest and its uses. One strain of thought was willing to confront the vast socio-economic and technological changes that made the biblical prohibition difficult to obey and sought to mitigate whenever possible, and to modify, its ramifications. The more conservative approach was to accept limitations on the prohibition but in turn to confine any burgeoning leniency within tight circumscriptions.

It was quite common during the Middle Ages for Jewish communities to be faced with the need to save lives, and sometimes with the need to save whole communities, through bribery and payments of exorbitant taxes. The Tosaphot and their school of thought evidently understood that unless they allowed the payment of interest, the men of capital in their midst would be ruined, for the interest was undoubtedly the major income from which they lived. Should there be no interest, they would constantly be compelled to dig into capital. Thus Tosaphot sought midrashic-biblical sanction to declare this a mitzvah. Tosaphot did not hedge and did not limit it to when there was only one wicked capitalist available who demanded interest. Karo's halakha was therefore soundly based on the tradition. On the other hand, the pietistic *Taz,* who no longer precisely understood the historical conditions which gave rise to the halakha, sought to limit its applicability. As a matter of fact, the limitation of applicability evident here was really part of an inaugural of what became "orthodox" halakha in the ensuing centuries. In effect this was the constant erection of restriction and limitation which gave rise to our crisis in halakha in the twentieth century.

The problem of interest, the *hetar iska* and the other modifications of the prohibition of interest have here been used to depict what can be done toward overcoming a crisis in halakha. For "overcoming a crisis in halakha" means merely to revise or update halakha in order to make it viable and to make possible continued loyalty to its original intent. To achieve this it becomes necessary at times not only to "interpret" a halakha for our day but to innovate practices which in effect abrogate the old ones. What was here shown to be true in a matter of "civil law" is no less true in questions of ritual observance. Our modern crisis calls for the "creative interpretation of the law, in opposition to the mere mechanical process of applying the law," which Dr. Cohen recommended as long ago as 1939. Yet when one reads more recent "guides" for standards in such areas of halakha as *kashrut,* funeral practices or Sabbath observance issued by the Rabbinical Assembly, the one body that should have followed Boaz Cohen's advice avidly, one wonders precisely how much energy we have applied to being creative during the past three decades. Dr. Cohen stressed, "The chief obstacles to such an interpretation would be the failure to comprehend the force and operation of the law, a bleak worship of its letter, an exclusive reverence for precedent . . . a certain elasticity is required if we mean to attain the ends for which the law exists."[28]

Frequently we lose sight of the *spirit of halakha* as a system. We concentrate on the mechanics of fulfilling it precisely. We forget that halakha as a system or a process is designed to expand piety and arouse the moral sense. When we turn our attention to particular halakhot, having lost this vision of the general goal of the system of halakha, we dissipate our energy in a fastidious loyalty to technicality. And too often this loyalty to technicality is only because the practice is buttressed by age or geographic diffusion, even when it has lost spiritual meaning. Yet as long ago as Talmudic times, in a discussion which purportedly took place in the fourth century between Raba and Rabbi Papa concerning the excessive piety of some Jewish ladies in regard to their separation from men when experiencing a menstrual flow, Raba lucidly referred to the need to recognize a distinction between an *issur,* a prohibition which is in accord with the requirements of halakha, and a *minhag* which might suit the private piety of some segments of the population.[29]

There is a lesson to be learned here for a sophisticated age when excessive restrictions and long-accumulated encumbrances have the opposite effect on the modern Jew to that which had been intended at the time when given practices emerged as *minhag.* Instead of enhancing modern spiritual life, they provoke neglect of religious observance. Too often the pithy although inaccurately understood Yiddish aphorism "a *minhag zerbrecht* a *din*" (a custom breaks, or takes precedence over, a law) has been used as a stranglehold upon our creative search for a viable mode of observance. It really means that *new* observances can take precedence over old ones even after they have hardened into law, and therefore serves as an excellent antidote for those opposed to change. Strangely enough, for instance, we also tend to overlook Talmudic sayings which would have significant relevance to us today and in certain quarters might tend to increase respect for a halakha governed by common sense, an interest in relevance and compassion. One example is the well-known formulation that we are lenient in matters of *avelut*, the observances governing mourning. We read in the Talmud that the lenient view of Akiva, that one mourns for only one day in the case of *shemuah rehokah*, when one hears of the death after thirty days, takes precedence over the view of the Rabbis, although usually one follows the majority when the individual is lenient and the majority more restrictive. It is explained that here the opposite is the case; and the halakha follows R. Akiva because halakha *k'divrai hamaikel b'avel*: the halakha follows the lenient view in matters of mourning.[30]

This, the supremacy of leniency, was also the explanation given in the Talmud for the views of Bet Hillel having been given precedence. The Talmud records the inquiry, "Why was Bet Hillel privileged to have the halakha established according to its view?" The reply was offered, "Because Bet Hillel was lenient and patient."[31] It may be argued that the Aramaic term used in this reply, *nohin*, need not mean "lenient" and that I here offer that translation only to sustain a preconceived notion. It would be instructive, therefore, to glance at the remarks of Rabbenu Hananel (980-1056) on the text. He commented that members of the Hillel school of thought were *nohin b'halakha*, which can only mean that they were easygoing or liberal in their interpretation of halakha.

One of the problems making for our inability to solve what Boaz Cohen called "the maladjustments in our religious life" is precisely our reluctance to appear "liberal" in spite of the Talmud's encouragement of that stance. Modern sloganism has usurped items which could mean something and made them into mere labels which either mean nothing or are used as misnomers for certain groups in Jewish life. In either case, these terms have been deprived of substance. "Liberal" is a word today identified with the so-called Reform movement, and so unless one is willing to risk that specific identification he is unwilling to use the term. The so-called Conservative movement, on the other hand, experiences a public expectation that it will live up to the term conservative in the negative sense, conserving that which has been handed down and departing from tradition at the risk of being regarded as reformist. One would think, at least in the light of what I have expounded in this chapter, that to be a "permitter" like Yose b. Yo'ezer or a "liberal" like Hillel would place one in good company and allow one to transcend the narrow definitions of any of the contemporary denominations.

Zvi Hirsch Chajes has evaluated the halakhic process and stated that anyone who violates a legal decision of Mishna or Gemara, regardless of how this decision was arrived at, "is as liable to punishment as he who breaks any of the laws of the Torah." Obviously this opinion was based on, or received its legitimacy from, the Talmudic saying that "anyone who violates the decisions of the sages is liable to capital punishment."[32] It may be safe to say, however, that such an opinion would no longer be accepted by anyone outside the official "orthodox" camps, if even there. We have come a far way from being able to agree with Chajes' judgment that "from none of these can one depart," which he states to be the case with the *gezerot* of the Talmud. He would have us accept Rav Ashi and his *Bet Din* as of "perpetual authority."[33] Among the *gezerot* Chajes would have us give such loyalty to as we would find difficult to accept today is the prohibition for a woman to go out of her home with certain ornaments on the Sabbath lest she take them off to show to a friend and become culpable for carrying in a public domain on the Sabbath. Another is the *gezerah* against taking or applying medicinal products lest a person be tempted to grind up drugs.[34] One could go on and on to cite *gezerot* that few halakha-loyal Jews among us could still seriously observe scrupulously in modern times. But that would be extraneous to the scope of this chapter. Yet if we accept the theory of "perpetual authority" we have no alternative. Evidently we must predicate our loyalty to halakha on other grounds than "perpetual authority." We must establish the premise of *contemporary* authority, for which, as has been shown in this and other chapters, there is a great deal of evidence in our Rabbinic-halakhic literature.

Takkanot which would have to be taken seriously if we gave credence to Chajes' point of view would be such as the one that clothes must be washed on Thursday and garlic eaten on Friday.[35] Reference is not made to these trivia irreverently or facetiously but rather in a mood of quiet desperation. They dramatize forcefully the problems involved in accepting traditional premises and the need to predicate our halakha upon more flexible foundations. Once we discard certain of the old premises we will be able to freely establish new criteria for the conservation of halakha and open new vistas for the future of the halakha.

We have seen how Yose ben Yo'ezer faced the challenge of crisis. Rabbi Yohanan b. Zakkai did the same. Among R. Yohanan's *takkanot* that would be relevant for consideration in our time was the one that permitted the sounding of the shofar on Rosh ha'Shanah occurring on the Sabbath wherever there was a *Bet Din*, after the cataclysm of 70 c.e.

Previously the Sabbath shofar-sounding had been confined to the Temple according to Rashi (Rabbi Solomon b. Isaac of Troyes, 1040-1105). Rashi interpreted the Mishna which stated that during Temple days they did not sound the shofar when Rosh ha'Shanah occurred on the Sabbath in the *medinah,* to mean that Jerusalem and its suburbs or environs were excluded. Maimonides, on the other hand, maintained that the prohibition on sounding the shofar in the *medinah* meant beyond the environs, and he described certain criteria for sounding the shofar throughout the Holy City and even outside Jerusalem on Sabbath-Rosh ha'-Shanah.[36]

This difference of opinion regarding the older practice highlights for us the fact that there was often an ambiguity in the classical literature which left open areas for medieval disputation.

The different interpretations that medieval commentators gave to classical statements also led in turn to differing halakhic conclusions, each conclusion always depending on the individual who made it. In the matter of sounding the shofar on the Sabbath, some of the less patient scholars simply took the attitude that there was no point in trying to establish the accuracy of the case in discussion, because it was no longer relevant at all. The shofar was simply no longer blown on the Sabbath anywhere.

It may be contended, on the other hand, that this should become a relevant matter. The shofar may be blown on the Sabbath wherever there is a *Bet Din* or its contemporary equivalent. It is difficult to assess why R. Yohanan set as a specific criterion the existence of a *Bet Din*. Perhaps for him and in that period the *Bet Din* marked the seat of religious authority in a community. With the cessation of a functional concept of *Bet Din* in modern times, the only meaningful institutional embodiment of Jewish communal religious authority is the synagogue. Consequently it might be of great spiritual value to reconsider the use of the shofar on the Sabbath. First it was sounded in the center of supreme embodiment of the religious life, Jerusalem. Then the Temple was cast down into a mound of ruins, and Jerusalem was ploughed under and sown with salt. Judaism had to respond to the existential reality. Therefore the symbolic essence of Jerusalem was transferred to wherever there was a *Bet Din*. The need for a similar process is no less real in modern times and in the context of our social institutions. The right or even the obligation to sound the shofar on the Sabbath should now be accorded to every synagogue. Halakha, if it is to serve as an instrument in the ongoing quest for the enhancement of life, will be wisely adjusted to newly arising forces. It should make no difference whether the forces operating to change Jewish communal life are political as in ancient Jerusalem, socio-economic as in the medieval question of *hetar iska* discussed previously, or, as is most pertinent in our times, a revolution in science or technology.

There can no longer be any question of the need to re-examine the *takkanot* and the *gezerot,* both the positive and the prohibitory enactments, or amendments to existing halakha which came into being more or less as "executive orders" rather than as legislation based on the reinterpretation of previous halakha, or negative decrees prohibiting some action which might have been considered permitted. A re-examination of these halakhot would also have to take under study the philosophy behind them and their motivation. As indicated earlier, many *takkanot* were based on the simple expedient of *mipnai darkai shalom,* "for the welfare and harmony of society," whether among Jews themselves or for the improvement of interfaith relations. Another standard given consideration by the Talmudists was *shalom bayis,* "domestic tranquillity." The ancient sages allowed such criteria as the honor of women, appreciation for God's favor and the protection of the defenseless or underprivileged to govern their attitude toward *takkanot.* These and other facets of the underlying philosophy of the halakha have already been expanded upon in other chapters of this volume. But this is a highly significant aspect of overcoming the crisis in halakha.

There is no question that the crisis in halakha is part of the crisis of religion in general. What too often besets us is our preference for clinging to nostalgias and taking comfort in habits that we are accustomed to regard as the sancta of Judaism. Yet the sages of yore did not have our reluctance or suffer from our diffidence to innovate and to apply the old sancta in new ways. It is not necessarily *more* "traditional" to reject change. On the contrary, a traditional approach to Judaism implies doing what the Rabbis of ancient Palestine and Babylonia did. They readily modified the ritual as well as other segments of halakha. One criterion which they used was radical sociological change. For example, in the attestation of tithes required by the Torah, the donor declared, "I have removed the sacred from my home and have given it to the Levite, the Ger, the orphan and the widow. . . ." From the time of Ezra the tithes were given only to the priests because the Levites refused to return to Judea. This was the custom followed in early Tannaitic times prior to the cataclysm of 70 c.e. Consequently Yohanan Kohen Gadol abolished the recital of these verses, because, as the Talmud reported, it was no longer being done in the manner prescribed by the Torah.

Here we evidently have an instance in which, first, a Torah halakha, the distribution of tithes, was abolished by the act of a human sage, Ezra, and as a consequence a Torah-ordained liturgical rite was abolished by act of another human sage, Yohanan Kohen Gadol. Yohanan also introduced other revolutionary interpretations of the inherited tradition of his time.[37]

Psychology too must be examined for its value in dealing with the crisis in halakha. We know that every individual is different. The ancient Midrash lauded the infinite wisdom of God in creating man with such incredible individuality that although "God has stamped every man with the die of the first man, yet not one of them is like his fellow."[38] Since each person has a distinct personality, each person should be given greater latitude in fulfilling his yearning for his Creator. Ritual life, man's expression of his relations or his devotions to his God, could lose nothing by providing for greater selectivity. Just as an athletic father cannot necessarily sire an athletic son, so an observant Jewish father striving to impose a given, inflexible regimen upon his child may not be contributing to his most serene adjustment to Judaism. But it is not adequate to withdraw from the fray and let each Jew handle his religious life as best he can. Rabbis and their synagogues, and especially their synagogue schools, must take a position in halakha, and when confronted with the question whether a given practice is right or wrong, permissible or forbidden, must venture a lucid response. Perhaps the time has come to profess a ritualistic selectivity, a philosophy of individuation as over against regimentation. Understanding this problem may help us to appreciate the definition of halakha as a *juristic principle* rather than a particular case. It is perhaps *ma'aseh,* the particular case, the particular action in a given situation, which is in more of a crisis than halakha as a process, principle or system. The juristic *idea* is something we all cherish. But it is the precise requirement of the moment, the *ma'aseh,* where we may have wide divergence. It is here that we can have no unanimity and that we require the right of selectivity.

The halakhic imperative of the future, therefore, is to reexamine our guiding principles, our basic halakha, in the light of the criteria already set forth by the Talmud: changing historic conditions, social revolution, civic and domestic tranquillity and interfaith harmony, the welfare of the underprivileged, the lessons of psychology and the host of other criteria and disciplines already discussed in this volume. From this re-evaluation of juristic guidelines in each generation we may arrive at a functional set of *ma'a'sim,* of usages, that will enhance the life and the aspirations of the dedicated Jew and the society in which he moves.

A CLOSING WORD

THE HISTORIAN Heinrich Graetz once wrote, "If the Talmud resembles a Daedalian maze in which one can scarcely find his way even with the thread of Ariadne, Maimonides designed a well-contained ground-plan with wings, chambers and closets through which a stranger might easily pass without a guide and thereby obtain a survey of all that is contained in the Talmud."

The nature of the Talmud described here as being a Daedalian maze has much truth to it. It is difficult for the scholar, not to speak of the layman, to find his way through the mass of material which is disorganized and quite unthematic. But while Maimonides appears to have given the mid-nineteenth-century historian a high degree of satisfaction, it is clear over a century later and as we prepare to enter the twenty-first century, a wholly new era and an utterly unforeseeable epoch, that Maimonides' Mishne Torah has become something of a medieval castle to the modern explorer, with all its thick walls, hidden passageways, excessive number of rooms and small closets no longer adequate for our broader expanse of vision and interest.

The time has come to reorder the gigantic mass of halakhic material and to extract the relevant elements of every facet of halakha still observed to some extent among all Jews. I am presently planning to do this in the field of bereavement, *Hilkhot Avelut,* but there is a serious necessity to have it done in relation to the Sabbath, the festivals, liturgy, marriage and divorce, and other areas of ritual and ethics that continue to play a role in modern Judaism. What may a Jew do or not do, if he is loyal to his faith, so far as ecological questions are concerned? Perhaps it is today as prohibited for a faithful Jew to smoke a cigarette or to use a detergent with phosphate as to partake of pork.

The task before us is great if one only considers the academic task. But it is all the greater because of the emotionalism involved in selecting extracts of halakha and suggesting what is relevant. Inevitably the process of extraction and selection will result in certain practices slipping into desuetude. This in turn will result in what some will call abrogation, which will then in turn call forth much abuse and controversy.

The whole tenor of this volume has been what I am sure some critics will call tendentious. They will be employing the word negatively, to cast suspicion on the book's objectivity, and by implication on its academic validity. Therefore I hasten to confirm this charge. This book *is* tendentious, and the purpose throughout is to attempt to open some windows in Judaism to allow a refreshing breeze to waft through the synagogue and the Jewish home. I am attempting to prove that there was a pronounced tendency throughout Rabbinic literature toward leniency, toward providing options for Jewish religious observance, away from dogmatism and one-track orthodoxy. It is to be deeply lamented that this book had to be written at all in 1971 to merely restate the obvious. The tendentious nature of this book is precisely to dig up the self-evident and document it for our generation and the future.

In every previous chapter I have brought forward examples of the leniency pursued in the halakha and of the legitimacy of diversity or options in Jewish observance. This is further shown quite cogently in a discussion of an old practice which may not have a great deal of relevance to our life style or to our mode of ritual life today. But it has potency for demonstrating to us the underlying thesis that Rabbinic halakha practiced leniency. In this sense it is extremely relevant, for we are still too frequently beset by arguments that we must not relax certain restrictions, such as photography on the Sabbath, or that we must not simplify certain areas of ritual which have meaningless strata of minutiae. What this passage will indicate is that the Rabbis chose not to pile restriction upon restriction and not to so hedge in an observance that they would in effect be stretching a one-day occasion to three days. Perhaps most significantly for our time, it demonstrates that they preferred to allow people a degree of self-expression in their piety.

The passage relates to festive days listed in the Megillat Taanit. This was a scroll which listed festive and semi-festive occasions in ancient times. It was the practice not to mourn or to fast on the days listed in the scroll. In time the scroll was abolished, but certain days, such as Hanukah and Purim, were retained. The Mishna in Taanit recorded two opinions regarding whether a Jew may mourn or fast on the day before and the day after a festive day like Hanukah or Purim.[1] One opinion, cited anonymously, maintained that we need not be concerned that a person will neglect the festive day if we permit him to mourn on the day after, but that he should refrain from doing so the day before so that he may approach the festive day in proper mood. R. Yosi held that he must refrain from doing so both on the day before and on the day after so as to be certain he will not intrude upon the festive occasion at all. Similarly, Anonymous was more relaxed on the question of fasting. He maintained that one may fast if he so wishes both on the day before and on the day after the festive occasion, while R. Yosi was of the opinion that he should not fast on the day before, but he may on the day after.

The clear distinction between Anonymous and R. Yosi was that Anonymous was less fastidious and restrictive. He was not concerned lest a more relaxed attitude toward the day in question result in a violation of the days' standards. On the other hand, R. Yosi apparently was quite insistent that a meticulous hedge be constructed so as to be certain that no violation would occur on the important day in question. This is not unlike the modern divergence one frequently encounters between those who feel there is no need to be overfastidious in ritual matters and those who persist in enforcing a very restrictive code lest the barriers come tumbling down.

Yet this passage is rather instructive. The Talmud proceeds to inform us that the third-century scholar Rab, head of the Academy at Sura, decided the halakha according to the more restrictive opinion of R. Yosi, and that his colleague in Nehardea, Samuel, decided it according to Anonymous.[2] The Talmud then

interestingly adds that when it was learned that R. Simon b.
Gamliel had advocated a policy even more lenient than that of
Anonymous, namely, that in both instances, mourning and fast-
ing, neither the day before nor the day after counted at all,
Samuel switched to the more lenient position.

Without our entering into a complicated analysis of this
passage in the Talmud, it is clear that in either case—whether
the halakha is decided in accordance with Anonymous or with
R. Simon b. Gamliel—the decision tends to the lenient. As a
matter of fact, the Talmud said explicitly that the halakha follows
either of those two, since they advocated the lenient point of
view. The Talmud was willing to trust to the discretion and judgment of the public and to avoid being overbearing in arranging
Jewish ritual life.

Perhaps an even more illuminating facet of this particular
passage and the conclusion reached by the halakhic sages is that
we have here another example of what has been noted earlier in
the book, that although normally a question of ritual halakha
followed Rab, here the halakha followed Samuel! The only explanation for this is further confirmation of the tendency toward
leniency that predominated in the Rabbinic halakha, even to the
extent of digressing from usual patterns. There was not unanimity
among medieval halakhists on whether Samuel should prevail
over Rab, but ultimately he did. We know inferentially that we
may fast or mourn, for example, on the day before or after a
festival or a semi-festival like Hanukah or Purim.[3]

The passage I have here described is not of great moment in
modern Jewish life. But for that matter, none of the religious
ritual is presently regarded as of great moment by too large a
number of Jews. Yet if we are to preserve Judaism, we have to
preserve some distinct form of it. And if Judaism is to be preserved with a sense of historical continuity and therefore historic
legitimacy, it is the halakha that must be preserved and in a form
which will become inspiring, meaningful and enriching. For the
halakha to be all this it must at a very minimum become viable.
It must assume a form that twenty-first-century Jews will be able
to accept and live by.

The task of putting the halakha into such a form is now several centuries late. Further delay can be fatal to Judaism. To assuage the anxieties of some that halakhic surgery may be as fatal to the patient as neglect, it should be emphasized that it is not surgery alone that has to be done but a revaluation of the patient's purposes and functions. Some surgery will be necessary to prune away layers of dead matter and useless strata of decayed substance. But transplants will also have to take place so that new life can be nurtured in coming generations.

This massive task may be undertaken in the spirit of the interesting remarks of a medieval scholar, popularly known as *Maharsha,* the acronym of his name and title. This was Rabbi Samuel Eliezer b. Judah ha'Levi Edels, who lived in Volhynia from about 1555 to 1631. At the end of the tractate *Yevamot* in the Babylonian Talmud he wrote a very illuminating comment on the subject of abrogating old halakha.[4]

In that passage Edels was apologetic for the idea expressed in the Talmud that the Rabbis have the power to "uproot," or abolish or abrogate, even a Torah rule. A number of examples are discussed in *Yevamot* and elsewhere. Edels was of the opinion that the intent of the Rabbis was not really to abrogate the Torah's rulings but rather to *fulfill* the spirit of the Torah: increase peace, expand the *benefits* of halakha and carry out the promises of the Bible expressed in such verses as "Its ways are ways of pleasantness and all its paths are peace."[5] In other words, Edels was employing a semantic device. The Rabbis were not destructive or negative; the intent was not to abrogate. They were constructive and positive; the intent was to preserve. Yet, as we all realize, and as the Talmudic sages themselves were aware, regardless of how you interpret the word, the effect was *akira,* abrogation.

It is in this same spirit that a great deal can be undertaken in our own time. No Rabbi and no Rabbinic body need feel zealous about abrogating any ruling, injunction or customary practice found in the tradition. They would merely process the tradition and select and evaluate, extract and suggest what Jews might still find spiritually meaningful, what is still of significant historical value, what best expresses human aspirations and most richly gives vent to human emotions. The evaluation would take into consideration the criteria we have discussed, projecting guidance for Jewish religious practice that would inspire and enhance the aesthetic sense, consider one's economic need, take under advisement contemporary intellectual currents, and preserve historical associations and values. The selection would enrich humanitarian principles, the ethic or moral imperative of the Torah and subsequent tradition.

The intent in the selection would be to preserve, enrich and expand religious life, not to decimate the Torah. The letter of halakha would give way to its spirit, as Edels explained in his reflections upon Rabbinic abrogation. But out of the subordination of letter to spirit would naturally arise a new letter of halakha to guide a new age and offer options not presently open to those who would pragmatically like to know what they can do, and how, to express Jewish religious forms without violating their intellectual standards or repelling their universalist approaches to life.

Eli Ginzberg has explained that his father, the great mentor of dozens of contemporary Rabbis, ". . . did not take any initiative to modernize the law. He saw no point in venturing on such a task, for whom could he hope to persuade?" He further claimed that his father felt Jews in the United States did not need new halakha, since they "had long ago denied its authority."[6] Perhaps Louis Ginzberg despaired. But on the other hand he had himself written, "It is only in the *Halakha* that we find the mind and character of the Jewish people exactly and adequately expressed."[7] Although I am planning a specific essay on Louis Ginzberg and the halakha, it is worth risking some repetition to indicate here that regardless of what Ginzberg did or failed to do about the halakha in twentieth-century America, he left a major legacy to us and a weighty responsibility by stressing throughout his lifetime the centrality of halakha for the Jew. He saw the halakha as the "converging point" of all spiritual tendencies in Judaism, and stressed that halakha is the medium used by Judaism ". . . to elevate through action and so strengthen man's likeness to God . . . it is the spiritualization of everyday life." But with all his reluctance to cause a tempest by actively pursuing revisionism in halakha, he taught us that "laws which govern the daily life of man must be such as suit and express his wishes, being in harmony with his feelings and fitted to satisfy his religious ideals and ethical aspirations."[8]

In a nutshell, the tendentiousness of this book is related to my desire to see Judaism live again. Halakha was made for living. If it has of late been inadequate, then the fault, as Shakespeare said, is not in the stars but in us. We have failed to do what the guardians of the halakha who preceded us consistently did: adjust the halakha to conform with the age. There are those who will argue that only a giant like Louis Ginzberg has the right to engage in serious revisionism. But Rabbinic literature teaches us that there are no exceptions. Religious authority and intellectual expertise are relative matters. "Jephtha in his generation is as authoritative as Samuel in his," we are taught in a famous passage, even though superficial examination might lead us to conclude that Samuel deserves the authority that belongs to a Prophet who encountered divine revelation, while Jephtha was a mere military leader with no special spiritual capacity. The Rabbis chose precisely two men of such wide disparity, as well as pointing to other similar pairs, to emphasize beyond a shadow of a doubt for all time that *authority is contemporary*. The Talmud explicitly stated so in an exegetical comment on the verse enjoining Jews to seek proper judicial advice. The Torah said, "You shall go . . . unto the judge that shall be in those days," and the Talmud innocently inquires, "Can it possibly enter your mind that you can go to a judge who is not in your own days?" The Talmud seizes upon that opportunity to stress that the Jew is to follow contemporary authority and not appeal to the past.[9] If our revered teacher Louis Ginzberg, of sainted memory, chose, for his own reasons, not to engage in an extensive program of halakhic revision, and if our revered teacher Saul Lieberman similarly chooses to devote his time to the pursuit of textual analysis and criticism rather than halakhic revision and development, this does not excuse their disciples from undertaking the task and doing so with alacrity and with the self-confidence the Talmud imbued in the halakhic sages of the past. Although the task is great and awesome and will invoke much opposition, it must begin somewhere. The Mishna has instructed us: though a task be great and it is not incumbent upon any one of us to complete it, nevertheless none of us is free to evade it.[10] It is my prayer that this volume at least marks a modest beginning in a new intensive effort to revise and update the corpus of our halakha, which is, after all, "our life and the length of our days."[11]

NOTES

PREFACE

1. Louis Ginzberg, *On Jewish Law and Lore* (Phila., 1955), pp. 78-79.

2. Ps. 30:13. All biblical references are to the *Biblia Hebraica*, ed. Rudolph Kittel and Paul Kahle (Stuttgart, 1952). Translations are my own. At times I translate in accordance with emendations that have been indicated in the Kittel-Kahle footnotes or in my seminary notes of lectures given by Prof. H. L. Ginsberg. In every case, however, the responsibility is my own. The verse in this note is an example.

The Septuagint here reads *Khvodee* in the Hebrew instead of our Masoretic *Khavod,* and I am therefore taking the word as it often is understood, not as "glory" or "honor" but as "person" or "being," and translating it simply as "I."

CHAPTER I

1. Lev. 18:5. "Observe my statutes and my laws that man ought to perform so that he may live by them. I am the Lord."

2. This is not to overlook the fact that there are other areas of the world where hundreds of thousands of Jews live and where there are presently other and parallel serious challenges. Among such geographic centers could be listed Latin America and the Soviet Union. In former times too there were more than three centers, but these three—Babylon, Spain and North Africa—during the early and middle Middles Ages were the sources of a permanent intellectual impact, as were Spain, Palestine and the Franco-German center during the later Middles Ages, and Central and Eastern Europe from the 16th century to World War I.

Similarly in the contemporary era the three centers I have mentioned—Israel, Western Europe and North America—are probably capable of a major intellectual impact upon the future of Judaism.

3. Cf. my article "Jewish and American Pragmatism," *Judaism* vol. 19, no. 2 (Spring 1970), pp. 191-95.

4. Job 1:21. The acknowledgment of our sins as the source of our misfortune was regularly prayed in the Musaph Amidah of the festivals.

5. Emil Fackenheim, "Fragment," *Commentary*, Aug. 1968. Cf. his essay "These Twenty Years: A Reappraisal," in *Quest for Past and Future* (Bloomington and London, 1968), p. 20.

6. Job 2:10.

7. Cf. my article "Halakha Is Not Law," *Jewish Spectator*, Feb. 1971.

8. Saul Lieberman, *Hellenism In Jewish Palestine* (New York, 1950), p. 83, note 3. I discuss this more extensively later in the book where I express a preference for halakha as meaning "a pattern of conduct." But this does not obviate Professor Lieberman's contribution toward helping us see the term as something other than "law." See chap. 11, and especially the discussion in note 2.

CHAPTER II

1. Ex. 19:4-8 and frequently throughout the Pentateuch and prophetic literature. Cf. Deut. 13:4, 18; 14:2; 27:10; 7:6; 26:18-19; Ps. 135:4; Mal. 3:17; Isa. 61:6; 62:12. I propose to take up the broader question of the origin of halakha in a future volume in which I will explore and discuss the transition period between the Bible and the Maccabean age, when what we call Pharisaism emerged.

2. Abraham J. Heschel, *God in Search of Man* (Phila., 1956), p. 217.

3. Louis Ginzberg, *Legends of the Jews* (Phila., 1946-54), vol. 1, p. 292, and vol. 5, p. 259, note 275. Cf. also vol. 2, p. 94. Cf. Midrash Rabbah Ruth 2:9 commenting on the biblical text Ruth 1:4, that when the sons of Elimelekh took Moabite wives, the "new halakha" that allowed female Moabites to Israelites, which was based on an exegesis of Deut. 23:4, had not yet been propounded. In the same Midrash, 7:7 and 7:10, we are told that Boaz was still unaware that a new halakha had been innovated permitting female Moabites and Ammonites. According to this Midrashic discussion, it is self-evident that the Rabbis were attributing the origin of the halakha to a specific historical period. When they defended the legitimacy of David's Jewish descent from Ruth (ibid. 4:6), they again called it a "halakha which has been innovated" and attributed its origin to the time between Elimelekh and Saul.

The "Noahide laws" referred to in my text consisted of seven basic moral imperatives which the Rabbis considered were binding upon gentiles. In the seventh chapter of Babylonian Sanhedrin is related the exegesis on which the Rabbis based their views. The seven commandments were (1) to establish a system of justice, (2) not to commit idolatry, (3) not to blaspheme, (4) not to commit incest or adultery, (5) not to kill, (6) not to rob, (7) not to eat flesh from a living animal. For all of this see the Babylonian Talmud, Sanhedrin 56a, and following pages. Cf. also the earlier statement in Tosephta Avodah Zarah 9:4 which has the "seven mitzvot of the sons of Noah" listed in the order I have here given them.

The extent of patriarchal observance of halakha and whether it encompassed only the Noahide laws or other practices as well is discussed in a number of Talmudic passages. Cf. Babylonian Yoma 28b, Hullin 101b and the Mishna Hullin 7:6.

4. Babylonian Talmud, Eruvin 21b, Baba Kama 82a, Sabbath 14b, Rosh ha'Shanah 31b and elsewhere.

5. Mishna Hagiga 1:8.

6. Babylonian Hagigah 11b. It is true that the Talmud attempts to limit the statement to the idea that if one performed an indirect Sabbath violation such as digging a hole not because he wanted a hole but to use the earth, he is not culpable for digging the hole. But this is not the clear sense of the Mishna. The Mishna's statement may be taken at face value, that there is "little Scripture and much halakha." The meaning was probably quite simply that the Torah prohibits *melakha* (usually translated as "work"). But there is no definition of *melakha* per se. Rather, the halakha related the concept of *melakha* to the activities conducted in the construction of the portable sanctuary in the wilderness. Thus it was self-evident, and probably troubling, that such a vast and complex corpus of Sabbath halakha had evolved. Yet, in accordance with the general Pharisaic approach to the evolution of halakha, the Mishna termed non-scriptural laws *gufai Torah*. The term *guf* in this context is undoubtedly related to the word in its meaning of "essence" or "substance" as in *Yerushalmi Berakhot* 3c, where the term is used of the Ten Commandments as constituting virtually the substance of the Shema.

7. Tosephta Sota 15:5, Babylonian Baba Batra 60b, Avodah Zarah 36a, Horee'yot 3b and frequently elsewhere. Cf. Yerushalmi Berakhot 3c, that certain scriptural portions were removed from the services in ancient times so as not to burden the congregation. Cf. note 1 to chap. 1.

8. Avot 1:17.

9. Babylonian Berakhot 5a, Megillah 19b, Midrash Rabbah Numbers 19:6. Cf. Rashi on Megillah 19b.

The classical conservative statement of the divine origin of all of the halakha is stated in a variety of ways by Moses Maimonides. See, for instance, his introduction to the Mishne Torah, where he explicitly affirms that all the mitzvot given to Moses at Sinai were already then and there accompanied by their elucidation. Cf. also his *Perush ha'Mishnayot* on Hullin, 7;6 (in Talmud editions, p. 100b), where he states that we do not observe any mitzvah because God revealed it to someone such as enjoining circumcision upon Abraham, but observe it only because God revealed it anew to Moses, and enjoined it again specifically at Sinai. He calls upon the student to realize the important principle embodied in the Mishnaic passage, that the sciatic nerve was prohibited at Sinai and not at the time of Jacob's wrestling with the angel. Maimonides averred that this signifies "whatever we refrain from or whatever we fulfill today we only do because God commanded Moses, and not because He commanded any previous prophet; for example, we do not refrain from eating a cut of meat from a live animal because it was prohibited to Noah, but because Moses issued the prohibition at Sinai. . . ."

10. Babylonian Talmud Temurah 16a; Avot 1:1. See also Yerushalmi Peah 15b. In the latter reference the term used by the Rabbis for Joshua's independent halakhic discoveries was *haskimah dato*: his deliberations "coincided" or "harmonized" with what was taught to Moses at Sinai. The term is to be understood as it is in many other instances, for example Babylonian Yevamot 62a. There we are told Moses acted independently three times, but *v'hiskimah dato l'da'at hamakom*: his mind or his reasoning or conclusions coincided or harmonized with the will of God.

11. Babylonian Gittin 60a.

12. See chap. 4 and the succeeding three chapters which elaborate upon it.

13. Babylonian Baba Metziah 59b, Temurah 16a, Eruvin 13b. Cf. Ginzberg, op. cit., vol. 4, p. 4, and vol. 6, p. 170.

14. A. J. Heschel, op. cit., p. 273.

15. Cf. the minutes and Decisions of the Committee on Jewish Law and Standards, available at the Rabbinical Assembly offices, 3080 Broadway, New York City. See especially the responsum on *Tnai Kiddushin*, which, to all intents and purposes, has introduced an annulment procedure which solves the *agunah* problem from now and into the future. The committee has permitted the marriage of a *kohen* to a divorcee or to a convert and has declared the restrictions of *mamzerut* (bastardy) "inoperative."

A responsum voted upon in 1970 suggested a conditional clause at the time of marriage which would in effect retroactively annul the marriage if *halitzah* was required. There was an alternative approach by myself to offer the officiating Rabbi the option to waive *halitzah* at the time the widow presents herself for remarriage.

The point here is that there is constant human intervention in the halakha, and I am urging more such intervention to increase respect for halakha and make it more viable.

16. This question of "static versus dynamic" Judaism is one that can be comprehensively studied in the general literature available on Pharisaic and Sadducaic Judaism. This juxtaposition and terminology, the static-Sadducee and the dynamic-Pharisee, and their relationship to contemporary Orthodox and non-Orthodox is, I believe, my own, taken up in some of my previous articles. Cf. Louis Finkelstein, *The Pharisees* (Phila., 1946), and Jacob Z. Lauterbach, *Rabbinic Essays* (Cin., 1951). Lauterbach's quotation regarding Pharisees being "masters of the law" is on p. 47.

17. I am here using the word *transcendentalist* with no reference whatever to its usage in Christian theology. I use it simply as a term that signifies the desire to "transcend," move beyond, the divisiveness and sectarianism in Jewish life by crossing all denominational lines.

18. Phillip Sigal, "The Problem of Halakha Re-examined," *Reconstructionist*, Dec. 30, 1955. It will be noted that in the course of this book I have fused that definition of halakha with the idea of halakha-as-conduct, the blueprint for human behavior.

19. The original practice was to permit marriages on Rosh Hodesh Iyar and Lag B'omer, the 1st day of the month of Iyar and the 33rd day of Sephira. In October 1949 the Committee on Jewish Law and Standards of the Rabbinical Assembly issued a report that modified this practice. The committee followed Gaonic tradition, which only prohibited marriages from the 2nd day of Passover until Lag B'omer, but not after Lag B'omer, a practice followed in medieval French Jewish communities. The committee, furthermore, permitted weddings on the 5th of Iyar, the day on which Israeli independence was observed. In 1956 this was interpreted more particularly to mean that weddings with music and dancing may take place from Passover through Rosh Hodesh Iyar, on the 5th day of Iyar, and from Lag B'omer to Shavuot, and that private weddings, without music and dancing, may take place even from the 2nd day of Iyar to Lag B'omer. In 1969 even festive weddings were permitted altogether, and with the exception of the weekend of the 27th of Nisan and including it, the Sephira was declared to be as the rest of the year.

In 1968, similarly, as regards the "three weeks" from the 17th of Tammuz through the 9th of Av, when Jerusalem walls were pierced and the battle culminated in the destruction of the city and the ancient Temple, the committee unanimously permitted weddings from the 18th of Tammuz through the 8th of Av. Only Tisha B'Av itself was unanimously exempted from the sweeping change. The committee still unanimously prohibits weddings on the 9th day of the month of Av. An overwhelming majority voted to continue the prohibition on the 17th of Tammuz, but an official minority position allows it, and so, as halakha, that is a permissible option.

20. Heschel, op. cit., p. 274.

CHAPTER III

1. Roscoe Pound, *The History and System of the Common Law* (New York, 1939), vol. 1, p. 18.

2. For a summary discussion of the development of medieval law and the role of individuals see C. W. Previte-Orton, *The Shorter Cambridge Medieval History,* 2 vols. (Cambridge, 1952). Cf. vol. 2, chap. 23, for Frederick II's work in Sicily. For the significant work of Henry II in England see vol. 1, chap. 19. More extended discussions can be found in *The Oxford History of England* and in histories of law; references are not given here as not germane to our subject.

3. Frederick J. E. Woodbridge, *The Purpose of History,* p. 23. Cf. also pp. 26 and 89.

4. Quoted by Lord John Acton in a footnote to his "Inaugural Lecture on the Study of History" (Cambridge, 1895). It is cited in Acton, *Essays in the Liberal Interpretation of History,* ed. William H. McNeill (Chicago, 1967).

5. Ibid., p. 316, note 35; p. 327, note 55.

6. For further discussion see chaps. 4, 5, 6 and 7 of this book.

7. The priestly benediction is prescribed in Num. 6:22-27. In the Jerusalem Temple the priestly blessing was pronounced from a *dukhan,* a special platform, after the *Tamid,* the regular daily and evening sacrifice. Cf. Mishna, Tamid 7:2 and Sotah 7:6. Babylonian Sotah 37b-40b has an extensive running discussion of aspects of the priestly rites and the original texts used in it. This rite, the blessing given by the priest with raised hands, for which reason it was called *nesiat kappayim,* the raising of the hands, was described in Lev. 9:22, where Aaron blessed the assemblage after the sacrificial service.

Cf. Ex. 3:15 for the opening phrases of the Amidah. The traditional assumption is that this opening portion of the Amidah was originated by the men of the Great Assembly. This is not the place to go into the question of who these men were or whether there was a body called the Great Assembly. It is a much debated and sparsely documented question. But assuming that attributing the opening blessing of the Amidah to them at the very least implies antiquity, we may further assume that it originated somewhere around 200 B.C.E. But because it was entirely an innovation at its origin it required the establishment of the kind of continuity we are talking about. In Babylonian Megillah 18a we have an attempt to reconcile two contradictory traditions. The first is that the Amidah was instituted by the Great Assembly, the other that it was instituted by Shimon ha'pakoli. (*Pakoli* means "cotton dealer." For use of this word cf. Rashi on Megillah 17b and cf. also its usage in Babylonian Shabbat

110b and Niddah 17a.) Shimon ha'pakoli was said to have received his instructions from Rabban Gamliel II at the end of the 1st century C.E., which leaves a disparity of some three centuries between the two traditions. The Talmud explains "it was forgotten" and had to be "reinstituted." This is not the place, however, to enter into a fuller discussion of the Amidah, although it serves as an excellent example of the evolution of the halakha of liturgy and possesses a rich mine of illustration and illumination to help us in our profound liturgical difficulties today. For a more detailed scholarly study of the origin of the Amidah see Louis Finkelstein, "The Development of the Amidah," *Jewish Quarterly Review,* new series, vol. 16 (1925/26), and Kaufman Kohler, "The Origin and Composition of the Eighteen Benedictions," *Hebrew Union College Annual,* vol. 1 (1924). Both these articles are now conveniently included in Jakob J. Petuchowski's collection of essays, *Contributions to the Scientific Study of Jewish Liturgy* (New York, 1970).

8. See Yerushalmi Peah 15b and other references. Cf. chap. 7 of this book.

9. Ibid.; and chap. 4 of this book.

10. For the etymology of halakha here touched upon see further Saul Lieberman's discussion of the term in his *Hellenism in Jewish Palestine,* p. 83 and note 3. For a more extended discussion of the question see chap. 11 of this book, especially note 3.

11. Mishna Avot 1:1. Cf. Lev. 18:30, which was interpreted in Yevamot 21a and elsewhere to give the sages the right to add injunctions to those of the Torah. Deut. 4:2, which admonished them not to add to the Torah or subtract from it, was not held to prevent halakhic evolution and innovation, since Deut. 17:11 supplemented Lev. 18:30 in providing confidence in contemporary authorities. It did not trouble the Rabbis at all that Lev. 18:30 was specifically related to the priests and had nothing to do with Rabbinic halakha. But it is important to see the other side of the coin: the desire to *limit* excessive additions to the basic halakha on the basis of Avot 1:1. Thus R. Hiyya and his son Hizkiah discouraged this kind of accumulation of restrictions. Cf. Midrash Rabbah, Gen. 19:3 and Babylonian Sanhedrin 29a. R. Hiyya derives the lesson not to suggest more than the original from the fact that Eve misquoted God and as a result was led to disaster. God had instructed man in Gen. 2:17 not to eat of the tree in the midst of the garden, and when Eve tried to stave off the serpent she added to the restriction (Gen. 3:3) by saying that God had said not to eat or to touch. Ultimately this enabled the serpent to prove to Eve that she would not die by touching, and consequently she could be sure that she might eat without fear as well.

Cf. *Avot de Rabbi Nathan,* ed. Solomon Schechter (New York,

1945), ms. 2, p. 2. See also the commentaries in Gen. Rabbah 19:3. Rabbi Samuel Yaffe Ashkenazi in his *Yefe To'or* is troubled by the contradiction between R. Hiyya's attitude and that of the usual accumulation of restrictions. Rabbi Zev Wolff Einhorn, in his *Perush Maharzoo*, offers the explanation adopted in our text, not to build the fence too high lest it topple upon the plant. See my further discussion of this in chap. 4.

12. Herman L. Strack, *Introduction to the Talmud and Midrash* (Phila., 1945), p. 6.

13. Babylonian Pesahim 66a. Cf. Yerushalmi Pesahim 33a.

14. Maharil was Rabbi Jacob b. Moses ha'Levi Moelln of Mainz, who spanned the late 14th and early 15th centuries. Cf. Shulhan Arukh Yoreh Dayah 376:4.

15. Deut. 26:13. Cf. Lieberman, op. cit., pp. 39 ff. The *takkanah* of Rabbenu Gershom banning polygamy is nowhere extant, as Salo Baron confirms in *A Social and Religious History of the Jews* (Phila., 1958), vol. 6, pp. 135-36. See also his note 156, where he refers to Louis Finkelstein's *Jewish Self-Government in the Middle Ages* (New York, 1924), pp. 23 ff. and 139 ff., for data related to this question. Cf. the responsa of Rabbi Asher (the *Rosh*), no. 43, 1.

16. Babylonian Berakhot 45a, Sabbath 40a.

17. See note 7 to chap. 2.

18. Cf. Babylonian Shabbat 14b, 15a; and see Rashi. Cf. Babylonian Avodah Zarah 8b. There is some difference of opinion among Talmudic scholars whether the motivation behind the leniency in the case of glassware was economic, with a view to reducing competition, or simply to establish the old rules for a new product so that there would be "continuity" in a changing environment. In either case, the *fact* is that the Rabbis considered the environment and acted to deal with a new product. Whether the stimulant was technology or economics, it was *external* and had the same result. But the reader is referred to my more comprehensive and documented discussion of the question of science and technology and the economic ramifications in chaps. 6 and 7 of this book.

19. I plan a more extensive study of the Sabbath question in a future volume. Meanwhile it will suffice to indicate what the basic sources are which can help us with modifying the Sabbath. Cf. Babylonian Pesahim 65a and Yerushalmi Yomah 1:1 for the principle on *shevut bamikdash*, "there is no rest in the Sanctuary," that is, all tasks may be routinely performed on the Sabbath. The term *shevut* was applied loosely to signify any act from which a Jew was to desist and which was prohibited only by Rabbinic halakha. Cf. Babylonian Betzah 36b, Sabbath 95a and other references. Throughout the Talmudic period the concept of *shevut* was used to expand Sabbath re-

strictions so as to forge a quiescent day. More and more activities were encompassed under its wings. This is shown quite extensively by the late Boaz Cohen in his essay "Sabbath Prohibitions Known as *Shevut*," found in a collection of several of his papers, *Law and Tradition* (New York, 1959), pp. 127 ff. Cohen shows that medieval scholars further extended the *shevut* prohibitions to many acts not so designated in the Talmud. See especially his note 82, p. 155. The burden of my position is that the concept of *shevut* ought to be employed toward *leniency*, reinterpreted with a view toward *liberalizing* the restrictions.

For the concept of *melakhah she'ain tzreekha l'gufah* see Tosaphot Babylonian Sabbath 94a, beginning with *R. Shimon Poter*, in reference to the Mishna on 93b. A related concept is *davar she'ain miskhavain:* when the person who performs the act does not want its result, but rather the prohibited result is merely a by-product of the act which is performed for another reason. For example, when a man drags a chair in order to sit upon it, the purpose of the act is to sit, and if the dragging causes a rut to be scratched into the surface, which is a prohibited act, he is not culpable. Cf. Babylonian Sabbath 29b, 41b and passim, and Ketuvot 5b. Furthermore, although usually the halakha is like Rav in matters of ritual (Babylonian Bekhorot 49b), in this instance it is like Samuel, who decided in favor of this halakha. Cf. Babylonian Sabbath 22a.

In these matters too, as in *shevut*, the burden of my argument will be to examine the halakha closely for avenues of liberalization to be derived from these principles. In Talmudic times these principles saved the Jew from punitive measures, and in modern times they can perhaps be applied in a more positive manner to open the windows upon the Sabbath and allow in fresh breezes which will enable a modern halakha-oriented Jew to enjoy the Sabbath to a greater extent than is now possible, or to win the uncommitted to halakha.

20. Babylonian Sabbath 133b; Yerushalmi Peah 15b. But see my later discussion and documentation in chap. 7. See also chap. 5 for the question of spiritual value inherent in halakha.

21. Mishna Sabbath 16:1; Babylonian Sabbath 116a; cf. 24a. See *Tiferet Yisra'el* on the Mishna, note 6. There is some confusion on this matter of reading Hagiographa on Sabbath afternoon. Some connect it with the custom of reading a prophetic *haftorah* at Sabbath Minha, which was prohibited by the Persians and later not restored. In Babylonian Sabbath 24a, Rashi cites a Gaonic source for this. Others held it was Hagiographa that was read. Cf. Tosaphot Sabbath 24a, B. Megillah 21a and Babylonian Sabbath 116b. In any case, Rashi's citation is now confirmed in a responsum of Natronai Gaon

published by Louis Ginzberg in *Geonica*, in Texts and Studies of the Jewish Theological Seminary, Genizah Studies (New York, 1968), vol. 2, p. 322. See Ginzberg's comments, pp. 298 ff.

22. Joseph Karo, Shulhan Arukh Orah Hayyim, Hilkhot Shabbat 344:12. See Ginzberg, op. cit., vol. 2, p. 216, for the right to change halakha when the reason for the halakha changes, or because of variations required for local needs. The text under consideration there is a responsum Ginzberg believed was written by the Gaon Natrronai. He decided Jews might do the work connected with the burial of a body on the second day of a festival because the reason for not doing so applied only at times and places when Jews were under Persian jurisdiction. See the text as published by Ginzberg on p. 220, line 3, beginning with *akhshav shebatlah*: now that Persian rule is over, even Ravina, who prohibited it, would concede it ought to be permitted. Similar situations frequently arise in the halakha, and I refer to many throughout this book and in the notes.

23. In 1970 the Committee on Jewish Law and Standards of the Rabbinical Assembly broke up over the inability to secure a unanimous vote to require the immersion of a candidate for conversion.

CHAPTER IV

1. Gen. 45:13-25. Babylonian Taanit 10b has the passage as a comment on v. 24, indicating that Joseph advised his brothers not to become preoccupied with matters of halakha. Tosaphot, beginning with *al tirgezoo*, cited a midrash as saying the opposite, "do not cease" from discussing Torah. Midrash Rabbah Genesis 94:2 also has this view but reads differently from the anonymous midrash cited by Tosaphot. In any case, there was apparently a tradition that contradicted Taanit 10b, for it is cited immediately in our passage. Cf. Sotah 49a. Our passage, however, reconciles the two readings by indicating that the one that says travelers can be saved from disaster by words of Torah refers to mere recitation of texts, whereas Joseph's travel advice was against becoming distracted as a result of profound analysis of complex matters. In either case, the Rabbis took it for granted that the *system of halakha* was primeval, or if we may put it another way, "aboriginal" with the Patriarchs. Joseph was considered a significant halakhist who had imbibed his knowledge from both Isaac and Jacob. See Louis Ginzberg, *Legends of the Jews*, vol. 2, p. 5, and vol. 5, pp. 325 f., notes 5 and 6. This view is expressed in numerous other sources relating to the patriarchal and even pre-patriarchal period.

2. The explanation of the criteria as I see them will follow in the next chapter. Here I would merely like to enumerate them, although in no particular order: (1) scientific data, as for instance in the

Kashrut halakha and elsewhere; (2) *dinah d'malkhuta dinah:* the acceptance of the current civil and criminal law in the land of residency, a very broad principle that freed the Jew from unnecessary resistance to government and the courts and even martyrdom; (3) *kavod ha'met,* to do honor to the deceased; (4) *kol d'mekadesh al datah derabbanan mekadesh:* when a person takes a wife it is in accordance with Rabbinic halakha and therefore (5) *afkinhu rabbanan kidushin minay:* the Rabbis may find reason to annul the marriage; (6) *hefkar bet din:* the court may declare property ownerless. With such principles as enunciated in 4, 5, and 6, the Rabbis made life in society possible when older halakha might have been burdensome. These, like the others, will be more fully discussed in the next chapter. To continue the enumeration: (7) *hidur mitzvah,* to beautify religious practice; (8) *mipnai tikun ha'olam;* (9) *mipnai darkai shalom* and (10) *mipnai shalom bayit:* all three basically directed toward harmony, including civic and domestic tranquillity, or in modern terms, interfaith and interracial relations—in sum the *general welfare* of society; (11) *communal solidarity,* or in today's terms, "Jewish identity"; (12) *leniency:* a tendency always to decide certain questions according to the lenient point of view as in questions of *avelut* (mourning) or *agunah* (a woman caught up in a dilemma preventing her remarriage); (13) the principle *ain gozrin gezerah she'ain yakhol rov tzibur la'amod bah:* not to enact a decree by which the majority could not abide; (14) economic viability and economic concern for both the community and for individuals; (15) *kavod ha'bree'yot:* respect for one's fellow humans, which would include concern for human psychology; (16) the protection of defenseless and underprivileged persons, which governed a whole range of social welfare legislation; (17) the status of women was consistently elevated and protected in line with the 16th point; (18) *remembrance:* the historico-sociological recall of the role of God in history, the expression of gratitude for God's favor in historic events and miraculous interventions, as well as to reflect upon communal tribulation; (19) historical change which swept away the circumstances under which certain aspects of the halakha were relevant, as when the events of time made the sacrificial cult and agricultural halakha obsolete, or later emancipation and modern national and political development made the practice of the old civil law irrelevant; (20) *minhag,* the usage of the people, was studied and taken under consideration; included in this sphere would be Rabbinic effort to examine patterns of piety and how a halakha would affect the personal religiosity of Jews; (21) conservation of life and property; (22) ethical concerns not already listed, such as the concept that the end does not justify the means, and therefore a mitzvah derived through a sin remains a sin and the mitzvah is not considered fulfilled. All these criteria or motivations of the halakha can be expanded into subdivisions, and other students of the halakha may add categories not herein enumerated. Thus such principles as the halakha following Hillel, or halakha in ritual following Rav and other similar formulations of method, could be utilized in a listing of the imperatives that underlay the Rabbinic complex of halakha.

3. Louis Ginzberg, *Students, Scholars and Saints* (New York, 1958). See the chapter "Jewish Thought as Reflected in the Halakha," p. 114; also "Isaac Hirsch Weiss," p. 236.

4. The acceptance of the "yoke" of the Kingdom of Heaven was another way of saying that the person had acknowledged the sovereignty of God's will in his life. Taking the "yoke" merely meant to ask oneself, What must I do? What is the direction in which I am to proceed? And he would then find in the same source that he is to be a humane person who practices compassionate deeds. Cf. Sifre, 323, ed. Louis Finkelstein, p. 372.

5. Louis Nizer, *My Life in Court* (Garden City, N.Y., 1961), p. 523.

6. Saul Lieberman, *Hellenism in Jewish Palestine*, pp. 86-87. See in general his chapter "The Publication of the Mishna."

7. Victor Tcherikover, *Hellenistic Civilization and the Jews* (Phila., 1959), pp. 80 ff. See also p. 437, note 112. Cf. Louis Finkelstein, *The Pharisees*, p. 580, and George F. Moore, *Judaism* (Cambridge, 1950), vol. 3, p. 10. For another view see Travers Herford's commentary on Avot 1:2. Babylonian Megillah 11a connects a Shimon haTzadik, Simon the Just, with the Maccabees. Cf. Mishna Eduyot 8:4.

8. Lieberman, op. cit., note 6.

9. When the Talmud records that in a controversial matter a sage interjects, *tnee*, it signifies he is emending the text to reconcile the disputatious data. Many examples of this abound in the Babylonian Talmud.

10. Lieberman, op. cit., p. 99, note 128.

11. R. Travers Herford, *Pharisaism* (London, 1912), p. 103.

12. For a general discussion of this halakhic literary activity of the Gaonic period see Louis Ginzberg, *Gaonica*, 2nd ed. (New York, 1968), vol. 1.

13. Ibid., p. 97. Ginzberg points out that the *Sheiltot* written by Rabbi Aha at the same time was written in Palestine, where the prohibition on writing halakha for publication had long since been abrogated, or perhaps Aha did not write until after Yehudai had abrogated the prohibition in Babylonia. Cf. ibid., p. 98, note 1, and the references there.

14. Yehudai omitted, for example, all of the Order of *Kodoshim* except for *Hullin,* which was still of practical use for the dietary

observances. He excluded *Hagigah* from the Order of *Moed* because it dealt with the festival animal offerings, and Sotah from the Order of *Nashim* because the institution of Sotah, the unfaithful wife, as legislated in the Torah was inoperative.

15. After I had written this passage on the term "code," I found that I had been anticipated in this by George Horowitz, in his comprehensive work *The Spirit of Jewish Law* (New York, 1963), p. 52, note 1. He pointed out that a "code" is a body of law determined by governmental authority, and that the *Mishne Torah* of Maimonides was a restatement of the law by a private person and should be compared to Blackstone's *Commentaries on the Law of England*. He then wrote, "This observation applies also to the *Tur* and the *Shulhan Arukh. . . .*"

16. Ginzberg, *Gaonica*, p. 203.

17. Cf. Ketuvot 56a and 84a. But even more relevant and more cogent is the example that follows in this chapter and is referred to in the next note.

18. The point involved here is the authority of Rabbinic halakha. The Rabbis regarded it as having equal force with the Torah. Babylonian Talmud Pesahim 30b; cf. 39b. Rabbenu Hananel's commentary on the text makes it clear that this principle was an accepted one. He wrote, ". . . and although *hametz* is Torahitic and forbidden wine is Rabbinic and all that the Rabbis enact is as if the Torah had done so"—and this would imply that glazed ware used for gentile wine which should be prohibited for use by Jews is permitted because the wine is cold. In other words, the Rabbis offer a rational explanation to permit that which should be prohibited, and to prohibit that which the Torah did not prohibit, and in either case it is on the strength of the principle that "whatever the Rabbis enact is as if the Torah had done so." See further on how "human authority" deals with "divine revelation," in chap. 2.

19. Mishna Avot 1:1. See further on this my discussion in chap. 3. See also *Avot de Rabbi Nathan,* version 1, chap. 1, p. 4, of the Solomon Schechter edition (New York, 1945). Cf. also version 2.

20. Gen. 2:17 and 3:3. Cf. Midrash Genesis Rabbah 19:3 for a slightly different version of the confrontation between the serpent and Eve but with the same point.

21. *Avot de Rabbi Nathan,* p. 5. R. Yosi concludes the passage with the statement "it is better to have a ten handbreadth fence that stands erect than one of a hundred cubits [that will be so top-heavy] as to topple." See also version 2, p. 3. And see chap. 3 of this book, note 11. Cf. Midrash Rabbah Genesis 19:3, and the *Perush Maharzoo* of Zev Wolf Einhorn. Cf. Samuel Jaffe Ashkenazi's *Yefe Toar* on the passage of the Midrash. He evidently noted that this places in jeopardy the traditional view of "building a fence" about the Torah

and defended the efforts to do so as not being contradictory. But in my opinion the traditional sense of the phrase is inaccurate.

22. Babylonian Sanhedrin 29a; cf. Genesis Rabbah 19:3.

23. Cf. my chapter "Halakha as a Modern Problem" and especially note 11.

24. Moses Isserles, Responsa, no. 21, cited in "Proceedings of the Rabbinical Assembly," 1950, p. 128.

25. The source for this quotation eludes me, but I have had it in my notes for many years.

CHAPTER V

1. Babylonian Talmud Kiddushin 40b, Baba Kama 17a and Yerushalmi Shabbat 3b.

2. See my discussion of the term *halakha* in chaps. 1 and 11.

3. Midrash Tanhuma, Shemini, and Genesis Rabbah 44:1.

4. Babylonian Sukkah 30a. The *lulav* is the palm branch carried in procession on Sukkot.

5. Cf. Gen. 17:7 for circumcision and Exodus 12 for the same general theme repeated in reference to the Passover observance. There is no such indication in Ex. 21:1-23:19, which may be the earliest codified general halakha, involving civil and criminal law as well as some aspects of ritual.

6. See the discussion of certain specific cases by Louis Ginzberg in his *On Jewish Law and Lore,* pp. 81-82. It might be argued that the only consideration in the sources, Tosephta Mahshirin 3:3-4, is the purity of the food rather than economics, but the fact remains that there were economic ramifications which are quite illuminating. Furthermore, I am inclined to agree with Ginzberg that the rulings in the Tosephta were for economic reasons and that is why in both cases the sages told the advocate of stricter halakha who expounded the banning of the imported foodstuffs that if he wished to ban for himself he might, but not for the public. If it were merely a matter of purity and impurity, the other sages would have been motivated by piety just as much as Joshua b. Perahya, who wished to ban the importation of Alexandrian wheat. But the others obviously felt that scrupulousness in matters of doubtful impurity should not outweigh the humane concern for the price of grain the poor would have to bear.

7. See note 2 of the previous chapter.

8. Other scholars, like Lauterbach, Ginzberg, Finkelstein, G. F. Moore, Saul Lieberman, Travers Herford, Zvi Chajes, Zeitlin and Rivkin, and a host of others, have made valuable contributions to "Pharisaism" and to the related sphere of halakhic origins or to the analysis and evolution of halakha. But a systematic, scientific and comprehensive study such as I am suggesting is still required.

9. The twenty-two criteria listed in my previous chapter (note 2) might conceivably be included under five general headings in the following manner: I, Religio-Humanitarian: *kavod ha'met* (respect for the dead); leniency; *mipnai tikun ha'olam, mipnai darkai shalom, mipnai shalom bayit* (the general welfare); *kavod ha'bree'yot,* or the dignity of man; the protection of the poor, defenseless and underprivileged; the elevation of the status of women; consideration for human psychology; the conservation of life. II, Historical: *dinah d'malkhuta dinah,* that the local general law has primacy; the identity of the Jewish community; historical remembrances of the role of God or of events; a consideration of historical-sociological change. III, Intellectual: the findings of science; reasonings within halakhic categories such as *kol d'mekadesh al datah derabbanan mekadesh* (one takes a wife in accordance with Rabbinic halakha): *afkinhu rabbanan kidushin* (the Rabbis may annul a marriage); the patterns of piety reasonably pursued by people; the existing *minhag* (custom) in terms of time and place. IV, Aesthetic: *hidur mitzvah* (beautifying religious acts). V, Economics: *hefkar bet din,* that the court can declare property ownerless and therefore has elements of social control that help in the realization of other criteria; general economic considerations regarding prices, wages and economic conditions of time and place, which sometimes overlap with the humanitarian concern for the poor and underprivileged classes.

10. The "Holiness Code" is considered by some to be Lev. 17-26. (See Robert H. Pfeiffer, *Introduction to the Old Testament* [New York, 1948], pp. 210, 239-50.) But I regard this as the biblical critics' way of inventing or supporting the notion of an "H" document in the Pentateuch. It seems to me that Lev. 19:1, "be ye holy," introduces the "Holiness Code," which consists of Leviticus 19. By the "Covenant Code" I have in mind what is often called, and is so called in Ex. 24:7, the "Book of the Covenant," perhaps the oldest book of halakha and probably encompassing Ex. 21:1–23:19. (Some Bible critics, e.g. R. S. Driver in *The Cambridge Bible Commentary on Exodus,* define the "Book of the Covenant" as Ex. 20:22-23:33, as does Yehezkel Kaufman in his *Toledot haEmunah haYisra'elt.*) Both the Book of the Covenant and the Holiness Code were possibly originally promulgated by Joshua after the entrance into Canaan (cf. Josh. 8:30-35 and 24:22-27), when for the first time a halakhic compilation would receive the status of a "code" by virtue of its being supported by an organized government with a judiciary and a law-enforcement agency. In any case, both exhibit the historic nature of halakha: their composition is a medley of civil and criminal law, ethical prescriptions and the halakha of domestic relations as well as ritual.

11. For the meaning of *karet* as being physically "cut off"—"ceasing to be"—cf. Sifre 112 on Num. 15:30.

12. Rashi on Babylonian Yevamot 90a, beginning with *Shev v'al taseh.*

13. The sustaining references to what I have here asserted are widespread throughout the classical literature, and I will therefore cite only several. The maxim *shev v'al taseh* is taken up in Babylonian Yevamot 89b through 90b, as is *hefkar bet din hefkar* and the parallel of Elijah. In Babylonian Gittin 36a-b the matter of Hillel's famous *prozbul* is discussed, and there too the rationale is given as *shev v'al taseh:* the creditor does nothing overtly to violate the Torah. There again *Rashi* explained what I have cited in the text of this chapter, that by doing nothing, "in this manner it is permitted to abrogate something from the Torah." See the passage *shev v'al taseh* in his commentary to Gittin 36b. A second rationale is given by Rabah, that "the court has the right to declare property ownerless," *hefkar bet din hefkar,* which is the standard formula to indicate that the Rabbis had total sovereignty in matters of civil law, and as *Rashi* put it in his comment on the text there, "in monetary matters one does not consider it abrogation of the Torah." All the sources can be consulted for a host of cross-references.

In Z. H. Chajes, *The Student's Guide Through the Talmud* (New York, 1960), chap. 13, pp. 103-10, we have a partial list of enactments whose binding force was relaxed by the Rabbis. Although many of these are no longer relevant and some may appear rather trivial from our standpoint, what counts for us is that the Rabbis radically transformed Jewish practice, overtly abrogating not only their own enactments but procedures and requirements of the Torah such as the "ordeal ceremony" of an allegedly unfaithful wife's drinking the concoction of the bitter water. (Cf. Num. 5:11-31 and Babylonian Sotah 47a.)

14. Babylonian Moed Katan 18a, Bekhorot 49a, and elsewhere.

15. Babylonian Gittin 33a. Cf. Babylonian Yevamot 114b and 122b.

16. For more detailed discussion see chap. 9, "The Future of Religious Divorce."

17. Tosephta Sota 15:5. Cf. *Minhat Bikkurim,* note 6, who suggests the reason for Rabbi Yishmael's opinion which I have cited in the text, a *zekher l'horban,* a reminder of the Holocaust. The Tosephta went on to inform us that *perushin* (sectarians) increased who did practice abstention from meat and wine for the reason of remembering the Holocaust. Incidentally, this happens to be an important source to indicate that *perushim* in the Talmud is not necessarily "Pharisees."

Cf. Babylonian Avodah Zarah 36a, where the same formula, "that we do not enact a rule for the public unless the majority can fulfill it," is given in the names of Rabbi Simon b. Gamliel and Rabbi

Elazar b. Zadok. Of interest is Rabbenu Hananel's text here, for he substitutes "Israel" for *Tzibur,* which would mean that one does not enact a rule unless one expects the *majority of Jews* to be able to fulfill it! Cf. Babylonian Horeeyot 3b.

18. Sifre Numbers 112, on Num. 15:31. It is cited this way in Babylonian Sanhedrin 90b and 64b, as well as in Kiddushin 17b and in numerous other places. In Yerushalmi Yevamot 8d and Yer. Nedarim 36c, however, it is given as "the Torah spoke in normal manner," i.e., presumably in the customary manner current in social usage.

19. Babylonian Baba Kamma 79b and Baba Batra 60b. In the latter we have the Tosephta Sota 15:5 (mentioned in note 17 above) extensively quoted, and the text uses Rabbi Ishmael as the source, although in other texts the saying not to enact a *gezerah,* a rule which the majority cannot abide by, is given in the name of Rabbis Simon b. Gamliel and Eleazar b. Zadok. The reference in Baba Batra is exceedingly interesting in its elucidation of the Tosephta and how Rabbi Joshua moderated the extremist sectarians by arguing that if they would not eat meat or drink wine because the sacrificial cult had been abolished, they ought to give up fruit, since the *bikurim*—first-fruit offerings—had been abolished, or drinking water since the water libation had similarly been abolished by the forces of history.

This is an instructive parallel for many instances in which the argument is used, Do not observe such and such because gentiles observe it. Thus it is argued not to use flowers at a funeral because it is allegedly a gentile custom. We should therefore also not use coffins or the 23rd Psalm. The lesson to be derived is that there is no need to prohibit upon ourselves "comparative" practices like giving up wine because the libations are not offered, or flowers because gentiles use them. Whatever we practice need simply be "Judaized," as Saul Lieberman has indicated with reference to the ashes used on a groom's head and other customs. Cf. Babylonian Baba Batra 60b, and Saul Lieberman, *Greek in Jewish Palestine* (New York, 1942), pp. 105-06. It should be clarified here that in all instances where sources are cited to illustrate the thesis of the chapter, as in the case before us, not *all* references are given, nor would *all* the references in the Talmud necessarily exhaust all the instances in which a principle was used over a period of perhaps seven centuries from 200 B.C.E. to 500 C.E. References are given only as illustrative support.

20. Mishna Gittin 4:2-7,9. In general, Babylonian Gittin 32-48 offers a rather extensive picture of the operation of this concept. Cf. 33a, where we see how the sages found two social purposes served by Rabbi Gamliel the Elder's enactment of an innovation "for improvement of society" (as we may, I am sure, translate *mipnai tikun*

ha'olam), the first being to reduce the likelihood of bastardy, the bastard being under serious disability, and the second being to reduce the incidence of abandoned wives, *agunot,* who cannot remarry. The section of the Mishna here referred to has a wide variety of innovations enacted by the Rabbis and comprehensive discussion of them ranging over sixteen pages of Talmud. A review of this material here would not serve the purpose of our subject and would only be pretentious. The student, however, is urged to study these passages for the enlightenment they shed on the Rabbinic approach to halakha and the many cross-references they yield for the same formulas in branches of halakha other than *ishut,* or domestic relations.

21. Babylonian Gittin 59b.

22. Midrash Tanhuma on Shemini, and Genesis Rabbah 44:1.

23. Babylonian Menahot 99a-b; Mishna Berakhot 9:5. Cf. Babylonian Talmud Berakhot 54a, 63a, and cf. Yevamot 89b and 90b for cogent halakhic examples of how they acted in this spirit.

Rashi on Berakhot 63a cited here gave Elijah on Carmel (1 Kings 18) as an example of violating the Torah for a higher purpose: he offered sacrifices on a *bamah,* an inappropriate "high place," in order to win Jews back to God. And on 54a Rashi is quite explicit about what the Rabbis meant: that there are times when we must violate the Torah in order to fulfill the will of God!

24. Maimonides, Mishne Torah Hilkhot Mamrim 2:4.

25. Mishna Sukkah 2:7, Bezah 1:5, Hagigah 1:2. Cf. also Rosh Hashanah 1:1, where Hillel favored the 15th of Shevat as Arbor Day to provide the unyielding less fertile soil of the poor a longer period to produce blossoms in contrast to the rich who, with better soil and more advanced agricultural methods, were able to observe the day on the 1st. Another possibility may be that Hillel preferred the 15th because he was from Babylonia, where produce ripened later, as we may infer from Babylonian Taanit 4b. In any case, the effect would be beneficial for the poor.

26. For burial practices modified by the Rabbis see Babylonian Moed Katan 27a. I will discuss these matters and their ramifications for our day more extensively in a projected book on *avelut,* which is now in preparation and will cover the halakha of mourning in historical terms as well as being suggestive for future observance. See also chap. 7 of this book.

27. See note 17 above. Cf. Maimonides Mishne Torah Hilkhot Mamrim 2:5-6 for its general application in areas beyond concerns of ritual. Cf., in addition to Talmudic references given in note 17, Babylonian Baba Kama 79b and Baba Batra 60b and my discussion of these matters in note 19 above.

28. Deut. 20:19. Cf. Babylonian Baba Kama 91b, Babylonian

Makkot 22a. Cf. Maimonides Mishne Torah Hilkhot Melakhim 6:8, 10, and his *Sefer ha'Mitzvot,* Negative Commandment No. 57.

29. Mishna Avot 2:18, Berakhot 4:4 and Babylonian Berakhot 29b.

30. Yerushalmi Berakhot 3c.

31. Babylonian Shabbat 82a, Yoma 85b, Mishna Yoma 8:6, Mekhilta, Lauterbach edition, vol. 3, pp. 197-98. Cf. Sanhedrin 74a, Pesahim 25a, Yoma 82a.

32. Mekhilta, Ki Tissa, on Ex. 31:14, Lauterbach edition, vol. 3, pp. 198-99. Cf. Babylonian Baba Kama 91b. The principle of *Bal tash'hit,* the prohibition on waste, is closely tied to the idea of the preservation of life.

33. Mishna Eduyot 1:13; Babylonian Shabbat 81b; Makkot 22b; Baba Metziah 83a; Mishna 7:1; Babylonian Berakhot 45b and Mishna 2:4 and Mekhilta on Ex. 21:20, 26, which refers these verses on punishing a master for beating a slave to a gentile slave. Cf. Mekhilta, Lauterbach edition, vol. 1, chap. 7, pp. 56-57, and chap. 9, pp. 69-70.

34. Babylonian Sukkah 30a, Berakhot 47b, Baba Kama 94a, Sanhedrin 6b. In Sukkah 30a, Tosaphot, beginning with *m'shoom,* points out that although the verse in Mal. 1:13 upon which the concept that a mitzvah *ha'ba'ah al yedai averah,* is unacceptable, refers specifically to the sacrificial cult, it applies to every mitzvah in the Torah. Tosaphot then cites the reference in Baba Kama 94a dealing with tithing to prove there is wider application. In Berakhot 47b the question involves public worship, and although there the Talmud permits an individual to violate a Torah verse to enable the public to perform its mitzvah of public worship, the Talmud is careful to clarify that mitzvah *d'rabim,* a collective mitzvah to be performed by a public body, is different, and may be made possible by an individual on his own initiative violating a verse for the *collective* welfare. But the principle would remain that an individual cannot receive merit for a pious deed performed through immoral or illegal means.

CHAPTER VI

1. Examples where the rituals of Passover and Sukkot are connected with history are Ex. 12:17, 27; 13:3 ff.; 13:13-16; Lev. 23:42-43. An ethical example is Ex. 22:20. These references could be multiplied many times over. In similar fashion, as will be evidenced in this chapter, later rituals were designed either to maintain the historical memory (Purim, Hanukkah) or to preserve the solidarity and communality of the Jews-in-history.

2. Cf. Louis Finkelstein, *Akiva: Scholar, Saint and Martyr* (New

York, 1962), pp. 251-52. Tosephta on Pesahim 3:16 indicates they did not say *barookh shem* in Jericho. This is undoubtedly an allusion to that Hadrianic period. But there is another version of the text cited both by Rashi on Pesahim 56a and by the *Minhat Bikkurim* on the Tosephta which reads that in Jericho they *did* say *barookh shem* in a loud voice. In other words, they were defiant of the Roman decree. In any case, the Babylonians no longer knew why *barookh shem* was said in an undertone, and gave an agadic explanation (B. Pesahim 56a).

3. The *Megillat Ta'anit* indicated days on the Jewish calendar when fasting, or both fasting and mourning, was not permitted because of some happy historical event. It is mentioned in Mishna Megilla 2 and cited in various tractates of the Talmud, such as B. Taanit 15b ff. and B. Menahot 65a. Some of the days in it noted minor triumphs of the Pharisees over the Sadducees; and once Pharisaic Judaism was established and entrenched these gloatings undoubtedly seemed inappropriate and were abolished. B. Rosh ha'-Shanah 18b already indicates that the days were obsolete as early as the 3rd century. Two of the days mentioned as "festive" actually became "fast days" later, the 3rd of Tishri being known as the Fast of Gedaliah and the 13th of Adar as the Fast of Esther. Many of the days celebrating happy events were undoubtedly regarded as repetitious of other days or contradictory to other days. Thus Iyar 7, which celebrated the consecration of the walls of Jerusalem, would appear bizarre when they observed the destruction of Jerusalem on Av 9. Hanukkah was undoubtedly retained, not so much to celebrate the restoration of Jerusalem as to celebrate the salvation of Judaism, a totally different thing.

This is not the place to analyze every date mentioned in *Megillat Taanit* to rationalize its obsolescence. Suffice it to say that the abolition of the Megillah does not run counter to the thesis which is self-evident in Judaism, of retaining historical remembrances in the liturgy and the ritual long after the event is no longer of great import. But when a ritual was introduced which did not mark a very central event that cut through to the heart of Judaism either as peril or as triumph, it did find itself destined for forgetfulness.

4. There are useful books for the interested reader, among them Isidore Epstein, *The Responsa of Rabbi Solomon b. Aderet of Barcelona* and *The Responsa of Rabbi Simon b. Zemah Duran* (New York, 1968), two volumes in one; a number of studies by Irving Agus: *The Heroic Age of Franco-German Jewry* (New York, 1969), *Rabbi Meier of Rothenburg* (Phila., 1947), *Urban Civilization in Pre-Crusade Europe* (New York, 1965); Y. F. Baer, *A History of the Jews in Christian Spain* (Phila., 1961-66); Abraham Neuman, *The Jews in Spain* (Phila., 1948). An invaluable work is Louis Finkel-

stein's *Jewish Self-Government in the Middle Ages* (New York, 1924).

5. The responsa literature of the 16th and 17th centuries is invaluable for this purpose. Ben Zion Katz, *L'Korot ha' Yehudim* (Berlin, 1899), uses responsa literature for a history of the Jews of Poland. Boaz Cohen, *Kuntres ha-Teshuvot* (Budapest, 1930), is a significant bibliography of this literature.

6. Solomon Freehof, *The Responsa Literature* (Phila., 1955), pp. 33-34; Agus, *Heroic Age of Franco-German Jewry*, pp. 16-18.

7. Shulhan Arukh Hoshen Mishpat 282. It is apparent from chap. 283 that the *Bet Din* might hold the apostate's inheritance in custody, either to await his repentance or for his heirs.

8. See Babylonian Talmud Gittin 10b; Baba Kama 113ab; Nedarim 28a; Baba Batra 54b, 55a.

9. A recent monograph is Leo Landman, *Jewish Law in the Diaspora* (Phila., 1968). While Rabbi Landman rejects the notion that Samuel articulated an *earlier* principle, I do not regard it as germane to my volume to conduct an intensive discussion of the matter. As a matter of fact, if Landman is correct that *dinah d'malkhuta dinah* is a halakhic principle *originated* by Samuel (p. 24) "to propose a *modus vivendi* for the Jew," he is sustaining the modernist position that halakha or the Oral Law is a human development and not a divinely revealed system. All of the vast halakha that was based on this principle could then certainly claim nothing beyond human authority.

10. Babylonian Baba Kama 113b.

11. Cf. Landman, op. cit., p. 124, and p. 207, note 1, for references; and chap. 10 and notes in general.

12. Shulhan Arukh Orah Hayyim 391:1. This was contrary to the ruling of others preceding Karo. R. Meier of Rothenburg of the 13th century, for instance, is quoted in Mordecai on Eruvin, sec. 509, that Jews cannot acquire ownership of a town by simply purchasing it from the sovereign authority but must take title to each property separately. Karo, however, apparently extended the halakha. He permitted the combination of "state law is binding" and "the state's agent has state authority" to allow Jews to "purchase" a town and erect an *eruv,* a "boundary" encompassing the town. In my childhood I well recall a Rabbi in Toronto, Canada, "purchasing" a sizable section of Toronto for this purpose. Either the telephone wires or the old trolley wires of the Toronto Transportation Commission running along Bloor Street were determined as the boundary on the north, with the Don and Humber rivers and Lake Ontario serving as boundaries on the east, west and south respectively. This *eruv* ritual, easing the Sabbath restrictions, was an obvious application of a formulation in civil law for "making religion convenient," an en-

deavor so frequently criticized in our time. The *Be'er Hetev* on this text of Karo, 391:1, note (a), indicates post-medieval decisions following Karo and the opinion of *Hakham Tzvi* that if Jews "possess" a street (and therefore a district or a town), he can see no reason why they cannot freely carry in that area. This has become the accepted orthodox way to avoid the restriction on Sabbath carrying and constitutes a highly interesting extension of a civil-law formula to ritual observance through what is essentially a legal fiction. It is highly instructive for our time in terms of using *dinah d'malkhuta*.

13. Mishna Yevamot 16:3. Cf. Shulhan Arukh Even ha'Ezer 17:29, 31, and commentaries. Landman, op. cit., p. 130, cites in his footnotes the comment of Ezekiel Landau in Eben ha'Ezer 46 that he differed with R. Joel Sirkes on this and held it was not because of *dinah d'malkhuta* but rather because the hangman does it. Obviously R. Landau was wary of using the *dinah* formulation to influence the ritual of remarriage and sought to divert us, and Landman cites this to further his contention that *dinah d'malkhuta* was not used to influence ritual. The fact nevertheless remains that the Rabbis accepted a form of testimony barred by the Mishna in a situation governed by the secular state law. The *Taz* (Rabbi David b. Samuel), note 43 on the *Even ha'Ezer* 17:31, cites an opinion that when the hanging technique makes for probable death one can testify upon seeing the hanging. The Sirkes opinion and Landau's opposition were already previously discussed in the *Pithai Teshuvah* (R. Abraham Hirsch Eisenstadt, 1818-68), and he adds, in support of the contention of Sirkes, that he has seen law books of some of the nations that do require, as *dinah d'malkhuta,* that the hangman break the neck. It is apparent that if *dinah d'malkhuta* was not used to directly modify ritual, it was used by some authorities to allow for an indirect modification of what they must have considered a harsh halakha which placed women in a constrained situation, most especially since the halakhic principle already existed that in such cases of *agunah* the lenient point of view was to be followed. References to the latter principle are scattered throughout the text and notes of this book. Cf. Babylonian Yevamot 88a and elsewhere.

14. See Landman, op. cit., chap. 10, for a discussion of possible cases where *dinah d'malkhuta* influences ritual *halakha,* all of which he dismisses. It is precisely the opposite which is my thesis here: *dinah d'malkhuta* always did, and may continue to, influence ritual halakha when and if desirable Cf. *Rutgers Law Review,* Vol. 3, No. 2, p. 266.

15. Babylonian Yevamot 90b, Gittin 33a and elsewhere. The Geiger suggestion is cited by Landman, op. cit., p. 214 and note 10.

16. Mishna Berakhot 9:5. See Rashi on the text. The Mishna reads "to everlasting," but a marginal correction reads "from ever-

lasting," and while our text reads "Sadducees" a marginal gloss suggests *minim*, "sectarians," in accordance with the Tosephta's reading, which may or may not signify the Sadducees. Cf. Berakhot 63a; Tosephta Berakhot 6:27; Babylonian Taanit 16b.

17. Babylonian Yevamot 39b.

18. Mishna Ketuvot 1:1; and cf. Babylonian Ketuvot 3a. Though the court sat on Monday, there was no *takkanah* to require marriage on Sunday, as this would occasion undue hardships for preparation of the celebration, the day before being Sabbath. Cf. Shavuot 7:1 for a number of *takkanot* with which the Rabbis reversed biblical halakha owing to the changing economic conditions of a totally new historical period. Z. H. Chajes, *The Student's Guide Through the Talmud,* offers several chapters in which he discusses enactments that were instituted and others that were repealed, and cites extensive sources. However, the thesis here pursued is that these reversals, like the enactments in the first place, were related to historical necessity or desirability.

19. Josh. 17:16, Judg. 1:27 and 1 Kings 4:12 refer to the town Beth Shean. This later changed hands many times during the Greco-Roman period. Cf. Hullin 6b and Pal. Talmud Demai 2:1; cf. Megillah 5b. See also Babylonian Avodah Zarah 35b, and Palestinian Talmud Avodah Zarah 2:9, 41d.

20. See fuller discussion in note 21.

21. Babylonian Gittin 33a, 73a, Yevamot 90b, 110a, Baba Batra 48b, Ketuvot 3a. Rashi elucidates that this power is held by the Rabbis because when the groom declares he consecrates his wife in accordance with "the law of Moses and Israel," he is declaring that he does so in accordance with the customs, requirements and obligations which the sages have instituted. When they declare this marriage null it is *retroactive*. As Rashi puts it, the Rabbis withdraw the term *kiddushin* (marriage consecration) that orginally defined the relationship of the couple.

Joseph Karo in Shulhan Arukh *Even ha'Ezer* 141:60 adopted the position of R. Judah of Gittin 33a that even after the abolition prohibition was instituted, if a man violated that enactment and did rescind his writ of divorce, it was validly rescinded, thus implying that the formulations I am here upholding as agents of change in halakha were not considered halakhic. But that the halakha was really like R. Judah and not like the opposing opinion of R. Simon b. Gamleil, who projected the futility of the acts of any court if someone could go elsewhere and have another court rescind its documents, is not clear in the Talmud. As a matter of fact, since both R. Ashur and Alfasi cite both opinions without comment, it appears that the second one had strong authority. Furthermore, R. Nissim on the text of Alfasi indicates precisely why R. Simon b. Gamliel's view is significant: because the Talmud has indicated the sages can annul the marriage. See Rabbenu Asheri on *Gittin,* chap. 3, sec. 4, and Alfasi 16b.

There was some dispute among authorities whether the power of the Rabbis to terminate the marriage was retroactive or as of the time they invoked the power. This is referred to in the notes called *Hokhmat Shelomo,* by R. Solomon Kluger of Brody (19th-century Galician scholar), on the *Even ha'Ezer* 141:60. He stresses the logic of its being retroactive, for otherwise it would be no special power and the fact that the husband consecrates the woman at the outset in compliance with Rabbinic rulings would be meaningless, since he can himself make a condition that the marriage will end at a certain time, or he can himself now terminate it without the enunciation of such high-sounding halakhic principles. Furthermore, in a case cited, Gittin 73a, the halakha is in conformity with these principles, that the Rabbis can declare a document a valid writ of divorce although Torahitically there is no warrant for it, because they can terminate marriage at will.

22. Deut. 15:9 enjoins the Jew from refusing to lend capital on the excuse that he may lose it during the seventh-year cancellation of debts. Ezra 10:8 is the verse upon which the sages relied for confiscatory powers. Cf. Babylonian Gittin 36b, Yevamot 89b.

23. Babylonian Yevamot 90b and Sanhedrin 46a.

24. Deut. 17:8-11. See my discussion of the question of contemporary authority in other chapters, especially "A Closing Word."

25. Professor Saul Lieberman discusses this subject in a cursory but enlightening fashion, and in his footnote references he provides a bibliography. Cf. his *Hellenism,* chapter "The Natural Science of the Rabbis." But he does not at all get into the halakhic questions taken up in this chapter.

26. The Gaonic decision on salt is in Shulhan Arukh Yoreh Dayeh 69:12. See also Babylonian Hullin 111a, Pesahim 76a, for the pickled item regarded as cooked. Cf. Shulhan Arukh Yoreh Dayeh 94:1, 98:4, 121:6, which are decisions without any clear mandate from the Talmud.

27. Babylonian Hullin 111b, Shulhan Arukh Yoreh Dayah 95:1; and cf. the *Kitzur Piskai ha'Rosh,* chap. 8 of Hullin, par. 29, where he reaffirms the halakha according to Samuel. Here is another instance of where a methodological rule, that ritual matters are decided like Rav, and not Samuel, is waived, so as to decide in favor of the liberal opinion.

28. Babylonian Niddah 24b.

29. Deut. 23:2, Yevamot Mishna 8:1, Babylonian Yevamot 70a, 75b, 76a and passim.

30. The subject of *minhag* really deserves a separate monograph. It is therefore dealt with only cursorily here.

31. Chajes, *Student's Guide*, p. 119. Cf. Mishna Baba Metziah 7:1, 9:1, and Baba Batra 1:1.

32. Cf. Mishna Maaser Sheni 3:4; cf. also Midrash Rabbah Esther 1:9 and Ruth 1:4, where R. Levi definies *medinah* as *eparkhiah*, a Greek term meaning "prefecture," "province" or even "city-state." The fact that in matters of ritual the local usage applied in terms of the *medinah* usage is evident in Babylonian Pesahim 51a, where a number of ritual observances are reviewed and the opinion of the *medinah* is reckoned with. Cf. Mishna Pesahim 4:1 for the same phrase *makom shenahagoo* as used in Baba Metziah and Baba Batra. Cf. Mishna Baba Metziah 7:1, 9:1, Baba Batra 1:1.

33. Babylonian Pesahim 51a. Cf. Tosaphot, beginning with *EE Atah*.

34. For the original phrasing of *minhag* vs. halakha see Palestinian Talmud Baba Metziah 7:1, 11b.

35. Joseph Karo, Orah Hayyim, Hilkhot Megillah 690:17. See Moses Isserles' notes on this passage and the comments of *Magen Avraham*, note 22, and *Be'er Hetev*, note 14. Cf. also Tractate Sopherim 14:18.

There are many other Talmudic and halakhic references on the strength and nature of *minhag* whose investigation and whose contexts might yield valuable lessons for our own time in terms of developing new *minhagim*, allowing old ones to lapse and correcting faulty ones that are only, as is stated in the above-cited reference to *Sopherim*, *k'toeh b'shikul ha'da'at*, errors in reasoning or judgment. Cf. Baba Batra 93a, Yoreh Dayah 89:1, 376:4, Baba Metziah 86b, Pesahim 50a-51b Palestinian Yevamot 12c, and Babylonian 112a. The latter omits the statement of Yerushalmi *"minhag* nullifies halakha" but is otherwise the same.

36. Tosephta Sotah 13:9, Mishna Maaser Sheni 5:13, Yerushalmi ibid. 56d, Babylonian Sota 48a. Cf. Ps. 44:14, 121:4.

37. Tosephta Makhshirin 3:2. The views of Louis Ginzberg are further elucidated in chap. 7.

CHAPTER VII

1. Cf. Lev. 18:3.

2. Examples of this are found in the funerary customs discussed in Babylonian Avodah Zarah 11a.

3. Mishna Yoma 3:9-10. Cf. Yoma 25b for Ben Katin's twelve brothers and 37a-b for the other material. Cf. Maimonides Mishna Torah Hilkhot Avodat Yom Kippur 3:1 and Bet ha'Behira 3:18.

4. Deut. 26:1-10; Mishne Bikkurim 3:2-3. Cf. the discussion of some of these points and Greco-Roman parallels in Saul Lieberman's *Hellenism in Jewish Palestine*, pp. 128 ff. and throughout. While

Lieberman points out that the Bible does not mention adorning the sacrifice, he fails to indicate the Bible does not even mention the bull. The biblical ceremony involved only a hand-carried basket of first fruits symbolically presented at the Sanctuary.

5. Deut. 12:11. The entire chapter Mishna Menahot 8 testifies to the necessity of *quality* in worship.

6. Ex. 15:2, Mekhilta on the verse, in Lauterbach edition, vol. 2, p. 25, Masekhet Shirata, Parasha 3, lines 40 ff.; Babylonian Sukkah 11b, 32a-b; Shabbat 133b, Nazir 2b and Baba Kama 9a-b. Cf. Shulhan Arukh Orah Hayyim 656:1. Cf. especially Isserles on not paying exorbitant funds.

7. Babylonian Yoma 39a, Hullin 49b and elsewhere.

8. A very brief bibliography of helpful literature follows: Adolph Buchler, *The Destruction of the Second Temple* (London, 1912); Louis Finkelstein, *Akiba: Scholar, Saint and Martyr* (New York, 1936);——, *The Pharisees*, vols. 1 and 2 (Phila., 1946); Zechariah Frankel, *Mebo ha'Yerushalmi;* Louis Ginzberg, *Introduction to the Palestinian Talmud,* vol. 1 (New York, 1941);——, *On Jewish Law and Lore* (Phila., 1955); R. T. Herford, *Pharisaism* (London, 1912; paperback reprint); Jacob Z. Lauterbach, *Rabbinic Essays* (Cambridge, 1954); George F. Moore, *Judaism,* 3 vols. (Cambridge, 1954).

9. Babylonian Shabbat 14b. Cf. also Avodah Zarah 8b. Ginzberg, *On Jewish Law and Lore,* pp. 79 ff., prefers the economic explanation. In my notes on the lectures on Avodah Zarah by Professor Saul Lieberman in class during 1951-52, I have record of an extended discussion in which Lieberman preferred the religious or ritualistic explanation. It appears to me that the truth is somewhere between. The sages recognized primarily that a new product must be dealt with. Since it was made of sand, it was similar to earthenware. (Cf. Shabbat 15b, where Resh Lakish makes that point.) But they allowed its purification, unlike earthenware. They were obviously dealing with it in terms of new technology. On the other hand, the pressure to decide the matter might conceivably have been the repeated questions put to them by consumers who had to decide whether there was any advantage in buying the glassware, and by earthenware and metalware manufacturers who may have repeatedly warned them of the danger to their local industries.

In a modern analogy of economic pressure applied we know the kosher butcher trade constantly warns of its decline if kosher meat were packaged and sold in supermarkets and this has long restrained the supervisory segment of the Orthodox Rabbinate from allowing this kind of free distribution of recognized, authenticated kosher meat.

10. Cf. Ginzberg, *On Jewish Law and Lore,* chapter "The Significance of the Halakha for Jewish History," pp. 77 ff. Cf. Mishna Sukka 2:7; Hagigah 1:2; Rosh ha'Shanah 1:1; Babylonian Ta'anit 4b.

11. Babylonian Moed Katan 27a-b. Rabbi Papa there indicates that what was used customarily was a *Tzerada bar Zuzah,* which is translated in the Soncino as "a paltry shroud that costs but a zuz." In a note the Soncino explains *tzerada* as coming from Latin *sordida,* meaning cheap or ragged. The *Arukh,* however, on Babylonian Baba Metziah 51b interprets the word as *kanvus,* that is, as Rashi also interprets here and there, "canvas," a coarse, unbleached cloth made of hemp or flax. "Canvas" is from the Old Northern French, and hence Rashi's usage of the word. Rabbenu Hananel interprets it as *haluk,* a garment. Cf. Maimonides, Mishna Torah, Hilkhot Avel, 4:1, and Shulhan Arukh Yoreh Dayah 352:1-2; 353:1.

12. Babylonian Taanit 15b. Cf. Maimonides, Mishna Torah, Hilkhot Taanit 1:5 and Shulhan Arukh Orah Hayyim 572:1.

CHAPTER VIII

1. Boaz Cohen, *Law and Tradition in Judaism* (New York, 1959).

2. Cf. ibid., pp. 9 ff. and notes, especially 23 and 27.

3. Babylonian Sotah 16a.

4. See Ex. 21:24 and Lev. 24:21. Cf. Mekhilta, ed. Jacob Lauterbach, vol. 3, chap. 8, p. 67.

5. Cf. Babylonian Sabbath 104a and Yerushalmi Eruvin 22c.

6. Cohen, op. cit., p. 30.

7. Babylonian Gittin 55b-56a. Cf. Babylonian Hullin 13b, which indicates that pagan pledges of sacrifices for the Jewish altar were acceptable. The term *anvatnuto* in the passage in Gittin is often taken to be "patience," as in the famous Hillel-Shammai story in B. Shabbat 31a. But it may also mean "overscrupulous" attention to detail in a positive sense. Its opposite, *kapdanut,* often used in contrast to it, also means "particular," but in a negative sense. In fact, these might be the meanings in the Hillel-Shammai story rather than the usual "patient" and "angry." Hillel took *care,* that is, he was especially *attentive* to the fine points and delicate sensitivities of his fellow humans, and so he offered conversion to pagans rejected by Shammai. Shammai was also very particular, but in a negative sense, being too meticulous about details without concern for the need of the person. I do not necessarily agree with the conventional estimate of Shammai's nature in contrast with Hillel because I believe there are many citations in the literature that can prove Shammai was very much like Hillel. But I am here only interpreting the text as it stands and not seeking to reconstruct Shammai's reputation.

8. Sifra on Lev. 16:30; see *Aharai Mot,* chap. 7, Weiss edition, p. 83a. Cf. Shulhan Arukh, Orah Hayyim 339:3, for Isserles' citation of the permission for and leniency toward dancing in the 16th century.

9. Babylonian Berakhot 4b and Eruvin 21b are two examples of the statement that "anyone who violates the words of the sages [*sofrim* is the term used in Eruvin] is worthy of capital punishment."

10. See Cohen, op. cit., chapter "Sabbath Prohibitions Known As Shevut," pp. 127-66. This chapter is a comprehensive discussion of the topic of *shevut*. It also reflects, however, how extensive the Sabbath restrictions become because of *shevut*, and helps us understand why the Sabbath law is so complex. Nevertheless, a very careful reading of this chapter will be quite rewarding, for it also indicates to us how large a proportion of the Sabbath law with which we are familiar is the result of arbitrary definitions of *shevut*, of judgments as to what constitutes "rest," based on the socio-economic and technological realities of that ancient period. See especially p. 139 for the example used in our text.

What this chapter proves beyond a doubt is that a totally new monograph is needed on the whole subject of *melakha* on Sabbath, on what should be proscribed within the Torah's concept, and what, in terms of contemporary society, should be permitted. Not only was the ancient Sabbath halakha a "mountain suspended from a hair," as the Mishna termed it in its time, but it is today of frightfully questionable spiritual value.

11. Cf. Ex. 16:23, Lev. 23:3 and especially Ex. 31:14-15, where both phrases are used in the same passage. See my discussion of the concept of *siyag*, a "fence," in chap. 3.

12. Mekhilta de R. Ishmael, ed. Jacob Lauterbach, vol. 2, p. 253, and vol. 3, p. 205. On the verse in Ex. 31:17, where the Torah says God "ceased His work and rested" *(shavat vayenafash), Avot de R. Nathan* has a comment in the name of R. Yosheyahoo that *shavat* refers to desisting from labor and *vayenafash* to desisting from thought!

13. Babylonian Shabbat 113a-113b. The scriptural text was Isa. 58:13: "If you turn your path from the Sabbath, refraining from fulfilling your objectives on my holy day . . . and shall honor it by refraining from carrying out your own pursuits transacting your business and arranging matters." (My translation of the last part of the verse is based on my lecture notes taken in the class of H. L. Ginsberg at the Jewish Theological Seminary in 1953. Prof. Ginsberg took *mimtzo heftzekha* as "transacting business" and *diber davar* as "arranging matters.") On Shabbat 113b *diber davar,* taken as "speaking thereof" (of prohibited activity), is interpreted to mean "one must not speak but one may think" about prohibited activities. This is codified by Maimonides in *Mishna Torah Hilkhot Shabbat* 24:1: "speech is thus forbidden, but thinking of business is permitted." Incidentally Tosafot on the spot takes the prohibition of speech to mean excessive conversation of any sort.

The main discussion, however, is on Babylonian Shabbat 150a on the Mishna 23:3 whether one may hire or make other business plans on the Sabbath. R. Joshua b. Korha said he may intimate to his associate without expressing the purpose that they ought to get together after Sabbath. This implies he is thinking about the business operation and yet it is permissible, on the basis of the verse in Isaiah. Rabbah bar Hannah in the name of R. Yohanan added that the halakha is as R. Joshua b. Korha expressed it, which is undoubtedly the reason for the Maimonidean decision regarding the reference on 113b. Cf. Tosephta Shabbat 18:6 for R. Joshua b. Korha.

14. Cf. Babylonian Shabbat 113a and 150a. These "divine matters" include such things as mathematical calculations related to a mitzvah, the designation of charity for the poor, the supervision of urgent communal affairs and even attending assemblies at such unlikely places as theaters, coliseums and basilicas. The scholars cited in this passage (bottom of 150a) are for the most part Amoraim, and this shows how emphatic later scholars were in relieving the Sabbath stringencies and making the day more rational.

15. Cf. Tosephta Shabbat 17:14.

16. See chap. 3.

17. Moses Maimonides, *Mishne Torah, Hilkhot Shabbat* 21:2-3 and 23:17.

18. Ibid., 15:22, 23:5. See Babylonian Shabbat 40b—41a.

19. Ibid., 21:28. Cf. 24:5.

20. Babylonian Pesahim 65a. Cf. Yerushalmi Yomah 1:1.

21. See Mordecai on Bezah 696, who cites Rabbi Joel ha'Levi, who permitted a Jew to tell a gentile to play music on the Sabbath at a wedding party because it was a mitzvah to have music at weddings. Cf. Tur Orah Hayyim 339 for R. Hai Gaon's permission for dancing, and for the decision of R. Solomon Luria see commentaries to Orah Hayyim 268:8. These examples could be multiplied manyfold.

22. I refer to his collection of essays *Law and Tradition in Judaism.*

23. For a good general survey of the Jews during the Renaissance see Cecil Roth, *The Jews in the Renaissance* (Phila., 1959). The Roth quotation is from p. 3 in that volume. See also pp. 28-30, and the relevant note on p. 342 for primary sources of Provenzal's responsum.

24. Reference to this and its relationship to the Sabbath and liturgy was made in chap. 3. See notes 21 and 22 there.

25. See Shulhan Arukh Orah Hayyim 690:18, where this position is cited by *Magen Avraham,* note 22, from a responsum of Moses Isserles, no. 21. He goes further and quotes Tractate Sopherim that if a *minhag* has no real evidence for it in the Torah (as is the case with many Sabbath restrictions), it is simply "error." Other commentators on the text also cite these points and do not refute them.

The *Be'er Hetev,* note 15, cites an opinion that if a practice is based on certain anxieties, and the anxieties are no longer current, it is not necessary to have a new *Bet Din* rescind the old practice and create a new one. Thus, in this field of recreation, the old anxieties about violation of travel, carrying or repairing are no longer current. Cf. Shulhan Arukh Yoreh Dayah 116:1.

26. Shulhan Arukh Orah Hayyim 308:45. Cf. 508:1.

CHAPTER IX

1. This chapter was published in a briefer form as "The Rabbis and Divorce" in the *Jewish Spectator* of October 1961.

2. Saul Lieberman, *Greek in Jewish Palestine* (New York, 1942), chapter "Pleasures and Fears," and especially pp. 105 ff.

3. The term *Get* according to Jastrow is a form derived from *hattat,* an "engraving," and hence a "document." It is commonly re-referred to as *Get Ishah,* literally a "woman's document," and hence divorce.

A recent development within the Rabbinical Assembly (Conservative) has made for much improvement. A *Bet Din* (court) serves on behalf of the Committee on Jewish Law. This *Bet Din* will carry out annulments of those marriages in which there has been a civil decree and in which cases the *Bet Din* has satisfied itself that after every recourse has been exhausted the husband continues to refuse to issue a religious divorce.

Furthermore, for marriages henceforth, the same group has introduced the *tnai kiddushin,* a new formula for use in marriages which gives the *Bet Din* the power of retroactive annulment in the event a husband or wife procures a civil divorce and the recalcitrant husband refuses a religious divorce.

Nevertheless, it must be understood firstly, that the public at large must still become fully aware of these reforms. And secondly, that many, including me, are of the opinion that reforms that overcome an evil *after* the fact, or that continue to embody certain inequities, are not adequate. What is really called for is a reform of the whole process of *Gittin,* of religious divorce, as will be suggested in this chapter. See note 16 below.

4. Mention of the decree of Rabbenu Gershom is found in the notes of Moses Isserles to Shulhan Arukh Even ha'Ezer 119:6. It is stated briefly in Responsa of R. Asheri, no. 42. The basic halakhot of *Gittin* here summarized are found in the following sources, among others: Deut. 22:13-19, 22:28-29; Mishna Yevamot 14:1, Ketuvot 4:9; Gittin 7:1 and 8:2; Babylonian Gittin 67b, 78a and Tosafot, *aino;* and Babylonian Yevamot 112b and 113. For the right of an insane husband to divorce in a period of lucidity see Yerushalmi

Terumot 1:1. For a brief summary of the halakha of *Gittin* see David Amram, *The Jewish Law of Divorce* (Phila., 1896).

5. In addition to references cited in note 4 see Babylonian Nedarim 91a, Ketuvot 63a, 77a, and Mishna Ketuvot 7:10 among numerous other references that could be cited on the general question of grounds for suit for divorce and the restricted powers of the court. There have been famous cases in Israel in which a recalcitrant husband may even accept fines and jail rather than follow the Rabbinic directive to divorce his wife. This accomplishes little, since the wife remains an *agunah,* unable to remarry. Interesting Israeli cases have been discussed in the *Israel Law Review.* See especially in the issue of April 1968 "The Recalcitrant Husband."

6. Lev. 21:7 ff. and Num. 30:10. A possible exception to this benevolent attitude in the Jewish Scripture might be cited from Mal. 2:14-16. But the interpretation of these verses may be subject to dispute. All the Prophet may be saying is that God hates *shalah,* the arbitrary, indifferent sending away of one's wife, dealing treacherously with her, but not necessarily a properly procured divorce in accordance with appropriate halakhic control. By the time Malachi came upon the scene, standards were changing. Women were acquiring rights they theretofore had not had. The Diaspora taught them much, and in both the Euphrates Valley and Egypt the rights of women were expanding. In Elephantine, as we learn from the papyri, women had the right to divorce their husbands by making a public declaration *ba'edah,* "in the congregation." Cf. Salo Baron, *A Social and Religious History of the Jews* (Phila., 1952), vol. 1, p. 113. What concerned Malachi was probably wanton divorce practiced by promiscuous men who were apparently unconcerned for morality or the future of religious life among Jews. This was an argument, not against divorce per se but against taking a loose attitude toward marriage, as was apparent in the post-exilic period, a situation also clearly seen in the books of Ezra and Nehemiah. As a matter of fact, the statement of Malachi can be seen as *favoring divorce law,* that is, as a support for promoting a rational, moral concept of divorcing one's wife only after giving due recognition to her rights, and to the morality of the alternatives the husband may imagine himself to be pursuing.

7. Deut. 24:1-4. Cf. 1 Sam. 18:27, 25:44; 2 Sam. 3:14 ff.

8. Deut. 24:1. Cf. Boaz Cohen, *Jewish and Roman Law,* p. 387, where he cites the Roman jurist Gaius as suggesting that the Latin term was derived from one of two ideas: either because man and wife had a diversity of opinion or because they went their own ways.

9. Deut. 22:13-19. Amram, op. cit., p. 42.

10. Deut. 22:20-29.

11. Cf. Babylonian Gittin 59b. See further my discussion of these motivations of the halakha in chaps. 4 and 5.

12. Cf. Moses Isserles on Even ha'Ezer 154:3. See note 4 above.
13. See chap. 3.
14. George F. Moore, *Judaism*, vol. 2, p. 127.
15. Cohen, op. cit., pp. 378 ff., discusses the question of gentile divorce law. Cf. Mishna Gittin 1:5 and B. Gittin 10b, and see Rashi's passage, beginning with *Elah bazman*, and again on *kraita*, where he interprets the Talmud's explanation for the halakha as being opposed to R. Simon. Cf. also Tosafot Rid on this passage for the role of *dinah d'malkhuta dinah*, as to why *Gittin* was not included under this principle.
16. The process used in the Rabbinical Assembly takes the form of an annulment. See note 3 above. The *Bet Din* (court) hears cases in which women must prove to the court's satisfaction that every fair means of moral persuasion has failed to elicit the husband's willingness to issue the *Get*. In the event, the *Bet Din* bases its subsequent procedure on a combination of ancient principles. These are *kol d'm'kadesh al daat d'rabbanan m'kedash*, "he who consecrates a wife does so on the basis of Rabbinic permission," and *afkinhu rabbanan kidooshin*, "the Rabbis retroactively nullify the marriage," since it was not done in accordance with their *da'at*, their intent, or in good faith. The idea is that since the Rabbis are the ones who sanction the union, if in their judgment the union has brought forth undue agony, they can retroactively withdraw their sanction. In Jewish law any child born of this marriage would not be a bastard, as only offspring of incest and adultery are so classed. See further on these ideas in chap. 6.
17. Mishne Avot 5:14.
18. Mishna Gittin 2:3.
19. Mishna Gittin 6:6; Babylonian Gittin 66a. There is a difference whether it becomes apparent retroactively that he expected to die and therefore did intend to divorce her so that she would not become subject to *yibum* or *halitza*, levirate marriage, or the procedure of freeing her from it.
As to the rules of "agency," cf. Babylonian Kiddushin 41a-b for the derivation of the law of agency and for the statement that "an agent is the equivalent of oneself." Cf. also Babylonian Nazir 12b and Nedarim 72b. The agent's power went no further than the assignment, and the assignor had great liberty in interpreting the agent's fulfillment of the assignment and the right to repudiate his action. It is on this basis that the instructions of a husband in *Gittin* were so carefully and scrupulously regarded. Cf. Hoshen Mishpat 187:4, Babylonian Baba Batra 169b and elsewhere.
As for the need for a "specialist" to deal with matters of *Gittin*, this is only a Babylonian development of the 4th century, as is evident from the injunction laid down by Rav Yehudah (citing Samuel)

in Babylonian Kiddushin 13a. That R. Yehudah was still insisting on it would imply that what he claimed was Samuel's original desire to centralize authority in matters of domestic relations had not yet become universal.

20. Mishna Gittin 2:5.

21. Mishna Gittin 6:7.

22. Mishna Baba Batra 10:3. Cf. Babylonian Talmud Baba Batra 168a. The Mishna was based on Deut. 24:1-4, which indicates the husband "writes and gives"; and the Babylonian Rabbis said, ". . . but now that we do not do it this way, the Rabbis placed the obligation upon the woman so that the husband will not procrastinate." Cf. Maimonides, *Mishne Torah*, Hilkhot Gerushin 2:4. See Rabbenu Gershom on the passage in Baba Batra.

23. Mishna Gittin 3:2. Cf. Babylonian Talmud Gittin 26a-b and Yerushalmi Gittin 44a-b-c. In the latter there is reflected a difference of opinion between R. Yohanan and Resh Lakish, with the halakha following the latter that a *Get* is *pasul*, null, when the basic relevant information, the *Toraif*, is fitted into the blank form, the *tofais*.

24. Mishna Gittin 9:8. Cf. Babylonian Gittin 64a. See further on this in chap. 6.

25. Mishna Gittin 3:6. Maimonides, Mishne Torah Hilkhot Gerushin 1:16.

26. This responsum is cited extensively in Rabbi Solomon Freehof, *The Responsa Literature* (Phila., 1955), pp. 138 ff. Rabbi Solomon Kluger of Brody, Galicia, lived 1783-1869.

27. Joseph Karo, *Shulhan Arukh* Even ha'Ezer, p. 154. Cf. the notes of Moses Isserles.

28. Note 17.

29. See notes 3 and 16 above.

30. Babylonian Baba Kama 15a. The Talmud also indicates two other areas of equality. Men and women were placed on a par for all forms of monetary or capital punishment. This in itself might imply that *dinin*, the third category, is *not* civil law only.

31. Cf. Babylonian Gittin 33a, Ketuvot 3a; also Cohen, op. cit., pp. 111 ff. Cf. Babylonian Yevamot 110a and Tosafot beginning *l'feekakh*, and Babylonian Baba Batra 48b, and many other references. See, for further discussion and references, chap. 6 and also chap. 5 and note 12 there. Cf. also Tosafot on Yevamot 89b, beginning with *keevain*.

CHAPTER X

1. The nuclear ideas of this chapter originally appeared as an article titled "Neurotic Fixations" in the *Jewish Spectator* of January 1964. Its halakhic substance was later incorporated in a responsum

written in collaboration with Rabbi Abraham Ehrlich for the Committee on Jewish Law and Standards of the Rabbinical Assembly in February 1969. Both those pieces have been substantially expanded here, and Rabbi Ehrlich bears no responsibility for the chapter's content or views.

2. Ex. 12; 23:14-19; 34:18-26.

3. Lev. 23. Cf. Num. 28:16-29:39.

4. Deut. 16:1-17. Cf. for this use of *atzeret* the Tregelles revision of Gesenius' Hebrew and English Lexicon under the words *atzar,* niphal no. 3, and *atzara* or *atzeret* as used elsewhere in the Bible.

5. Yehezkel Kaufman, *Toledot ha'Emunah ha'Yisra'elet,* 2nd ed. (Tel Aviv, 1952), vol. 1. Cf. especially pp. 47-142 and 185-220 on the dating of the various strata and the evidence he adduces for dating JE as the earliest code, P including part of Exodus, the bulk of Leviticus and the Laws of Numbers, as next and as very early, and D as the latest corpus of law although as the first book to be canonized in the emerging "Torah." H. L. Ginzberg, in an essay "New Trends in the Study of the Bible" (Essays in Judaism Series, no. 4, Jewish Theological Seminary), accepted the general outline of the Kaufman position, as I recall vividly he did to a great extent in the early 1950's when I studied Bible with him. On p. 21 Ginzberg writes: "For Kaufman claims—and it is beyond me how one can disagree with this . . . For Kaufman demonstrates brilliantly that P is earlier than D. . . ."

Accepting this premise, that Leviticus is older than hitherto believed, it can be further assumed that the general approach of the halakha from the beginning of the more organized kingdom after the time of David was well reflected in chap. 23 of Leviticus. Furthermore, if we accept the thesis of Yehezkiel Kaufman in its broadest outlines and look upon the Exodus Covenant Code as the earliest pre-monarchic formulation of the then extant halakha, it is understandable why no mention of a "holy assembly" is found in the Exodus sources for the festivals. The more highly developed Priestly Code, on the other hand, expressing the post-conquest and early monarchic period, while not yet emphasizing the centrality of Jerusalem, probably reflects the festival halakha as it existed from then to the end of the biblical period. It contained all the necessary ingredients: agricultural, historical and spiritual. And it omitted an ingredient which was not considered mandatory: the pilgrimage.

6. Excerpts of the Herxheimer essay are found in a sourcebook of documents on the origins of Reform Judaism: W. Gunther Plaut, *The Rise of Reform Judaism* (New York, 1963), p. 197.

7. It is my conviction that the prohibition repeated in numerous instances throughout the Pentateuch, not to do any manner of "work" on Sabbaths or festivals, whether the word *avodah* is used or *melakha,*

always signified one's *occupation*, the gainful employment in business, industry or profession that one engaged in, and had nothing to do with the expenditure of kinetic energy.

8. Mishna Rosh ha'Shanah 2:7. There is no definitive view on the meaning of the various titles used in the Palestinian Rabbinate, such as *Nasi, Rosh Bet Din* or *Av Bet Din*. All the sources and discussion of the matter are highly conjectural. There is a good deal of information and documentation available in Hugo Mantel, *Studies in the History of the Sanhedrin* (Cambridge, 1965). The same uncertainty as obtains for the definitions of the presiding officers holds true for the nature and function of the body that is variously referred to as *Bet Din* and *Sanhedrin*.

9. Tannaitic references indicating the authority in calendar matters being exclusively vested in Jerusalem and later in Yavneh are scattered. But Mekhilta 2 provides one, in the Lauterbach edition, vol. 1, p. 22. Another, indicating the legitimacy of Yavneh based on Deut. 17:8-11, is found in Sifre, Shoftim 153, Friedman edition, p. 104b, and in Yerushalmi Sanhedrin 11:4. It is apparent that the Rabbis of the post-70 era were seeking a way to decentralize the powers previously vested in the Jerusalem Sanhedrin just as the right to worship had been decentralized. They therefore fell back on these verses of Deuteronomy not only for chronological help, that the authorities of each generation are the final authorities, which is what had followed for halakhic evolution in general, but also to establish geographic validity, that halakha may go forth from places other than Jerusalem even in those matters where authority has been vested in the Jerusalem Sanhedrin. Naturally, at that time they specified Yavneh. But as Yavneh was successor to Jerusalem, so would any center that had the Sanhedrin become the legitimate successor to Yavneh, just as halakha could be studied and decided anywhere and was acceptable in accord with the interpretation given to Deut. 17:9 in Sifre. Yerushalmi Shabbat 4:2 indicates that questions were sent to Yavneh after 70. To emphasize the legitimacy of Yavneh in matters exclusively vested in the Sanhedrin, the shofar was sounded there when Rosh ha'Shanah occurred on the Sabbath, as it had been in Jerusalem. Cf. B. Rosh ha'Shanah 29b. Then, after the Sanhedrin was removed from Yavneh to Usha following the Bar Kokhba debacle after 135, Usha received the same legitimacy.

10. Cf. Yerushalmi Sanhedrin 1:2 for removal of the intercalation to Galilee. Use of the title *Nasi* ceased around 425, but it is disputed whether Gamliel VI or VII is to be considered the last Nasi. Cf. Mantel, op. cit., p. 2, note 4, for various listings of the men who held the office. Cf. note 18.

11. Mishna Rosh ha'Shanah 1:4.

12. Mishna Rosh ha'Shanah 2:2; Babylonian Rosh ha'Shanah 22b.

13. A quick survey of the basic scriptural passages indicates the following: Ex. 12:16 does not use the term. It says simply *kol melakha,* "any form of *melakha* shall not be performed" on the first and seventh Passover days. In Ex. 23:14-19 and 34:18-26 there is no mention of work except as regarding the Sabbath, in 34:21. Leviticus 23 repeats the formula *kol melekhet avodah:* is not to be performed on the first and seventh of Passover, on Shavuot, the first of Sukkot and on Shemini Atzeret. Again in Deut. 16:1-17 the simple term *kol melakha* is used without *avodah* for the seventh day of Passover. The prohibition of neither *melakha* nor *avodah* is mentioned for the first of Passover, Shavuot or Sukkot, nor is Shemini Atzeret recorded at all. It is not my contention that the variety of regulations or the differences in terminology have any significance at all. Leviticus 23 can be accepted as the governing passage so far as I am concerned. And here *melekhet avodah* is proscribed for all the standard biblical festivals. The new JPS translation of the Torah (Phila., 1962), translates the phrase *melekhet avodah* as "work at your occupation," that is, the Torah is prescribing "you shall not work at your occupations" in all the instances where that term appears in Hebrew.

This is an illuminating translation and would open great new vistas in halakha if the Rabbinate were to pursue the ramifications of so understanding the terms.

14. Babylonian Bezah 3a-5b constitute a major source for the basic background to various aspects of Yom Tov Sheni.

15. Yerushalmi Eruvin 21c, Babylonian Bezah 4a.

16. Salo Baron, *A Social and Religious History of the Jews* (Phila., 1958), vol. 6, p. 269.

17. Moses Maimonides, Mishneh Torah, Hilkhot Yom Tov 1:22, 24; Hilkhot Avel 10:10. Cf. Keseph Mishna on the text of Hilkhot Yom Tov and his citation of Nahmanides.

18. See note 17.

19. Rabbi Mordecai Waxman, ed., *Tradition and Change* (New York, 1958), p. 49.

20. Shulhan Arukh, Orah Hayyim 496:1.

21. Cf. Baron, op. cit., vol. 8, p. 369, note 52.

22. B. Bezah 6a.

23. B. Pesahim 51b, 52a. Cf. Maimonides, Mishna Torah Hilkhot Yom Tov 8:20.

24. Maimonides, ibid.

25. B. Pesahim 52a and Rosh Hashanah 23b. Cf. *Rosh* on Pesahim, chap. 4, sec. 5. Some read not "Biram" in this text but rather "M'be Rav," that is, R. Nathan went from Sura to Pumbedita. In any case, it is apparent that R. Nathan did not observe the second day, and he was in the Diaspora. Cf. also Moses Mielziner, *Intro-*

duction to the Talmud, p. 49, for biographical material on the dates of R. Joseph, who excommunicated R. Nathan.

26. See Korban Netanel, note 8, on the *Rosh* referred to in the previous note.

27. Cf. Baron, op. cit., especially vol. 5, p. 30, and p. 305, note 35.

28. Rabbinical Assembly Proceedings, 1927, p. 48.

29. Mishna Eduyot 1:5; and cf. Ikar Tosaphot Yom Tov, note 9. See Solomon Schechter, *Studies in Judaism,* 1st series (Phila., 1911), pp. 192-93. See chap. 2 above for further discussion of the right to change halakha.

30. Moses Isserles on Shulhan Arukh Orah Hayyim 339:3.

31. Tosephta Rosh ha'Shanah 1:17, Deut. 17:9 and Eccles. 7:10. For the term *parnas* as communal leader see Sanhedrin 92a, where it is just as likely to be a *religious* leader as a "manager" or secular administrator. In Babylonian Berakhot 28a, in any case, it applies to R. Gamliel in his position as president of the Academy, that is, the spiritual leader of the halakhic forces of the time, and is used in the context of a quarrel over halakhic matters. That is the famous passage telling of his deposition and reinstatement, and deserves further study in relation to the halakhic process. See also chap. 2 above and other discussions of the question of contemporary authority throughout this book where the subject is often extensively annotated.

32. *Rosh* on Babylonian Bezah 5, halakha 4.

CHAPTER XI

1. This chapter is based on my article "Halakha in Crisis," *Jewish Spectator,* Apr. 1966.

2. Salo Baron, *A Social and Religious History of the Jews,* vol. 2, p. 32.

3. See my article "Halakha Is Not Law," *Jewish Spectator,* Feb. 1971.

4. Saul Lieberman, *Hellenism,* pp. 83-84, note 3. *Halakha* used in Ezra 4:13 and 7:24 is interpreted in the Babylonian Talmud Baba Batra 8a as *arnona.* In turn this word is defined by *Rashi* as a produce tax, really an "income tax." By Tosafot it is interpreted as a tax paid to help support the royal court as it traveled from city to city. Tosafot related the word to *hailekh,* "a traveler," as in 2 Sam. 12:4. Rabbi Gershom on the Baba Batra text defined it as *mas karka,* a land tax. That a land tax could give its name to a "pattern of conduct" requires some imagination because on the surface it would appear to have the characteristic of exactitude and fixity, which would not correspond to the idea of flexibility and change embodied in halakha. Nevertheless, a tax too must be seen as possessing flexibility and

change, and like halakha, as conforming to the needs and challenges of the environment. All these considerations have led me to rethink the term halakha and to conclude that it is best related to the concept of "guidance" for religious practice.

Prof. Lieberman is in effect adopting the meaning of "tax" for *halakh* and accepting the possibility that the same term used for "tax" may also designate a set of religious practices. His analogy to this is the usage and growth of the term "canon." If Tosafot was correct in the etymology of the term, the idea of tax is derived from the root "to walk," and signifies a "travel tax," the primary idea being the "walking," or, for us, the *pattern,* and not the tax. Even the connection between the term *ilku* with the idea of a "boundary" which Prof. Lieberman commented on would not be amiss in this context, since the "boundary" of an area might have been determined in ancient times by the owner walking around the area he possessed.

Prof. Lieberman further relates the term with Deut. 19:14, not to move a fellow man's boundary mark, based on *Siphre* (ed. Louis Finkelstein, p. 227), which offers as one interpretation the idea that one should not reverse a halakha and decide that that which has been considered pure is impure, or vice versa. However, the word halakha is nowhere mentioned in that context, and therefore the fact that *Siphre* chose to call such a reversal a violation of "not to remove a marker" would not necessarily mean that halakha is connected with that concept any more than with the tax. But by implication it could well be so connected, as with "travel tax."

In some of my previously published articles I adopted Professor Lieberman's approach to the term halakha uncritically and without the present explanatory qualifications. What I am presently pursuing is not an abandonment of that idea but a combination of all the usages of the root and its forms to indicate the unifying factor in the concepts of tax, boundary marker and our term halakha as "guidance" or "patterns of conduct." One can continue to see the term halakha as a "boundary marker" in the positive sense of connoting "guideposts." It seems the most common derivation of the word, from *halakh,* to walk, and the idea of a "marker" can be reconciled in the concept of halakha as a "guide to practice," the "walk-way" or the "pattern of conduct" for a Jew to follow. Thus Deut. 30:16 is a reminder that the Jew is to "love the Eternal your God by walking in His ways." The verb "to walk" is *la'lekhet,* or as in many variant texts cited by Kittel, *v'la'lekhet* (to love and to walk). The "ways" of God are His mitzvot. The Jew is commanded to walk in His ways, *v'lishmor mitzvotav,* "by observing his mitzvot." In Gen. 18:19 we read that God had confidence in Abraham that he would teach his progeny "to observe the way of the Lord." Halakha is therefore the intellectualized guidance to keep us on the "way," or to avoid overpassing the marker, and if a translation of the word is necessary, best is "pattern of conduct" or simply "practices."

5. *Dinah d'malkhuta dinah.* Cf. Gittin 10b, Baba Kama 113a and elsewhere. This principle of the sovereign law taking precedence is attributed to Samuel, the Babylonian Rabbi of the 3rd century. But in my opinion it was merely formulated by him and was undoubtedly earlier. The statement is, after all, an explanation after the fact, and the rule was probably Tannaitic. For a further discussion of this subject see chap. 6 and relevant notes.

6. Palestinian Talmud, Moed Katan 3:7.

7. Neh. 8; 10:30.

8. Jacob Z. Lauterbach, *Rabbinic Essays,* chapter "Midrash and Mishna" (Cin., 1951).

9. Louis Ginzberg, *The Legends of the Jews* (Phila., 1954), vol. 1, p. 141. Cf. notes on vol. 5, p. 166, note 64, and notes on vol. 6, pp. 446-48. Cf. Yerushalmi Peah 17a, Hagigah 76d.

10. See note 8 above.

11. Yose b. Yo'ezer was a member of the first *zug,* "the pair" of sages who headed academies during the 2nd and 1st centuries B.C.E. There is much legendary material about him, but it is possible that the account in 1 Macc. 7:16 that he was executed among the sixty put to death by Alcimus is correct. That was in 162 B.C.E.

12. Mishna Avot 1:4.

13. Mishna Eduyot 8:4. Cf. Babylonian Avodah Zarah 37a and Maimonides, Mishne Torah, Hilkhot Mamrim 2:8. See in general the halakha in Mamrim for provisions that allow for the abrogation of neglected *gezerat.* In halakha 4 he used the analogy of a physician who amputates a limb to save a life for the right to disregard a halakha in order to bring the masses back to religion. Thus the great need in our own time is to cut through the encrustation of restrictions if we are ever to attempt to win people back to respect for a viable halakha. His formulations in halakhot 5, 6 and 7 are also of current interest.

14. Babylonian Talmud, Pesahim 17b.

15. Babylonian Bezah 6a. See Rashi there.

16. Lieberman, op. cit., pp. 129-30.

17. Ibid. See chap. 7 of this book and relevant notes.

18. Saul Lieberman, *Greek in Jewish Palestine* (New York, 1942), pp. 91 ff.

19. Ibid., p. 97.

20. *Shulhan Arukh Yoreh Dayah,* Hilkhot Milah 363:5; 365.

21. David Avudraham, Kempler edition, *Sefer Avudraham* (undated), based on Prague edition of Ezekiel Landau, 1784, p. 191. Cf. Maimonides, *Mishne Torah Hilkhot Milah,* chap. 3.

22. Boaz Cohen, *Law and Tradition in Judaism,* p. 19, note 59.

Cf. Babylonian Gittin 56a. See also chap. 8, and especially note 7, in this book.

23. See my chapters on these questions, "The Future of Religious Divorce" and "Rejoice on Your Festivals."

24. Cohen, op. cit., pp. 62 ff.

25. Ex. 22:24 and Lev. 25:36-38 record the Torah's prohibition of usury. The Mishna in Baba Metziah 5:1 defines it, and in 5:4 indicates a form of business arrangement which is also prohibited because of appearing to be usury. The Mishna states that one cannot offer a merchant the capital to retail a product in return for half the profit unless, in addition, he paid him as a worker. On Babylonian Baba Metziah 68b, Rabbi Judah b. Illai reduces this "payment" to a mere dry fig, a token salary. This Mishnaic halakha and its lenient interpretation by Rabbi Judah b. Illai became the source for the medieval *hetar iska*, which I discuss further in the text of this chapter.

26. Shulhan Arukh Yoreh Dayah, 160 passim. But see especially par. 22 and the commentators.

27. See 1 Kings 18 and Midrash Tanhuma on Mishpatim. Cf. Babylonian Avodah Zarah 26b and Tosaphot there, beginning with *Ani Shoneh*. Cf. Shulhan Arukh Yoreh Dayah 160:1.

28. Cohen, op. cit., pp. 72-73.

29. Babylonian Talmud, Niddah 66a.

30. Babylonian Talmud Moed Katan 20a, 18a, 19b and elsewhere; cf. Eruvin 46a. See also Maimonides Mishne Torah Hilkhot Avel 7:1 and *Shulhan Arukh Yoreh Dayeh* 402:1.

31. Babylonian Talmud Eruvin 13b. Cf. Rabbenu Hananel.

32. Z. H. Chajes, *The Student's Guide Through the Talmud*, p. 35. Cf. Babylonian Berakhot 4b.

33. Chajes, op. cit., p. 79.

34. Babylonian Shabbat 59b, 111a, and cf. Shulhan Arukh Orah Hayyim 328:1.

35. Babylonian Talmud Baba Kama 82a.

36. Babylonian Talmud Rosh ha'Shanah, Mishna 4:1, 29b; cf. Maimonides, Mishnah Torah Hilkhot Shofar 2:8. See *Magid Mishne* of Rabbi Vidal de Tolosa (14th century) on the text of Maimonides in which he points out that the view of Maimonides is disputed "but since it is no longer here nor there, for whatever was, was, I will not expand upon it." In other words, the shofar is no longer sounded anywhere on the Sabbath, and the question is therefore irrelevant. I believe, however, that this question should be reopened. *Lehem Mishna* (Rabbi Abraham Hiyya de Boton of Salonica, 1560-1609) on the same text points to a contradiction in *Rashi*, that in one instance he excludes Jerusalem during Temple days and in another says that the sounding of the shofar in Jerusalem took place even without a *Bet Din* in session, unlike Yavneh, which recognizes that

the sounding of the shofar *was* done in Jerusalem and not in the Temple itself. Tosaphot on Rosh ha'Shanah 29b attempts to introduce a chronological argument, but one may adopt the view of *Magid Mishne* and say the whole matter is irrelevant.

Furthermore, *Migdal Oz* (R. Shem Tov ibn Gaon, Spain, 1283-1330), on the same text, asserted that generally the usage of *Mikdash* in the Mishna refers to all Jerusalem and *Medinah* to the rest of the cities and towns. He therefore sustained the view of Maimonides.

The relevant point here is that there is room for honest differences of interpretation and that these lead to different conclusions for halakha. Ultimately it depends on the person in charge of deciding which way the halakha will go, and this is a very human process.

37. Deut. 26:13 ff. Babylonian Talmud Sotah 47b, Yevamot 86b.

It is not clear in our sources whether Yohanan Kohen Gadol was the father of the Maccabean progenitor Mattathias and lived at the same time as Yose b. Yo'ezer, pre-165 B.C.E., or whether he is to be identified, as some prefer, with John Hycanus, who lived a generation or two later, or with some other Tannaitic figure. Although his exact identity remains shadowy, his significance, like that of Yose b. Yo'ezer and R. Yohanan b. Zakkai, should not be underestimated in the history of halakha and as a guide in our own contemporary crisis.

38. Mishna Sanhedrin 4:5.

A CLOSING WORD

1. Mishna Ta'anit 2:8; Babylonian Ta'anit 15b, 18a.

2. The Talmud identifies Anonymous with Rabbi Meier because the Rabbis functioned with the assumption *stam mishne R. Meier,* "an anonymous mishna is a citation of R. Meier." This was probably because he was an early collector of Mishnaic material and his work was incorporated into R. Judah the Prince's.

3. Cf. Moses Maimonides, *Perush ha'Mishnayut,* on this Mishna text. He explicitly states that although Purim and Hanukah are still observed and were not abolished with all the other dates in the scroll and it is therefore forbidden to fast on those days, there is no prohibition to fast on the days before and after. He thus follows R. Simon b. Gamliel. During the Franco-German era fasting and mourning on the day before and after Hanukah and Purim seem to have been prohibited by some authorities. Cf. *Piskai Tosafot* on Ta'anit, no. 46. But it is clear in Tosafot itself on 18a, beginning with *Rav,* that it was permitted to fast before Purim during that period. And it is clear in Rabbenu Hananel on the text that the halakha was in accordance with R. Simon b. Gamliel because "he was more lenient."

4. Babylonian Yevamot 121a, *Maharsha,* p. 18a, beginning with *v'amar shalom* at the end of the tractate.

5. Prov. 3:17.

6. Eli Ginzberg, *Keeper of the Law* (Phila., 1966), pp. 237, 241-42.

7. Louis Ginzberg, *Students, Scholars and Saints* (New York, 1958), p. 117.

8. Ibid., p. 236; also p. 117.

9. Babylonian Rosh ha'Shanah 25a, b; Tosephta Rosh ha'Shanah 1:17.

10. Mishna Avot 2:21.

11. Cf. Deut. 30:20, on which is based the line I have paraphrased from the *Ahavat Olam* prayer in the Evening Service, which in turn constitutes the second blessing preceding the Shema.

BIBLIOGRAPHY

The following does not constitute a reading list in halakha; therefore dozens of worthwhile secondary volumes or collections of responsa are not included. The list includes only some of the main sources consulted in the course of the development of this book, while others may be cited only in the notes. Generally I have listed only those to which the average reader might have relatively ready access.

All the primary classical Rabbinic literature was consulted. This includes the Tannaitic literature, and both the Babylonian and Palestinian Talmuds, as well as the commentaries, commentaries upon commentaries and marginal notes included within the volumes of the edition I used. Pagination and references for this literature, except for that specifically listed below, are based on the edition published by Shulsinger Brothers, New York, 5708 (1948). The references for the following sources are given from that edition: Tosephta, Rabbenu Gershom, Rabbi Hananel, R. Nissim, R. Asher b. Yehiel (the *Rosh*), R. Isaac Alfasi, Rashi, Tosefot, Mordecai, Maimonides' *Perush ha Mishnayot*, and any of the other standard commentaries and marginalia cited in the note.

The biblical text used was *Biblia Hebraica*, ed. Rudolph Kittel and Paul Kahle (Stuttgart, 1952). The other editions of classical literature used were:

Avot of R. Nathan, ed. Solomon Schechter. Reprinted New York, 1945.

Mekhilta de-Rabbi Ishmael, ed. Jacob Lauterbach. 3 vols. Phila., 1949.

Midrash Rabbah. New York, 1952.

Midrash Tanhuma. Warsaw, 1910.

Mishna. Warsaw, 1863.

Sifra, ed. Isaac Hirsch Weiss. Vienna, 1862; reprinted New York, 1947.

Sifre, ed. Meyer Friedman. Vienna, 1864; reprinted Israel, 1968.

Sifre, Deuteronomy, ed. H. S. Horovitz and Louis Finkelstein. Berlin, 1939; reprinted New York, 1969.

The following editions were used for the medieval halakhic references, and it was also from these editions that such commentaries as the Taz, Shakh, Magen Avraham, Keseph Mishne, and Lehem Mishne, and a host of others, were cited:

Karo, Joseph. *Even ha'Ezer.* Reprinted Tel Aviv, 1953.

————. *The Shulhan Arukh, Orah Hayyim.* 2 vols. Reprinted New York, 1951.

————. *Yoreh Dayah.* 3 vols. Reprinted New York, 1953.

Maimonides, Moses. *Mishne Torah.* The 14 divisions in 5 vols. Reprinted New York, 1968.

Among the secondary sources were:

Amram, David W. *The Jewish Law of Divorce.* Phila., 1896.

Baron, Salo. *A Social and Religious History of the Jews.* Phila. and New York, 1952-69.

Chajes, Zvi H. *The Student's Guide Through the Talmud.* New York, 1960.

Cohen, Boaz. *Law and Tradition.* New York, 1959.

Finkelstein, Louis. *Akiva: Scholar, Saint and Martyr.* Phila., 1962.

————. *Jewish Self-Government in the Middle Ages.* New York, 1924.

————. *The Pharisees.* 2 vols. Phila., 1946.

Ginzberg, Louis. *Geonica.* 2 vols. Reprinted New York, 1968.

————. *Legends of the Jews.* Phila., 1946-54.

————. *On Jewish Law and Lore.* Phila., 1955.

————. *Students, Scholars and Saints.* New York, 1958.

Horowitz, George. *The Spirit of the Jewish Law.* New York, 1963.

Landman, Leo. *Jewish Law in the Diaspora.* Phila., 1968.

Lauterbach, Jacob Z. *Rabbinic Essays.* Cincinnati, 1951.

Lieberman, Saul. *Greek in Jewish Palestine.* New York, 1942.

————. *Hellenism in Jewish Palestine.* New York, 1950.

Mantel, Hugo. *Studies in the History of the Sanhedrin.* Cambridge, 1965.

Moore, George F. *Judaism.* 3 vols. Cambridge, 1950.

Schechter, Solomon. *Studies in Judaism.* Phila., 1908-24.

Tcherikover, Victor. *Hellenistic Civilization and the Jews.* Phila., 1959.

INDEX

Abraham, 27, 31, 58

Abrogation of Halakha, 34, 51, 56, 77, 80, 103, 129, 134, 152, 156, 173, 174, 190-192, 199, 202, 203, 205, 206, 220, 224, 228, 247

Abyeh (4th cent. Amora), 99, 164

Action-Symbols, 42, 54, 69

Adultery, 83, 240

Aesthetics (see also Hidur Mitzvah), 45, 53, 54, 74, 75, Chapter VII, 206, 223

Afterlife, 93

Agada, 27, 30, 31, 58, 182, 228

Agency, Laws Of, 145, 146, 148, 149, 240

Agunah (a Woman Unable to Remarry), 34, 77, 78, 91, 141, 146, 212, 219, 226, 230, 239

Akiva, Rabbi (2nd cent. Tanna), 29, 31, 37, 38, 62, 78, 146, 194

Alexander the Great, 183

Alexandrian Jews, 164

Alfasi (R. Isaac of Fez, 11-12th cent.), 30

Amidah, 44, 86, 210, 214, 215

Amoraim, 29, 59, 115, 122, 123, 127, 146, 147, 237

Annulment, 95, 152, 212, 223, 232, 238, 240

Apostate, 87, 135, 229

Arbor Day, 112, 226

Ashi, Rav (5th cent. Amora), 195

Assi, Rabbi (3rd cent. Amora), 163, 164

Auschwitz, 20-23

Authority (see also Contemporary Authority), 25, 30, 32-34, 36, 54, 65, 66, 95-97, 129, 151, 152, 160, 164, 170, 171, 173-175, 178, 182, 195, 197, 221, 241, 243, 249

Avelut (Death and Mourning), 50, 59, 75, 77, 81, 91, 113, 185, 194, 201, 203, 204, 218, 219, 226, 228, 235, 249

Avodah (see Melakha)

Avudraham, David (14th cent. Spanish scholar), 188

Babylonia, Babylonians, 16, 21, 50, 113, 164, 171, 180, 181, 198, 209, 226, 240

Baby Naming, 187, 188

Bar-Kokhba, 86, 123, 243

Baron, Salo, 165, 216, 239

Bastard (see Mamzer)

Bereavement (see Avelut)

Bet Din (court), 135, 146, 148, 149, 160, 164, 173, 175, 196, 197, 229, 238, 240, 243, 248

Bet Hillel (School of Hillel), 32, 80, 112, 124, 194

Bet Shammai (School of Shammai), 32, 80, 112, 124

Biblical Criticism, 155, 156, 223, 239, 242, 244

Birth, 133, 186

Breslau Rabbinical Conference, 157

Burial (see also Avelut), 81, 113, 218, 226

Calendar, 94, 98, 160, 161, 164-172, 228, 243